E-MARKET
DOMINANCE

E-MARKET DOMINANCE

 How to use the Internet to
win and keep customers

BRIAN ASH & **TOM LAMBERT**

THE McGRAW-HILL COMPANIES

LONDON·BURR RIDGE IL·NEW YORK·ST LOUIS·SAN FRANCISCO·AUCKLAND·BOGOTÁ
CARACAS·LISBON·MADRID·MEXICO·MILAN·MONTREAL·NEW DELHI·PANAMA
PARISSAN JUAN·SÃO PAULO·SINGAPORE·SYDNEY·TOKYO·TORONTO

Published by
McGraw-Hill Publishing Company
Shoppenhangers Road, Maidenhead, Berkshire, SL6 2QL, England
Telephone: 01628 502500
Fax: 01628 770224
Web site: http://www.mcgraw-hill.co.uk

Sponsoring Editor:	Eizabeth Robinson
Production Editorial Manager:	Penny Grose
Desk Editor:	Alastair Lindsay
Cover by:	Kate Hybert
Produced by:	Steven Gardiner Ltd

British Library Cataloguing in Publication Data
A catalogue record for this book is available from the British Library

McGraw-Hill

A Division of The McGraw·Hill Companies

Designed by Claire Brodmann Book Designs, Lichfield, Staffs.

1 2 3 4 5 BB 5 4 3 2 1

Printed and bound in Great Britain by Bell & Bain Ltd, Glasgow

ISBN 0077 09807-2

For my mother Doreen Ash for all her wise support over the years. Sadly she died only weeks before this book was completed.

For David and Carole as always. With grateful love and great pride. And for my mother, Bette Lambert for a lifetime of love and support.

CONTENTS

FOREWORD

Since the mid Nineties we have been talking loosely but enthusiastically about the New Economy. Our enthusiasm is justified, but if we want to enjoy the benefits of the Internet we should apply some careful thought to how we will benefit from greater global business opportunities at lower cost, providing better value to our invaluable customers wherever they may be.

The laws of economics have not been repealed. The creation of a profit is an essential pre-requisite of business survival, growth and prosperity. If we get it right the rewards will be enormous for the individual, the firm, the nation, and eventually the whole world.

Reecent spectacular nose-dives by over-hyped 'dot-coms' should serve as a timely warning, but should not be allowed to stifle creativity or entrepreneurship. Pasteur once said that 'chance favours the prepared mind'. Prepare your minds for the kind of success that only the New Economy can offer. Support your wonderful e-commerce idea with a comprehensive, robust and flexible 'go to market' strategy.

This book distils the expereince of two veteran business professionals who, between them, have worked in most parts of the world and practically all the important business sectors. It is a 'how to do it' manual based on the real world as much as cyberspace. It combines the most promising aspects of the new with the most fully proven tools and techniques of the familiar business world. Use it wisely and not only will you win the battle for new markets, but your people will win security and satisfaction, your investors will enjoy extraordinary returns and, most important of all, your delighted and loyal customers will become the best advertisement and the most vocal advocates that your business could have.

Gerald Allen
Managing Director
Coastal Sites UK Ltd

PREFACE

When two writers work in tandem it is a little like playing a disjointed game of ping-pong at a distance. Chapters and ideas have flown through the ether by e-mail, to be batted back with changes or better ideas or be smashed into oblivion. In the latter stages Elizabeth Robinson, our publisher, made the match triangular with incisive comments and suggestions about the manuscript. Eventually we reached a stage where the book is, or at least should be, seamless. Somewhat to our surprise, we are still friends. Apparently a greater percentage of friendships founder on the rocks of collaboration than in marriage. We leave it to the interested reader to establish who actually wrote what, but Brian is the expert on the Internet while Tom has written copiously on marketing here and elsewhere.

Research suggests that the average buyer of business books reads to page 29 after which he or she puts the book aside with the intention of completing it at a later date which for many is like the tomorrow that never comes. In this the reader has much in common with the writer who writes until a degree of numbness affects the brain, then ponders sadly on writer's block and chronic carpal tunnel syndrome and wishes that the advance had not been banked. Books, however, finally do get written and sometimes read.

HOW TO USE THIS BOOK

This book should be read through initially from beginning to end, preferably using some form of speed-reading or skimming. We suggest that, since it is your book, you would feel free as you read to make your own comments in the margins. (Tom is a scribbler on the page, Brian is somewhat neater, having retained the benefits of an early Roman Catholic education, and tends to use small 'Post-it' notes for comments and ideas.) Since this is a totally practical book the important thing is that you can easily find the information that will enable you to make money as quickly as possible, with the least time spent on re-reading what you already know.

We advise you to make no assumptions concerning your knowledge of either e-commerce or market dominance. The former is a rapidly moving feast while the latter is widely misunderstood even by specialists. So please check out the book as a whole before homing in on those sections that need what Winston Churchill called 'action this day'.

This is not a book for 'techies'. It is for those in businesses great and small who intend to prosper using the Internet as part or all of their strategy. It, like the Internet itself, is not about technology. It is about sales and marketing, profits and prosperity. It is aimed fairly and squarely at the entrepreneur and the businessperson. Above all, it is a 'how to do it' book.

This book will give you all you need to market profitably in the coming Information Era. We urge you to read it today and implement its 'how to' approaches starting tomorrow.

Enjoy the journey.

Brian Ash   Tom Lambert
London   Roselle
United Kingdom   United States
brga@hotmail.com   www.tom-lambert.com

WHAT IS E-MARKET DOMINANCE?

☞ E-Market Dominance is the only complete, ethical and effective approach to market dominance in the age of e-commerce

NATHAN GOLDBERG, Director, The Institute of Practical Marketing

We are living in a world our parents find hard to recognize. The speed of change has become so great that people of all ages and all levels of education have difficulty in coming to terms with it. Many of the technological advances trumpeted some thirty years ago have failed to materialize. At the same time things barely dreamed of less than a decade ago are now everyday realities. The business cycle spins ever faster. Companies great and small burgeon, decline and disappear in a vortex of volatility. Callow youths, fresh out of post-grad school, throw vast sums of other people's money at dot.com start-ups that have never made a penny of profit and for the most part, never will. Globalization as interpreted by the major conglomerates regularly fails while globalization, in the sense of someone somewhere plotting to lure and retain your best customers through lower costs and higher productivity, is an every-day reality. The Internet has made competition truly global.

Most of us live longer, live better, yet feel ourselves to be increasingly subjected to the stress of having to work harder because we will not or cannot work smarter. The idiocies of 'dumbsizing' come and go like the tides as the bootleggers of asset stripping and junk bonds are replaced by the hatchet-wielding billionaires of corporate hara kiri. Corporate executives, who should be aware by now that past acquisition sprees merely made clear their shortcomings (when they fail to follow Tom Peters' advice to 'stick to their knitting') are hitting the acquisition trail again. Not for horizontal nor for vertical diversification, but to get their hands on another company's customer databases, in order to cross-sell sometimes congruent, sometimes incongruent goods and services.

The customer is at last coming into his and her own – the Web is seeing to that. Offers can be compared on-line. Prices and services become increasingly transparent, costs can be reduced significantly. Customers are in a newly informed position that enables them to claim their share of the action.

At the same time, the more discerning of them are recognizing that there is more to life than the ordering, delivery and enjoyment of the product or service. They want to conserve what they can of their coveted and scarce time, and they are increasingly willing to pay a premium to those who can save that valued resource for them.

We are entering an entertainment-driven business environment. Doing business today needs an element of 'experience'. Shoppers demand greater involvement with their suppliers and the goods they buy. They look for relationships with their suppliers in a more comprehensive way than ever before. Suppliers prepared to build and sustain such relationships are rewarded through lower costs, higher sales, higher profits, more committed customers and employees, and ever-stronger advocacy for their business at every level. More than ever before, the business that truly puts the customer first prospers and grows, while those around them fail. Consistent customer delight is the key to market dominance. And regardless of Microsoft's much publicized troubles, market dominance – whether you set the rules of engagement for a segment, sector, niche or for the global market – remains the only sure way to survive and prosper in the face of truly global competition.

E-Market Dominance is a comprehensive programme that enable a business to attract and retain loyal customers at minimum cost. Unlike the many fads, fallacies and foul-ups routinely peddled by consultants, it is an approach that can readily be implemented by the business itself.

It is a way of working smarter, not harder, that reflects the pressures on time and attention of business and customer alike. It builds and sustains key relationships with the right kind of customer by first providing methods to attract more and more customers of the desirable type, then by winning and keeping a greater share of each customer's buying power. It enables one-on-one communication with every worthwhile customer. It even eases the perennial problem of ditching those customers who are more trouble than they are worth without adversely affecting the image and reputation of the company. It uses proven methods and techniques in new situations and in new ways. It takes full account of the effects which information fatigue has had on the marketer's ability to arouse attention, awareness and desire. It is psychologically sound and makes creative use of our growing understanding of customer behaviour, expectations and desires. Finally, it will make a massive positive difference to *your* business because it can be used by any company, with or without virtually unlimited cash resources, at virtually no cost. For it is the ultimate in no cost/low cost marketing.

WHAT IS THE URGENCY?

If you are in business, a brief summary of the most up-to-date forecasts should make it clear why E-Market Dominance is an essential skill for you right now. Look at the following projections:

PROJECTED GROWTH OF E-MAIL AND USE OF THE WEB

- By 2005 e-mail marketing will have increased in value to $7.3 billion (4000% growth in just five years).
- In the US in 1999 each e-mail subscriber received on average 40 business e-mails; by 2005 they will receive 1,600.
- The attention deficit that now strangles at birth so many direct mail and advertising campaigns will hit the Web within five years.
- Current research shows that customers are 49% more likely to buy if the marketing effort is synergistic. (E-Market Dominance is the only truly synergistic approach which is relevant to present and future circumstances.)
- By 2003 US business intends to spend almost half of its total advertising budget on the Web.
- Opt-in e-mail (the provision of a mandate to provide information) is increasing at a rate of:

Year	Growth
2000	52%
2001	66%
2002	70%

- Total e-mail is growing at a rate of:

Year	Growth
2000	29%
2001	33%
2002	34%

Sources: Jupiter Research, eMarketer Report

PROJECTED GROWTH OF ON-LINE HOUSEHOLDS IN EUROPE

	1998	2002
Germany	3,600,000	15,200,000
United Kingdom	3,200,000	9,700,000
France	800,000	4,000,000
The Netherlands	600,000	2,500,000
Italy	400,000	2,200,000
Sweden	700,000	1,600,000

continued over

Finland	300,000	800,000
Denmark	200,000	700,000
Norway	300,000	700,000

Source: Jupiter Communications, New York

Note: This report lacks figures for Spain, Portugal, Belgium and Greece, but the interested reader will find The Economist Intelligence Report on 'e-readiness' summarized in Chapter 1 provides information on international opportunities for online trade covering the next five years at least.

In short, aggressive competition and info-clutter will grow even faster than the astounding expansion of the Web itself. Now is the time to become established as a potentially global player before it is too late or too expensive. This is one time when being early to market will be crucial. To be early to market with the low-cost, proven but new tools of E-Market Dominance will be the most reliable path to on-going prosperity in the face of the toughest, most active and finally most desperate competition the world of business has ever known.

CASE STUDIES

Let us make clear our position on case studies. We could tell you what happened in General Widgets last year, last month or even last week as if it is an object lesson but it will be of very limited value. You are almost certainly not working for General Widgets. The chances are you do not have, nor wish to have, customers with the profile preferred by General Widgets in the recent or distant past. Besides, you are looking forward, not back.

We could show you a classic case study like *Polaroid France* to establish the principle of the non-transferability of a marketing plan, but for all we know the successor of the 'Swinger' may now be the number one selling camera in France. Logically it can be argued that if a marketing plan is not transferable, which we believe is the case, there is little to be gained from reading about an unsuccessful attempt at transfer. The plain fact is that any past success or failure is unlikely to be directly meaningful to you. You are not in the same business, nor in the same markets, nor will you be reading this at the time something occurred. So in general a reasonable response to any case study is 'so what?'

Our case studies have been selected because they:

- Enable us to back up an argument from the main text unusually concisely, saving your valuable time when you want to review the odd point;
- Establish an important principle using real world data;
- Help us review key points of a chapter;
- Prompt you to do a little lateral thinking about how you might adapt and adopt other people's ideas that have led to success.

The case studies do not necessarily invite you to analyse the situation and assume a role. Rather they will spur you to re-analyse your own situation and build your own solutions, so they are relevant to your enterprise right now. In short we intend them be useful rather than academic, applicable rather than entertaining, timely rather than historic.

CHAPTER ONE

IT IS NO LONGER BEYOND YOU

☞ An ounce of implementation is worth a ton of theory
MIKE DAVIDSON

☞ Truth may be stretched, but it cannot be broken, and always gets
above falsehood, as oil does above water
MIGUEL DE CERVANTES

☞ Those who are first on the battlefield are at ease
SUN TSE

☞ Control your destiny or someone else will
JACK WELCH

WHAT YOU WILL LEARN IN THIS CHAPTER

☞ The Internet creates a level playing field for large and small enterprises.

☞ All companies ought to be planning to dominate their carefully chosen markets.

☞ Your commitment can work miracles.

I have no intention of using arcane language or recondite terms (get me!) in this chapter, but a few well-known words are used so loosely that they have become virtually interchangeable. It is useful, therefore, to define how they are used here before we go any further.

- **Market sector** A well-defined group of buyers who will purchase your products or services. Often given evocative names such as 'empty nesters', 'baby boomers', 'hedonists', or my personal favourite, 'swingers'.
- **Market segment** Those parts of the market place with needs and wants that you have analysed with care and which your products and services are specifically designed to satisfy.

- **Niche** A narrowly defined area of the market specified in terms of products or services or buyer characteristics, where there is little or no competition and buyers are prepared to pay premium prices.

Now to business. One of the great challenges and greater opportunities of the Internet lies in the fact that it has the greatest potential to change business and trade since the invention of the wheel. It undoubtedly has the capacity to transform the way that we do business. This has little to do with the technology; it is almost entirely, as Marcus Bicknell has said, a matter of marketing and selling. For the first time, resources are not the be-all and end-all of competition: the Internet can be used to make small look and feel bigger. It is already being used to make the big look elephantine and unwieldy. The Internet is the ideal way to bind the customer to you for life. If you can attract and retain the right customers, you can set the rules by which your competitors must play. If you can give your customers all they want, your competitors will be forced to follow your lead – in a usually vain attempt to win business from you.

Customers seldom welcome the risk of changing from a supplier who genuinely exceeds their best expectations. In these circumstances the competitors' only card is price. They have the costs of playing the game according to your rules, but they have to offer low prices for products and services of equal or higher value. This is why, as Chris Prahalad and his team in Boston and Gary Hamel in London have shown, competition can be forced to lose money chasing you and either settle as a less-profitable small-time player or withdraw. The Internet enables you, whether you are great or small, to dominate your chosen markets, sectors, segments or niches.

IT COULD BE YOU

A great marketer died a short time ago. He was not recognizable as a business tycoon, but he was in his way as successful as MacDonalds or Coca Cola. Billions in virtually every country in the world enjoyed his products. He was, of all things, a cartoonist. His simple but beautiful drawings and his deep understanding of the gulf between the world-view of children and of their parents made him a legend and a multi millionaire. His name was Charles Schultz. His product was the celebrated antics of Charlie Brown, Lucie, Peppermint Pattie, Linus, and most important, Joe Cool aka Snoopy, the world's favourite beagle. I write of Charles Schultz in part because of the pleasure his work gave to so many people (it is a sad pleasure to add my little piece to the celebration of his life), but mainly because he is a perfect example of our belief that, if you are world-class, you can dominate your market. If you can dominate your market you can create the rules by which others must play. If you set the rules, your competitors have no choice other than to spend a fortune in playing catch-up. If catching up is too costly they have few alternatives other than withdrawal.

Your business can be world-class. If you have one happy customer you are doing something right. By leveraging your strengths you can set the rules by which others have to play and when they play by your rules, you win and go on winning. A General Electric, a Microsoft or an Intel does it on a grand scale. Many small enterprises do it one small step at a time using the Internet for what it is best at: building and sustaining mutually satisfying relationships. Here is how it's done.

- First and foremost, ensure that the decision makers in your firm share a burning desire to be the very best in the business.
- Build a clear vision of exactly where you want to be in six months, a year, three years, ten years hence. A vision so compelling, so inspirational, that it will get every one of your people to the barricades when needed.
- Communicate that vision until everyone has a shared view of a future that they lust after. Have them tell you what's in it for them, and challenge them to go out and get it.
- Find out what would attract the best people in the business to you, and go and do it.
- Regard your vision as achieved and 'walk the talk' of success.
- Be sure that you know your customers' real needs. Don't think in terms of products or services, but of customer satisfactions you deliver through your products and services. Specify where you beat competition and build on your advantage. Work on your strengths before worrying about your weaknesses.
- Identify those sectors, segments or niches where you are or can be the best.
- Build a strategic plan and use bench marking of the best in any industry to enable you to leapfrog the competition.
- Analyse all customers in your market and establish who are worth dealing with and who are more trouble than they are worth.
- Politely, pleasantly, but very firmly dump those customers who give you hassle rather than profit. Let your competitors steal them. Let the nuisance customer weaken your competitor, not you.
- Analyse your competitors by name in a head-to-head comparison between your offering and theirs, strictly in terms of how well you each satisfy the most important customer wants. Remember in the days of sexual equality that what used to be M.A.N. (Whoever has the Money, Authority and Need), is now W.O.M.A.N. (Wants Over-ride Money, Authority and Need).
- Identify the competition's customers you would give your eye-teeth to

serve and focus your sales effort on them, using your relevant strengths to win and keep their business.

- Commit yourself totally to doing everything better, faster and cheaper every day. Find the best sources of information and advice, and implement what you find.
- Set standards of real customer service that make competition shake with fear.
- Turn your best customers into advocates for your business. Develop a systematic approach to referrals.
- Use your website to give your customers everything that they want by way of information, entertainment and service – but keep it simple.

And, in Winston Churchill's words:

        ❝Never, never, never give in.❞

I have spent the last few years helping both small companies and huge corporations all over the world do the above. The ones who have indeed done them have two things in common:

1   That burning ambition I wrote about above.
2   They take pleasure, as they say in the US, in 'kicking ass'.

If those two descriptions fit you the Internet gives you a unique opportunity to make your dream come true. This book will tell you all you need to know about how you can use the Internet to dominate your markets. For E-Market Dominance is the only way to an *ethical* dominance strategy!

WHAT IS HAPPENING OUT THERE?

The world of business is becoming more volatile. As it does so, a whole range of changes have been set in train. Here are some of them:

- Public services are increasingly required to act as if they were businesses.
- The essential factor in success is more and more the acquisition and application of knowledge.
- We struggle to learn how to manage the human imagination.
- World trade booms and global competition grows ever quickly more dangerous.
- Success becomes more profitable and failure carries greater penalties.
- Organizations increasingly have to deal efficiently and effectively with the aftermath of the fads, fallacies and futilities which have dogged business over the last thirty years.

- People on whom success depends are driven, in spite of much talk of 'stake holding', further away from the goals of the organization.
- The gap between 'haves' and 'have nots' continues to widen and the socially almost fatal game of creating an underclass and keeping them under spreads through the advanced nations.
- We struggle to turn information into knowledge and knowledge into wisdom by adding the hunches, beliefs and feelings of our people to accurate data and then applying that knowledge appropriately in a rapidly changing world.
- The transfer of technology and resources between continents becomes ever easier.
- New markets and new concentrations of productive and economic power emerge and, too often, quickly decline.
- The need to get goods and services to the market place faster becomes ever more acute.
- Customer and consumer expectations increase and change ever more quickly.
- More and more businesses assume there is value in making major investments in the least stable emerging markets.

In short, as everything which characterizes the present and foreseeable future of the business world, becomes faster or more extreme, the need for a robust strategy with a sufficiently distant planning horizon changes from being useful to being critical. And there is more ...

DOMINANCE IS THE ONLY GAME IN TOWN

In their brilliant and groundbreaking book, *Competing for the Future*, Gary Hamel and Chris Prahalad made an unanswerable case for strategic dominance as the only way to be sure you control your own destiny in business. But there remains a lack of understanding of how to do it in the real world. Recent developments in the American courts, where it seems that Microsoft is to be victimized for giving a service to its customers and failing to give to its competitors its confidential business information, have added to the confusion. General Electric and, in particular Jack Welch, are rightly promoted as the exemplars of *Control Your Destiny – Or Someone Else Will*. But every firm is not General Electric and every leader is not Jack Welch.

Businesses large and small need tools, not admonitions. This book is written to explain *how to*, step by step, and to provide you with all the tools you need to succeed through E-Market Dominance. E-Market Dominance is the best; the most customer-centred, the most effective, the most economical way of creating sustainable market dominance through consistently delighted customers. Nothing better enables you to control your own future better than developing and keeping loyal customers. At no time in history has the opportunity been more accessible to companies large and small. You must initiate and sustain dominance thinking in your organization. You must use your customers and employees to become and remain number one in your chosen markets. It is a first-past-the-post situation. You must be number one, or the number one will crush you. 'We are second so we try harder' won't cut it any more. Now the last can truly become first – if they wish it. If they don't wish it they will not survive.

In a recent survey of major businesses less than 30 % could take and respond to an order placed via their wildly expensive web sites. Only 25 % are even thinking about using B2B to improve their procurement. Around 80 % see e-commerce as at best a minor add-on to their business. Mike Mazarr asks an interesting question:

> ❝How many of these folks will still be around a decade from now?❞

Number one in the marketplace does not have to mean first to market

There are a number of advantages to being first into the market:

1   You become recognized as *the* supplier of the product or service that you were first to develop.
2   You have an opportunity to make it so difficult and expensive for competitors to enter the market that they lose money and withdraw.
3   You have a strong possibility of being able to charge premium prices and make exemplary returns before competition finds its feet.

So why do the innovators so seldom come out on top in the long run? If entering a market place shouting 'me too' doesn't work, why do companies who enter late with 'me too' products frequently overtake those who once had the market to themselves?

Here are some of the reasons for this:

1   First to market companies are often product rather than service driven, for as long as they remain the only game in town, first to market will attract all who want, and can afford, their offering.

Too often this means that

2   Early success leads to complacency, the belief that 'we have the formula for success – we cannot fail'.

So that

3   Emergent customer desires are often ignored on the basis of 'we are number one, we know better than the customer what the customer really wants'.

CASE STUDY

Bedford Truck, a British subsidiary of General Motors, was the world number one manufacturer of trucks and buses. When the European trucking industry changed so that journeys became transcontinental, the need for a different kind of truck emerged, Bedford thought they had the answer. American trucks are almost by definition transcontinental, so why not use the American power train?

The reason why using the power train was inappropriate was complicated, but in very simple terms it came down to the customer's need for fuel economy. In America fuel was, and is, cheap; that is not the case on the European continent. The fuel consumption figures for the new Bedford truck were such that the trucking industry would not buy this truck at any price. Sadly, Bedford thought they knew better than the customer. A once great company paid the ultimate price. Many do: that is why the average life of a mature company is now measured in years rather than decades.

Here are some more reasons:

4   The organization is designed around the product. It cannot be responsive to changing customer demands even if it wishes to.
5   There is pressure to recoup development costs as quickly as possible. This means all customers are welcome – the good, the bad and the ugly – and that leads to retaining customers who are simply more trouble than they are worth.
6   Revenues, rather than profits, become the key measure of performance – another reason why bad customers are never jettisoned. Top companies who thrive consistently over many years are ruthless in weeding out the unwanted customer.
7   Expenditure on research and development is high and is focused on what is technically feasible rather than what will sell.

Some years ago Matsushita developed a small screen television to entertain 'home-makers' (are we being politically correct? – wow), while they were doing the jobs in the kitchen which can reasonably be referred to as 'drudgery' (is 'drudgery' a politically correct word? Are we now in the business of pretending that peeling spuds is somehow inspiring?).

The small, portable television that emerged, very late from R&D, was both beautiful and state of the art. It had every conceivable bell and whistle. It also had a price tag more than double what market research had shown to be the expectation of the market, and came out of the R&D department too late to be in the market-place for the peak selling season.

R&D engineers hate to let products go if they don't carry all the state of the art refinements that can be built into them. So market opportunities are lost. The pharmaceutical industry was for many years the worst example of this tendency. Research chemists (with PhDs and an abiding belief in scientific values) were reluctant to pass products to chemical engineers (with MScs and considerable scien-tific training). These in turn were not happy to turn things over to production engineers (master's degrees in engineering), who hated to pass their late-delivery baby to Production (some of whom, God help us, had no degrees at all).

This is the danger that any business faces if the love of their product exceeds the love of the customer.

So what should you do if you are first to market?

First you need to have a strategic plan in place that will enable you to develop and sustain strategic dominance through the development of loyal customers into enthusiastic advocates (see the schema over the page, figure 1.1). You must remain genuinely customer-centred at all times. That means designing or re-designing the organization to really be able to communicate and respond to customers quickly and effectively. Today's technology provides the tools.

Second, just as you need to be merciless in getting rid of customers who are more trouble than they're worth, you also need your salespeople to bring in highly profitable new customers. Do not let them swan around 'servicing' the one's you already have and acting as order takers. Rather, assess your people's training needs and use the assessment as a training opportunity in its own right. But make sure your training works. There is solid incontrovertible evidence that the transfer of learning to the workplace can be raised from a miserable 2%, to better than 90% through peer coaching (see Lambert's Laws of Training over the page too).

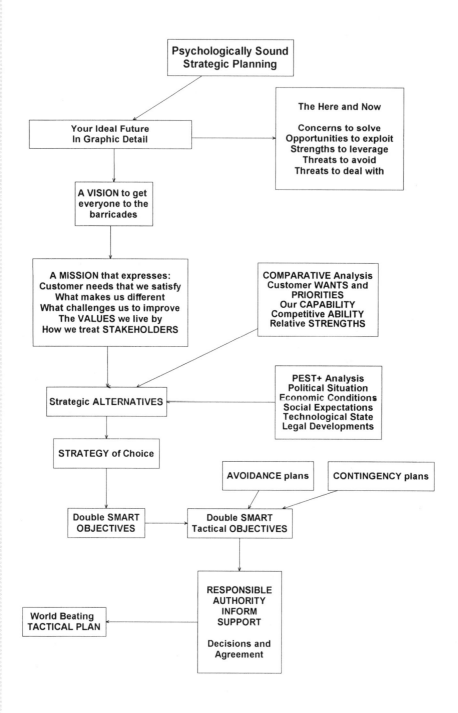

FIGURE 1.1   What strategic planning can do for you

LAMBERT'S LAWS OF TRAINING

· ·

☞ The sorry state of education and training means that, in effect, you confront panzer divisions with the home guard.

PETER MORGAN

☞ Those skilled in defence hide in the deepest depths of the earth, those skilled in attack manoeuvre in the highest heights of the sky. Therefore they can preserve themselves and achieve complete victory.

SUN TSE

The Internet has yet to prove its value as a medium for training although the potential is clearly great. Some laws of training apply to all media:

1. All training and development should lead to measurable outcomes that contribute in a pre-planned way to the attainment of strategic goals. And those outcomes must be routinely tested in the real world of work.
2. Training and development objectives must define precisely what the participant *will* do after training. Not what they 'will be able' to do; 'will be able' is a cop out.
3. Those who are to perform together must be trained together.
4. Where work teams cannot be trained as a unit, groups of at least two must train together to ensure the development of a learning club. The club must always be open to new members.
5. All employees must be taught the skills of peer coaching and given the time and encouragement to use them.
6. Managers must be role models of desired behaviours and professional coaches of the peer coaches.
7. Trainers must be fully advised of how the desired programme fits with company strategy and of the expectations of post-programme performance.
8. Trainers must be flexible in meeting the participants' behaviour goals.
9. Trainers must be committed to their own lifelong learning strategy.
10. Core competencies must be leveraged to develop new products, services, use of resources, and above all, new ways of doing business.

Contrary to what politicians may claim, you do not necessarily need more training. You need better training. When business experiences high-quality training that develops skills and knowledge critical to the strategic plan, and ensures that people exercise and hone those skills, then and only then will business demand more training.

Keep a tight rein on research and development costs. R&D should be market and strategy driven. Otherwise the horse is following the cart. The same goes for other costs: be frugal with all expenditure. Research by Arie De Geus of Harvard shows that long-lived companies, those that prosper for centuries rather than a few years, are flexible, learning communities which are careful always to have money available to pursue market opportunities as they arise.

Never let your people, at any level, believe they have the one unassailable formula for success. The world is changing too rapidly for any formula to work for long. A changing world demands that companies change if they are to succeed. The Internet must deliver new interests that will ensure that customers come back again and again.

Finally, involve everyone in the business in the marketing and strategic process, and do nothing unless it obeys Lambert's Laws of Business:

- There is a compelling strategic or tactical reason for doing it.
- It will pay for itself in a reasonable time.
- It can be explained in clear, easy to understand and inspirational words to those who must make it work.

And if you are not first to market?

You need to do all of the above and more. Start by developing a strategic plan that will enable you to dominate a carefully chosen niche, sector, segment, or global market. This involves identifying the aspirations of the most desirable customers in that market with precision, and comparing your capability to deliver those aspirations with that of your competitors. You should build on your strengths in relation to market needs. So identify those key, profitable customers who you can capture from competition by exploiting your strengths and competencies and leveraging competition's weaknesses.

Next, seek and gain a mandate from these customers to consistently supply them with information, entertainment and opportunities that are personal, expected, relevant, and useful. Use your competencies to rapidly respond to customer needs, wants and desires, and build effective strategic alliances to acquire more new high-quality customers.

Acquire an understanding of technology to the degree you must – that is, to the level you can use it to make money and secure the ongoing prosperity of the business in an increasingly volatile market place. Use your technology to enable you to treat each customer as an individual. You need to serve all customers with such responsiveness to their needs that you establish the rules for doing business in your chosen markets. This means keep it simple: simple for the customer to get what they want and to buy and go on buying.

First to market or 'Johnny come lately', this is what E-Market Dominance gives you the power to do at lowest possible cost.

INTERNATIONAL TRENDS

Since Faith Popcorn's first book, *The Popcorn Report*, made trend analysis popular and highly profitable, the soothsayers and doomsayers have committed themselves to unrelenting labour. The difference between trend analysis and futurism is that trend analysis takes what is and extrapolates from there, whereas futurism takes a look at what may be and guesses what might become of it – in the happy knowledge that whether right or wrong their prognostications will have been long forgotten by the time reality re-asserts itself. To put that another way: futurism is interesting, entertaining and sometimes mind-blowing, while trend analysis illuminates what is happening early enough for serious business people to plan how to exploit the opportunities emerging trends offer.

The Internet accelerates and accentuates global change. The Internet entrepreneur needs to think seriously about trends with one question in mind: 'what could be in this for me?' Professor David Myddleton famously said that 'forecasts are what would have happened if what did happen didn't'. Trend analysis, on the other hand is a reliable guide.

A number of global trends have been identified by such analysis:

- A shift from producing goods to producing, processing and distributing information. Clearly the Web has been and will continue to be crucial to the development and dissemination of information. It will, wisely used, enable the transformation, to quote Nonaka and Tacheuchi, of information into knowledge and knowledge into wisdom.
- Growth in personal care activities, counselling, health and beauty care, and tourism, with emphasis on spiritual and psychological needs.
- Global competition in domestic markets. Somebody out there somewhere wants your customers and the Internet is giving them the opportunity to approach them at minimum cost.
- Localization. The Internet is providing firms large and small with all the marketing advantages of acting as if they were just down the road.
- A shift from centralized decision making toward devolution and greater local autonomy. For the international conglomerate the Internet offers new ability to assess best practice and incorporate it in every aspect of the business. Is there any reason why the same should not be true of the small business? After all, whether your major competitors are around the corner or at the other end of the earth the Internet allows you to see precisely what they are doing and to compare their best with your own. If ever there was an opportunity to leapfrog competition, no matter how big, rich or powerful, this is it.
- A shift from governmental provision of social care toward self-help and care in the community.

- A shift from formal hierarchies to informal networks bound by a shared perception of common interests. The Internet provides exciting opportunities to turn common interests into low-cost/no-cost sales.
- Growing inequality of resources between the northern and the southern hemispheres. But the resources of as yet 'underdeveloped' nations will increase and in terms of numbers the growth of buying power will open massive markets. It is an interesting irony that with the accelerating spread of the Internet there will be people who have not made a telephone call before they are using the World Wide Web.
- Growing inequality between rich and poor in the so-called 'developed' nations.
- Consumers having a vastly greater range of options to choose from than ever in the past.
- Greater transparency and more opportunities to compare prices and offers.
- Time and convenience are becoming increasingly important buying motives among those with disposable income, but with too many demands on their time.
- Growth of religious fundamentalism.

Any of these trends may create new market opportunities – or threats. Keep your eyes on developments and always be ready to adjust your strategy to fully exploit worthwhile trends or to defend yourself. E-Market Dominance and the contact it provides with loyal customers will inform you of the trends that are essential knowledge to you and for your business.

ESSENTIAL QUESTIONS FOR EVERY BUSINESS

☞ Any fool can provide easy answers. It takes a genius to ask
the easy questions.
ALBERT EINSTEIN

☞ Capital isn't scarce; vision is.
MICHAEL MILKEN

☞ I have taken more out of alcohol than alcohol has ever taken
out of me.
WINSTON CHURCHILL

Easy questions and hard answers

Before I visit a client who wishes to plan a dominance strategy, I ask the top team to analyse their business in some detail. This saves them both time and money when we meet. A key question is 'what is your business really about?' It is surprising how few can answer this apparently easy question without a deal of soul-searching. The problem is that if the top team are unsure or divided on this question there is no way on earth that they can communicate the big, inspiring picture of their business to employees, customers, suppliers and investors be they on the Internet or off it. The team needs to decide what their answer is and, more importantly, turn that decision into action.

The same goes for other 'easy' questions, which are really about how you conceive your business. Here is a list of such questions:

CONCEPTUAL QUESTIONS

What business are you really in?

How do others see you?

Are you innovators or augmentors?

What are your thinking patterns?

What are your resources?

What are your assumptions?

Do you reward creative thinking
– and the associated risk-taking?

How does the future look?

What are the appropriate risks to take?

How do you develop your goals?

What are your alternatives?

Should you consider starting over?

Do you have the courage to confront
what the marketplace is telling you?

Answering such 'easy' conceptual questions is harder than you might think. Here are some questions I ask the top team so they do not accept easy answers to them:

HARD QUESTIONS

1   Is there consensus in the top team about whether the company is:
    (a) thriving or surviving?
    (b) growing or stagnating?
    (c) leading or following?

2   Are you in danger of calling agreement consensus when it is merely group-think?

3   Do you have and believe in a vision – or have you just strung together a few fine-sounding words?

4   Do you share an absolute determination to be the best of the best and become the organization that shapes the future of your industry?

Once these hard questions have been answered, we can move on to questions about strategy:

STRATEGIC QUESTIONS

What is your best current strategy?

What do you want to happen?

What is the organizing principle?

Are you too complex for easy focus?

What segments, sectors or niches are you aiming at?

What attracts you to these?

What are your resources?

What are the trends?

How good are the omens?

Are you proposing high-risk innovations?

How does your proposed strategy limit and control the level of risk?

What special factors influence your your business environment?

What are the consequences of your current strategy?

Who are you addressing?

How ready are you?

What processes do you have for feedback, evaluation and review?

What are your future strategic options?

Would you be comfortable as low-risk trend followers?

Once again you need to beware of coming up with too easy answers to these questions of strategy. Time for some more self-examination:

MORE HARD QUESTIONS

1   Are you thinking far enough ahead?

2   Have you organized the business to ensure that you can build or acquire the competencies and competitive strengths you will need?

3   Are the things you are doing today thought through so they contribute to the achievement of the strategy?

4   Do your present actions at the very least ensure you will be in the market place, strong and fully resourced when the great day of opportunity dawns?

5   What are your specific reasons for believing you can survive up to your planning horizon?

6   Have you created a 'story' around the future you want, which you can articulate and live every day? (Current psychological research by Howard Gardner of Harvard suggests that people – employees, customers, suppliers, strategic allies – all respond most positively and fully to corporate stories and myths.)

MINI CASE STUDY

Three of the great pragmatic story tellers of our generation

- RICHARD BRANSON, when planning to enter a new industry or a new market, tells and re-lives the story of 'Jack the Giant Killer'. It is more credible to believe that a privileged son of a comfortable family is well able to punch his weight when he takes on opposition from any organisation. His battles are those of corporate baron versus corporate baron.

- WINSTON CHURCHILL told, or had others tell for him, the story of the brave white knight standing courageously alone against overwhelming odds. This in spite of the fact that he was so subject to depression that he would take to his bed for days in moments of crisis and was habitually the worse for drink by ten in the morning. I love his saying 'I have taken more out of alcohol than alcohol has taken out of me'. It was probably no less than the unvarnished truth.

- JACK WELCH constantly lives the story of personal and corporate invincibility combined with the highest possible standards of public service. He promotes himself as a practical and pragmatic visionary. It is a little difficult to see him in that role when you take into account the deliberate or accidental dumping of toxins into the Hudson River.

The important thing about these stories is not whether they are true or are not. It is that they are believed. The three people quoted share a genius for 'walking the talk'.

So now for a final list of questions about tactics, to see how well you walk the talk.

TACTICAL QUESTIONS

What are the key activities?	What standards of performance are
Where are the bottlenecks?	necessary?
What kind of managers do you need?	How do you increase productivity?
How do you maintain control?	How do you get/give feedback?
What is your power base?	How do you allocate resources?
How do you communicate the	How do you avoid blame-fixing?
vision?	What is the right management style?
How do you walk the talk?	How do you build commitment?
How do you maintain your values?	How do you decide on useful
How do you stay focused?	measurement?

How do you communicate change?	How do you recognize the need for objectives?
How do you celebrate success?	How do you clearly differentiate
How do you reward desired behaviour?	between efficient and effective behaviours?

You don't have to go into a retreat to think about questions such as these. The real successes of this world make such thought a constant activity – a few minutes at a time. One good idea that results from considering these questions may be worth a great deal. The practice of thinking about building and using that thinking as part of the E-Market Dominance process will provide a life time of prosperity.

A CONVERSATION WITH A CONSULTANT

☞ Marketing and innovation, these are the drivers of profit in a business. The rest are costs.

PETER DRUCKER

We said earlier that it is at least as important to plan your success on the Internet as it is in the 'real world'. The cost of getting on line may be modest but the opportunities are not. You owe it to yourself to think things through carefully. These days, when I advise a corporation's senior team on developing a new business strategy, the Internet is an important feature I ensure they all take very seriously.

Here are some of the questions I typically ask to make sure my clients are planning for online success and are not assuming that a Web presence is simply more of the old routine. Consider each question carefully. The additional business and the profits it will bring will make you glad you took the time.

As you will see, I ask lots of questions. The first list is for those of you who do not yet have a website, the second for those who do. The third is for both, for it is about identifying market opportunities for all operators, be they in the dirt world or cyberspace.

I.   IF YOU DO NOT YET HAVE A WEBSITE . . .

- In an ideal world where anything is possible, what would you choose to accomplish through your Web presence?
- What is your objective for increased sales in the first year?
- How will a website support the achievement of this goal?

- What are your specific cost-cutting goals?
- How do you expect to measure the economies of being online?
- How will your people become more productive?
- How will you enjoy low-cost/no-cost entry into new markets?
- How will you switch from make and sell to sell and make?
- What products or services can be delivered online?
- What intermediaries can you stop having to pay?
- What are you doing to make your best customers more loyal?
- Some experts believe that online business will take off and will grow at a cumulative rate of at 30 % a year for the next five years. What are you doing to ensure you can handle the distribution and customer service problems that could arise if your business grew that fast or faster? (At this stage clients grin and say: 'That's a problem I would like to have to deal with when it happens.' To which I rather bad temperedly reply, 'Never mind the problem. What's your solution?')
- What are your goals for customer-service improvements?
- How will you measure your improvements in customer service?
- What motivates your best customers to buy?
- What motivates them to buy from you?
- What motivates others with the same or better potential to buy elsewhere?
- Who do your best customers also do business with or get information from on the Internet?
- What are your goals for doing joint ventures on the Internet?
- Can you list the Internet chat rooms, publications, newsgroups that your best customers participate in?
- What do your best customers say about you and your service online and off it?
- How do your best customers perceive your business?
- What precisely are your competitors doing online and what are you doing to ensure a competitive edge?
- As they change how will you stay ahead of the pack?
- What is the profile of your best customers?
- What future needs of your customers will your online presence enable you to satisfy?
- How do you plan to identify changing customer needs and expectations more quickly than your competition?
- How are you building right now the competencies that you will need in the most profitable markets of the future?
- What is your online marketing budget?

- What is your advertising policy?
- How many Internet PR pieces do you intend to have published each month?
- Who will publish them?
- Why will they publish your stuff?
- What are your growth limitations?
- What about order processing and fulfilment, e-mail capacity, credit-card processing and security, distribution and delivery, customer service and customer delight? What concrete steps have you put in place today to ensure your optimal future growth potential?

II. IF YOU ALREADY HAVE A WEBSITE . . .

- Who outside the company has checked your website for speed of loading and ease of use?
- Do the headlines on each page sell to the customer as well as to the search engines?
- What are the specific benefits you use?
- Are all contact details on each page?
- Do you give all potential customers clear and compelling reasons to give you their e-mail addresses for further information?
- If I visited your page looking for X, what specifically would make me want to permit you to keep in touch with me?
- How do you measure website traffic?
- How do you measure the sales per visitor?
- What keywords do people use to get to your site?
- What other sites or newsrooms do they come from?
- How often do you check the search engines to ensure you are in the top ten?
- How do you make the required changes when you find you are slipping?
- How many times each day do your people check e-mails?
- How often do you check your auto-responder messages to customers to be certain they are still relevant?
- When was the product or service information you are currently sending out last updated?
- Where do you display customer testimonials and how do you use them to build a prospect's confidence in you as the preferred supplier?

III. IDENTIFYING OPPORTUNITIES: DOWN AND DIRTY
MARKETING
. . . .

☞ Defence is for times of lack, attack is for times of plenty.

SUN TSE

☞ Those who render others helpless without fighting are best of all.

SUN TSE

- How do you capture all customers, prospects, suppliers, distributors, affiliates, prospective affiliate promoters, and joint-venture partners' e-mail addresses?
- Where would you find a list of, say, potential joint-venture partners if you wanted to do it personally in a hurry?
- What is the average purchase per visit?
- What is the purchase lifetime of the average customer?
- How frequently does the average customer buy?
- What parts of your range are 'cash cows'?
- How are they promoted?
- What parts are 'stars'?
- How are they promoted?
- What items are 'question marks' at present?
- How are you keeping the costs of market testing them within bounds?
- What do you do to ensure that you can lose 'dogs' without losing customers?

Note: Cash cows are established product lines that generate high revenues without further investment. Stars are high-potential product lines that still require considerable investment of money and effort to market, but which are selling well. Question marks are possible future stars but at present need thorough market testing to justify a high investment of time, creativity and money. Dogs are slow-moving low-value lines that probably cost more to supply than they generate in profit. It is probably a good exercise to look at clients and customers using the same definitions and the same nomenclature – but not in their hearing!)

- What specifically do you do to lengthen the product life cycle of cash cows and accelerate the wide acceptance of stars?
- What is your policy for getting rid of customers who are and will remain more hassle than they are worth?

- How often do you communicate with your customers?
- How do you personalize communications?
- What is in your signature file for e-mails?
- Which host/beneficiary deals are bringing in the most business?
- Which are bringing in the most profitable business?
- Which are competition's most profitable customers?
- What is your strategy for capturing them?
- What is your unique selling proposition online?
- What is it in the dirt world?
- What is your referral system?
- How do you reward referrals?
- If you could improve one key aspect of your marketing at a stroke, what would it be?

I cannot pretend this is an exhaustive list of the questions I ask in any specific situation. Good questions lead to supplementary questions and they only have relevance in the light of what has already been discussed. Similarly, not all the questions listed will be the key questions to which your specific situation and strategy demands full and careful answers. However, they should be relevant and at worst will remind you of the important questions you ought to be asking yourself.

In any case, from a marketer's viewpoint, whether you market on line or in the local flea market, there are some questions you must always keep in the front of your mind. Here they are:

IV.   MARKETING FOR ALL . . .

- Who is my best type of customer?
- What do these customers need?
- What do they want? (Remember: WOMAN – Wants Overcome [lack of] Money And Needs)
- What motivates them to buy?
- What motivates them to buy from a specific supplier?
- How can I give them more of what they like?
- How are their interests, needs and desires changing?
- If they want A today could they be persuaded to want B tomorrow?
- What is the lifetime value of a customer?
- How much can I spend to attract the right customer?
- How will I delight and go on delighting my customers?

- How can I dump those who are more trouble than they are worth without damaging my reputation, credibility and image?
- How can I make the best, most economical use of emerging technology to delight and go on delighting my customers?

Ten tips for the small (and large) business website

Finally, here are my top ten tips to get your websites working well.

1 Identity: be clear from the customer's viewpoint about who you are and what you offer.
2 Take a pride in your expertise, but don't try to push what customers don't want.
3 Be creative, but never cloud the purpose of your business with cleverness for its own sake.
4 Constantly look at what works for others, adapt and adopt the best that your creativity and budget can manage.
5 Build customer loyalty and you will build employee loyalty without effort.
6 Deliver more than you promise.
7 Remember customers on line are short on time and attention, not money.
8 Make it easy for people to buy on line.
9 Avoid pop-up advertising and 'get off my site' banners that distract customers from their purpose.
10 Be consistent. Market the same way when you're fat, dumb and happy. Ensure that your messages always reflect the image you want. Ensure that the customer is never confused by conflicting messages.
11 Make it easy to contact you.

(OK, we know that's eleven, but always deliver more than you promise.)

Make no mistake about it: dominance is the only real game in town, on the Internet or off. If you don't specify your markets and then establish the rules of engagement, someone else will. If they do you will be in an increasingly expensive spiral of attempting to catch up with the leaders. They never stand still, so catching up is virtually impossible. At best it is the most expensive option. Put that way it is no option at all. You may not fully appreciate it as yet, but through the Internet you have been handed a golden opportunity to leapfrog the best in your business. This book is written to explain in detail how you may exploit that opportunity. You may as well go for it, if only because if you don't when someone, somewhere does, you will be the loser. The cost of losing is becoming higher by the day. On the other hand, the rewards of winning are greater too. Market dominance, especially e-market dominance, is one game that is definitely worth the candle.

WHAT YOU WILL HAVE LEARNED IN THIS CHAPTER

☞ The Internet creates a level playing field for both large and small companies. This may be a short-term phenomenon whilst the commercial world wakes up to the immense power the online world can command.

☞ The Internet opens the opportunity for relative newcomers to become the dominant players in their markets. The ability of site visitors to compare alternative suppliers can mean that the leaner, more nimble e-start-up can out-price, out-perform and maybe even out-last the conventional business trying to convert to an online environment.

☞ Half-hearted commitment to the new technologies just will not cut the mustard. On the other hand, many opportunities presented by the new online world are limited only by your imagination and energy. Give it all you've got!

CHAPTER TWO

THINGS DON'T WORK LIKE THEY USED TO DO

☞ Those who are first on the battlefield are at ease.

SUN TSE

☞ Far and away the best prize life has to offer is the chance to work hard at work worth doing.

THEODORE ROOSEVELT

WHAT YOU WILL LEARN IN THIS CHAPTER

☞ You will understand why traditional marketing techniques give less reliable results than they once did – and why things will get worse.

☞ You will know how to increase the response to your traditional marketing efforts.

☞ You will have practical guidance to help you choose between different marketing tactics.

☞ You will understand why, although there are new, effective and exciting approaches to marketing (which this book will explain in detail), you still need to understand and use traditional methods to some degree – and know how to use them well.

☞ You will build the knowledge, skills and competencies of offline techniques to leverage your e-business.

BEFORE WE GO TOO FAR

We may need to market in the real world before we can get people to look at our cyberspace offering. This is becoming both less effective and more expensive. So to save money and avoid disappointment we need to be smart when it comes to old-fashioned dirt-world marketing.

This morning a realization struck me like a club. I am not too smart. I was making my breakfast (a healthy meal of various fruits, bran flakes and milk) when I wandered from the kitchen to my bedroom. I stood by the bed, wondering what I was doing there. A piece of doggerel came into my mind:

> 66 I find I'm much perplexed by fate.
>
> Come here and tell me girlie
>
> Is it that I'm maturing late,
>
> Or simply rotting early? 99

Slowly I remembered. I needed a knife. Now I don't keep knives in the bedroom. I haven't deteriorated that far. That is what brought it home to me. I'm simply not very bright.

This novel understanding of the simple fact that I have shortcomings brought into my mind a number of examples of just how dotty I've become. I wander off and forget where I'm going, let alone why. I almost quote Ogden Nash and other poets, but get the details wrong because I can't remember where I put the book. I push on doors marked 'pull' and when they fail to open I push harder. In short I act just like the marketing industry. Let me explain what I mean before my brain softens altogether.

Ever since some unknown bard composed another piece of doggerel:

> 66 He who whispers down a well
>
> About the goods he has to sell
>
> Never makes as many dollars
>
> As he who climbs a tree and hollers: 99

marketers have sought to shout louder and more luridly than each other. Back when my poetic hero Ogden was bemoaning the sprouting of billboards all over the United States there was something to be said for metaphorically shouting louder than your neighbour. In some of the less undulating states of America there might even be a small frisson of pleasure to be gained from the occasional sight of a garish outdoor advertisement as you travelled, relatively slowly in your model 'T'. A bigger, brighter, brasher billboard might even make your day by relieving some of the boredom of a journey across Iowa or Nebraska. Today in many states billboards line the road in such gratuitous abundance that we make an almost conscious effort to ignore them as we speed by. Like Ogden Nash we begin to fear that, thanks to their unwanted prodigality, we may 'never see a tree at all'.

It is the same with television advertising. There was a time, my children, when with the birth of commercial television, old fogies like me sat mesmerized by a tiny black and white picture watching with wonder and rapt attention anything that was offered. Television advertisements became the staple of our culture. We all agreed that a Double Diamond worked wonders and that you were never alone with a Strand and proved it by sharing, in the playground, slightly rude jokes with the advertisers' tags as tag lines. But it is not like that any more.

Today we are bombarded with advertisements as never before. The advertising profession 'knows' that frequency builds brands, that brands build trust and trust builds sales. So, at massive cost, they show ads over and over while we mindlessly surf the seventy or more channels now available to us simply to get away from them. But like me in my dotage, marketers push harder on doors marked 'pull'. The advertising becomes more entertaining in an attempt to capture and hold our attention, but in that entertainment the message is lost or non-existent. I happily stop my channel hopping for a moment to watch the ongoing war between that gangster-like lizard and the frogs, but I don't drink the beer. And there is a limit to the number of times that I'm prepared to watch the same little skit. In the US we are bombarded by upwards of 3,000 commercials every day. They try cute little tricks to stop us reaching for the remote, such as blending the advertisement so closely into the programme that we find ourselves confused as we are transported from an apartment in rainy Seattle to an anonymous beach where a gorgeous young woman in a red bathing suit is cavorting about after consuming her healthy breakfast cereal.

We may be confused, but not for long. We soon reach for the remote or wander off to the kitchen for a Millers Light or an unhealthy doughnut. I'm sorry to have to say this of my peers, but you have it wrong my friends: frequency doesn't work any more. Like the fad of job rotation which flourished back in the 1970s, it may sometimes briefly entertain, but most of the time it's just money down the drain.

There are two basic types of advertisement. One is known in the trade as a 'tombstone'. This is the glossy or super-smart advertisement that serves no other purpose than to bring the brand to our attention. When we see a low-angle shot of the latest luxury car and the lovely lady such cars are supposed to attract, we are not expected to break the piggy bank and rush off to the nearest dealer to place our order. We are expected simply to sigh longingly as we gaze, at car or girl according to taste, and dream of the day when we may get our hands on the car, the girl, or both. Howard Shenson used to say that such advertisements made a point through being pointless and he may well have been right. His argument ran something like this: 'Such advertisements make us believe that the companies are successful. They must be successful because how else could they afford to spend so much money to so little purpose?'

The second type of advertisement is known as a 'haemorrhoid ad'. It is so called because it says, in effect, 'If you have a pain in the butt, or elsewhere, we have the ointment'. Haemorrhoid advertisements are seldom glossy. They make little money for the agency. They give no pleasure to the creative types. They just sell the product.

They only sell, of course, under certain conditions. First they must be placed where they will reach those who have the right sort of pain in the appropriate place. In short, they must reach those who are in the market for what you offer.

'Reach' is a word beloved of advertising agencies. Reach is expensive. Reach brings in lots of commission. What it doesn't do is bring in lots of sales. Say 'reach' to an advertising man and he will smile the gentle smile of one who sees his bank balance spiralling upwards. To him 'reach' means placing your advertisement where it will be seen by as many people as possible, the vast majority of whom will have not the slightest interest in you or your offering.

In the US there is one day each year when you may be certain that not only is the whole country glued to the television, but we are all watching the same thing. Whether we like football or not, the Super Bowl Final brings us together in social gatherings in which we shout at the players and the officials, argue about every play, drink copiously and eat vast quantities of junk food which no considerate person would throw before hungry swine. The US is, for this one occasion, truly one united nation – though whether 'under God' is debatable. All you have to do to have your advertisement shown to the whole population is to shell out a few million dollars. So advertisers pay vast sums. What do we, their public do? We take the opportunity to slip out to the bathroom or get another beer or another twinkie from the kitchen. We turn on our friends and explain to them in simple language why it is that, if ignorance is truly bliss, when it comes to understanding football, they must be the happiest people alive. I, as a British rugby enthusiast, try to explain to an uncomprehending gathering why the tackled player should have passed or set up the ball for a ruck or maul before his three hundred pound opponent slammed him to the ground. We 'wash our hands', we consume, we drink, we lecture, and we fight. The one thing that we don't do is watch the super-glossy, super-clever, and mega-expensive advertisement. (Unless, of course those lizards and frogs come on, when we say: 'Hey this is clever!' as we swill down a different make of beer.)

At best 'reach' as used by advertising agencies means that you can visualize the potential audience as inhabiting a huge triangle. To the agency the bigger the audience the better; their interest is in the size of the audience not its quality as potential buyers. Those few, those very few, that gallant band of brothers who might, just might, be interested in what you have to sell are a tiny minority in the sharpest point of the apex. They are expected to turn the spotlight of their attention onto what you have to offer for long enough to get the urge to part with real money in exchange for the satisfactions that you promise.

It used to work that way perhaps, but no longer. So the agencies push ever harder on a door that doesn't open that way, and advertisements become glossier, increasingly clever, more expensive, more frequent and less effective as they add to the almost unbounded clutter that is modern marketing. Reach, frequency and tombstones are what advertising professionals offer to their corporate clients and the more they offer them, the less good they do.

BUT SURELY A BUSINESS NEEDS TO ADVERTISE?

A business needs to communicate. It needs to inform all those people who might buy the goods or services that it offers what those goods and services are and what they do for the customer. Sometimes the way to do this is through advertising and sometimes not. Let us lay down some ground rules.

GROUND RULES FOR ADVERTISING

1 Only use paid advertising when there is clearly no better alternative.
   Press releases, direct mail, word of mouth, seminars, conference presentations, point of sale promotions, articles in trade journals, letters to the editor or networking may be better and will certainly be cheaper.

2 If you must advertise make sure that a high percentage of those who will see your message have an interest in what you offer.
   Avoid being seduced by the agency view of reach. Reach has to mean that you place your advertisement only where it will be seen by a large number of potential customers rather than getting the idle attention of uninterested passers-by. Media are comprehensively listed in *BRAD* (*SRDS* in the US) and *Willings Press Guide*. If you have designed the proverbial better mousetrap these publications will guide you to *The Mouse Haters Gazette* – if there is such a recondite publication.

3 Design advertisements that lead the customer to take action. Haemorrhoids are undoubtedly unpleasant, but given the unenviable choice between haemorrhoids or a tombstone, I think I might learn to live with them.

THE KEY STEPS TO SUCCESSFUL SENSIBLE-BUDGET ADVERTISING

1 Choose your medium with care

Look at the analysis of the traditional media over the page. Having identified appropriate media organizations from *Willings*, *BRAD* or *SRDS*, contact them and ask for a 'media pack'. This will tell you:

- The demographic breakdown of the readership or audience.
- The numbers who buy the magazine or service.
- The numbers who read, watch or listen to the publication or service.
- What those readers, listeners or viewers are interested in right now.
- What they are arguing about on the 'letters' page or elsewhere.
- What is likely to excite the editor or production team by raising new issues – contentious or otherwise. (They generally prefer contentious.)

The traditional media

1 Newspapers
Dailies, weeklies, Sundays and local free sheets.

Advantages	Disadvantages
Wide readership	Circulation pattern may not cover all prospects efficiently
Readers are actively seeking information	Publication pattern may not suit your needs
Advertisements are easily torn out and kept for future reference	News and other ads compete for reader attention
Credibility can be high	Restricted ability to target prospects
Illustration is getting easier and less expensive	
Ads can be positioned to select readers (sports pages ... business section)	
Wide choice of ad size and cost	
Geographically and demographically selective (from the *Financial Times* to the *Muggletown Monthly Advertiser*)	

2 Magazines
Leisure, academic, hobbies, economics, politics, general interest, home and garden, politics, trade journals, soft pornography, business, regional, nature ... the list is endless. If the people who constitute your market share an interest, there is sure to be at least one magazine that caters for them.

Advantages	Disadvantages
Effective targeting	Scheduling inflexible – long lead time to publication
Prestige	Lacks immediacy, which in turn can suggest lack of urgency for response
Full-colour potential	Camera-ready artwork can be expensive
More readers than circulation may suggest (Have you too seen a compelling ad while in the doctor's waiting room?)	
Ads can be supported by articles, letters to the editor and press releases	
Good deals are possible if you buy space close to deadline	

3 Radio

Advantages	Disadvantages
High frequency at relatively low cost	No pictures on the radio (except those splendid pictures of the imagination)
Very flexible	Lacks permanence
Cheap to produce tapes	Usually highly localized
Can be very creative	Cannot put across detail effectively
Low cost per listener	

4 Television

Advantages	Disadvantages
High impact – sight, sound movement	Production costs high
Sometimes memorable	You can't 'do it yourself'
Convincing demonstration of product or service convincing	High transmission cost
Closest approximation to face-to-face communication	Desirable spots super expensive
High credibility – 'as seen on television'	Prospects channel hop or go and put the kettle on when ads are screened
Can be entertaining and memorable	Impact depends on frequency
	Difficult to target prospects
	No 'message' in 30 seconds or less

With this information you can make an informed decision about these questions:

- Is this the right medium for you?
- Might a cheaper approach than advertising get better results?
- Could paid advertising and editorial work in tandem?
- Should you become a radio or television personality?
- Might you usefully offer the editor a regular column or an 'agony aunt' piece that may turn you into the world's first 'mousetrap guru?'

2 So you decide to advertise

Design your advertisement with care.

- Create a heading or headline which will get the attention of every reader, listener or viewer who is in the market for your product or service: 'Do *You* Hate Mice?' Make sure you speak to your potential customers personally. Remember that the word 'you' is the strongest word in the advertising lexicon. Speak to your customers as if in a one-to-one conversation and grab their attention quickly. They haven't a lot of time to spare.
- Make a promise: 'The new Acme Mousetrap will rid your home of mice more quickly, cleanly and cheaply than any competitive product.' 'New' is another powerful word, but it must mean what it says. We are all tired of 'new and improved' – meaning same old stuff in a different box.

MINI CASE STUDY

In the US the Lufthansa marketing team has based its recent advertising strategy on the fact that too many companies claim 'new and improved' after doing very little. The airline makes that point and then simply lists the improvements from the customer point of view. Not so obviously clever as some campaigns perhaps, but effective in one of the world's most competitive marketplaces.

- Provide credible evidence that your promise will be fulfilled. 'Professor Felix Kattzenpuss of the Vienna Institute of Mouse Annihilation says "in tests nine out of ten mouzes preverred zis method of execution."'
- Tell the customers precisely how to get the benefit of your product or service while they remain excited by it. 'Ring toll free 800 Mouse today while limited stocks last.'
- You may wish to provide an incentive to call immediately. People are greedy, selfish and short of time. (Much more about this later.) 'The first

one hundred purchasers will receive, completely free of charge, the Acme patented mouse interment shovel.'

3 Count what you get for your money

Remember that any advertisement must generate at least enough additional profit to pay for itself and for the next advertisement. If that is all it does, it is a failure. If it produces less it is an abject failure.

TEST IS AN IMPORTANT FOUR-LETTER WORD

When possible any marketing initiative should be carefully and simply tested before it is rolled out. For example, a direct-mail piece and the list of potential customers to which it is being sent should be tested before a full mailing campaign is initiated. If you send out one hundred sales letters and less than two sales result, take a careful second look at the message, the price and the list. With advertising such a low-cost test strategy is not usually an option. You do the best you can, you pay your money and you keep your fingers crossed. So when you must advertise, check the content first and after the event the results, with scrupulous care.

Pre-testing your advertising copy

Having carefully selected your medium, so you have the highest probability of reaching the greatest number of people with whom you need to communicate – those with the need or desire for the benefits that you offer and money to satisfy their desire – pre-test your copy. Start by looking at the Copy Checker schema on the next page (figure 2.1) and then at this check-list of questions:

PRE-TEST CHECKLIST
. . . .
1   Does the advertisement demand immediate, favourable attention?
2   Is the headline powerful enough to dominate the infoclutter (the excessive 'information' to which we are subjected daily) that surrounds it?
3   Am I offering real benefits that are clear and desirable to my chosen audience?
4   Is the message concise but unambiguous? Does it address a known need or desire?
5   Is the layout clear and easy to read, without wasting too much money on so-called 'white space'? (Black print on a white background remains the easiest to read, while reverse printing takes time and people are no longer generous with their time. For pictures, colour is fine, though expensive. For the text it is not so good. You might like to exercise your own judgement on the recent

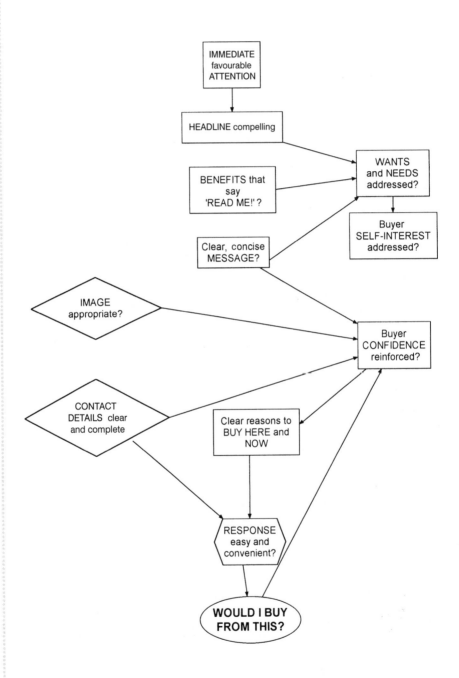

FIGURE 2.1   The Copy Checker

> BT advertisement, featuring a large, expensive blank square with a message
> around its border suggesting that BT can help you to think out of the box.)
>
> 6 Is the image of the firm conveyed appropriate and positive?
> 7 Would the stimulus to action now work even on those with only a lukewarm
>   interest in my offering? (Am I appealing to people's self-interest?)
> 8 Is it absolutely clear how to respond?
> 9 Are the simple things like address, telephone number, e-mail address and fax
>   number accurate and easy to find?
> 10 Does the advertisement show why you should buy from me rather than my
>   competitors?
> 11 Would I spend my own money on what is offered in this advertisement?
> 12 How would I rate the overall impression created? What will be the 'gut'
>   response?

Only if the answers to each of these questions are positive does your advertisement stand a realistic chance of competing for attention and action in the 'noise' which surrounds every piece of present day communication. Being 'good enough' doesn't cut it any more. We are in a world that is overloaded with messages. Yours must give people a compelling reason to give you some of their very limited attention. The most compelling reason to attend is 'here is something I want to know about – and I want to know now'. People are selfish, greedy and in a hurry. Entice them, play to their greed and make it snappy.

Testing the effectiveness of advertising

The more clutter there is to clog up the workings of the so-called 'information economy', the more important it is that you check carefully to ensure you know which marketing investments are giving the quickest return. If you have placed an advertisement, always measure the response. For the printed word there have been three traditional approaches to measurement.

The first is to get customers to return your advertisement with their order. You can do this by offering a small but valuable gift to those who clip and return the advertisement. This approach will not give you the whole picture – some will ignore all incentives to get the scissors out – but in general it will give you an idea of where they saw your announcement. This is particularly important if you place advertising in more than one publication at a time and need to know which gave you the best results. It has the advantage that if you forget to place a code on your advertisement to show what publication it appeared in, clippings from different papers or magazines will have different copy on the reverse which helps you to run them to earth.

The second approach is to include a coupon to be clipped and returned with the order. Coupons can be coded or you can check the reverse as explained above. Either way you will have a strong indicator of where you are getting the best bang for your buck. You can ask that buyers quote the name of the publication when they place an order. This is frequently done and it is often of very doubtful value. Many people simply see too many publications to be sure where they saw something as ephemeral as most advertisements. You may end up collecting the names of papers or magazines where you have never bought space. In the extreme case this can be useful: if large numbers of your buyers indicate that they read a publication which you have not used, there may be even larger numbers of readers of that publication who would buy your product, but who do not read the publication where you have placed your advertisement. It is unlikely you will get enough errors to put you on the right track, but if you do it is wise to use the information, even though it is in a sense, false. Because radio and television advertisements can't be clipped, it is better to ask where people heard or saw your offering promoted than to assume that any increase in sales relates directly to the advertisement.

One of the wonderful advantages of the Internet is that these tests become automatic. This is great because they are still essential.

If your advertising fails to bring in sales

Do not put all failures at the door of marketing. It is perfectly possible to get people to beat a path to your door only to drive them away again with poor sales skills or bad service. Here are some possible causes of the failure of your advertisements to bring in sales, allocated to both symptoms:

Causes of advertisement failure

Poor Response	Symptom Great interest, poor subsequent sales
Message too vague	Poor offer
Insufficient frequency	Inappropriate sales techniques
Ad too small to compete	Lack of sales skills
Wrong medium or wrong publication	Depressed economy
Placement of ad poor	Wrong stage in buying cycle

Bad timing of transmission
   – wrong audience
	Poor promotional material
	   or poor follow up

No demand for product or service	Style of follow-up material inappropriate

When times are hard and prospects few, the strategic decision is often taken to increase the marketing budget and go for a greater share of a depressed market. This may work for the mega-corporation with virtually bottomless pockets. For the small firm it may simply speed its demise. There are wonderful low-cost approaches to marketing that place the small firm almost on an equal footing with the giant: indeed the rest of this book will tell your company, be it large or small, exactly what to use and how to use it to generate highly profitable sales in good times and bad. But first, let's complete our survey of traditional marketing practices and advice on how to make conventional marketing techniques the foundation for super success.

SO WHAT IS DIFFERENT IF YOU ADVERTISE ON THE INTERNET?

To begin at the very beginning, where so many are getting it depressingly wrong you have the chance to get it right. Advertising agencies have conned business into believing that building a Web site is a brand exercise – that is why you see what are essentially tombstone advertisements in electronic form. They may be beautiful to behold, but you can't buy on them. A study quoted by Marcus Bicknell of CMGI (owners of more than 60 Internet companies, including giants like AltaVista) shows that 83 % of visitors to corporate sites in Europe go away never to return, because they can't actually buy. Advertising on the Internet is about building revenues and profits. It does not bombard people (unless you opt for those silly and intensely irritating 'pop-up' ones; rather, people choose to look at it. If having looked they think 'so what?', all that creativity, all those smarts, are wasted.

Web advertising should be haemorrhoid advertising. It should say 'forget the brand, you want this, you may even need this, and you want it now, so here's how you get your hands on it'. The other key difference is that technology allows us to measure the effects of advertising right down to the customer level. The old agency concept of reach goes out the window. What businesses want to know now is:

- How many customers bought?
- What exactly did they buy?
- How much did they buy?
- Did they come back to buy more?
- Have they happily agreed to provide us with pertinent information that enables us to serve them better?
- Have they agreed to receive more information or entertainment?
- Are we likely to have their business for life?
- Do they keep coming back?

Putting it bluntly, the so-called 'creatives' of the agencies are on the hook and wriggling. At last advertising is being measured for its results and not for the intangibles loved by the agencies, such as 'how many people think they saw the advertisement and think they remember it?'

Once you are on the Web you can analyse the market place as never before. Or to be more accurate, there are companies out there who will do it for you. You may want to look at the following sites to get a better idea of what is being achieved. Some of those listed both sell and track advertising on the Internet. Others track e-mails.

www.nielson-netratings.com

www.flycast.com

www.adknowledge.com

www.enliven.com

www.doubleclick.com

www.mediametrix.com

www.mediaplex.com

The Web makes it possible to test advertisements to see if they are bringing in additional business as they should. Never forget that even free advertising is not worth having unless it brings you measurable business results and online profits. The message is clear: test, test and test again and take full advantage of what the web makes possible to build your business now and in the future.

Brian Ash is the expert in this field: you can look forward to his chapters on how to go about making massive profits on the Web. But before you start collecting the cash you need to be sure your approach to traditional marketing is sound.

SIT RIGHT DOWN AND WRITE YOURSELF A LETTER

As infoclutter has caused the effectiveness of advertising to fall, the traditional marketer's faith in direct mail has risen. Strangely, one of the worst ideas thought up by the 'show me a bandwagon and I'll drive it' school of consultancy to damage business reinforced such faith for a while. Down-sizing improved the chances of getting your mail into the right hands as more executives found themselves forced to take on the onerous task of opening their own mail. By 1999 52% of marketing spend in the US was devoted to direct mail. Direct mail can be very effective. New variations on the direct mail theme make it very effective indeed, but for the moment let us concentrate on the old traditional old-fashioned approaches.

First, look at the following list of advantages and disadvantages of direct mail. Then read the research case study.

DIRECT MAIL

Advantages	Disadvantages
Messages can be directed at a highly selective target group	Total dependence on the quality of the list
Mailings can be highly personalized	Bought lists need constant updating
Messages can be long and and full of information – research makes it clear that long copy sells	Some rented lists can only be used once
Timing can be totally flexible	We have come to hate 'junk mail'
Can keep you in touch with valued customers and build referral and repeat business	You have, according to research, no more than eight seconds to catch the reader's attention
Can sometimes 'piggy back' with non-competing material	Getting attention is only half the battle, only maintaining it wins the war
	Average response rates are low 0.5 % is common, 1 % is good, 2 % is sometimes regarded as a marketing miracle.

RESEARCH CASE STUDY : Telemarketing

Research has shown that there are ways to raise low response rates to direct mail. Some years ago the American Marketing Association conducted an experiment. Identical mailings were sent to carefully targeted experimental and control groups that were equal in size and potential. The control group received the mailing in the normal way. The experimental group was sent the same promotional material but it was preceded by a telephone call to the recipient with the objective of persuading him or her to look out for it. (A member of the opposite sex to the recipient generally made the call. In most of us the near compulsion to keep a promise to a member of the opposite sex is strong.)

After the mailing was received a follow-up telephone call was made to establish the recipients' response to what they had read. The control group's response rate was under 1 %, while that of the experimental group was over 15 %.

As I write this, The Institute of Practical Marketing is replicating this experiment. Having recommended the approach I was interested to receive an e-mail this morning telling me that their response rate so far is an almost miraculous 90%. Clearly it cannot stay at that level – the programme is in its early stages – but their experience is certainly confirming the effectiveness of the approach.

It is educational to consider just what happened in this case. Like most of us, the experimental group probably disliked junk mail. Their usual response to it was probably to bin it without even opening it or to glance at it, and decide it held no interest for them. But that telephone call had persuaded them to look out for this mailing, and the vast majority of us keep our word – especially if doing so is neither onerous nor expensive. So for starters it is almost certain that more people read the message. But there is more to it than that. Psychology teaches us that when we do something out of the ordinary we justify our changed behaviour to ourselves any way we can. More people read the mailing, but more importantly they read it with the intention of finding something worthwhile in it. In short they sold themselves on the message.

Unless you can afford massive mailings a 15 to 1 response ratio is almost certainly worth the additional cost. This is particularly true for those who take our advice and test their marketing initiatives with small numbers. A few thousand telephone calls will stretch the budget of all but the biggest spender, but a couple of hundred brief calls, even if repeated, can be carried out relatively quickly and cheaply.

Using new marketing methods we can produce response rates of between 35% and 70%. We will tell you how as we proceed, but there is no escaping the groundwork and that groundwork may include old-fashioned direct mail.

Roses, roses all the way

Before looking at the new ideas in Chapter 7 it may be useful to see how some very clever people have overcome the problems of direct mail. One of the most successful mailings of all time before E-Market Dominance was discovered is described in the next case study.

CASE STUDY: INNOVATIVE DIRECT MAILING

The bane of the mailing expert's existence is the gatekeeper or dragon – the personal assistant who dumps unsolicited mail in the bin rather than bother a busy boss with it. If, and only if, you can get your message past the gatekeeper and into the hands of the intended recipient can you make a sale. This innovative approach noted that:

- Most PAs in this sexually unequal world are still women.
- Most women like flowers and regard red roses as particularly romantic.
- Romance and mystery go together and are great, though harmless, fun.

This mailing was aimed at chief executives with the intention of getting them to a meeting to assess a new and exciting concept. The campaign went like this:

Step One

A single long-stemmed red rose was mailed to each gatekeeper. It had a gold-edged card attached bearing no message, only the lady's given name. The card was attached to the rose by a green ribbon.

Step Two

Three days later a gold-edged envelope with an identical ribbon and addressed to the chief executive arrived in the mail. Inside was an invitation card matching the one attached to the rose in every way except that it bore details of the proposed meeting and was therefore larger. The PAs, in the main, went further than simply passing the invitation to the boss. They drew his or her attention to it and treated it as if it was very special. The response rate for attending the meeting was 78 out of 100. Putting that another way, 78 busy business opinion leaders attended the meeting, assessed the concept and bought into the idea. More importantly, they became advocates who praised the idea to their business contacts, leading to many more unsolicited sales.

The firm with that idea about how to sell was a marketing consultancy, but every entrepreneur should be prepared to think through successful approaches with the intention of building their own creativity.

Consultants are better than most ... but they must do better

In 1997 the Direct Mail Information Service researched 38 mailings from different consultants. If consultants offer their clients anything worth buying they ought to be able to do better than most in promoting their wares. Fortunately their results were an improvement on the 0.5% to 2% we have learned to expect. They scored on average a response rate of 5.3%. Of course, consultants seldom use mailings to sell a product or service: they sell a meeting with the potential client. So you would expect a higher response rate than the norm on two accounts:

1   It is an easier sale.
2   Consultants should be good at doing what they teach others to do.

An idea from an acknowledged master

Drayton Bird is a genius of copy writing. You might expect him to emphasize that the copy is the only thing that counts. He doesn't. His Drayton Bird Partnership says that a number of factors contribute to mailing success. They say that you can improve your success by a factor of up to 58 times if you get it all right. In his expert opinion this is what counts, and how much:

- The Mailing List   (factor $\times 6$)
- The Offer   (factor $\times 3$)
- The Timing   (factor $\times 2$)
- Creativity   (factor $\times 1.35$)
- Response Mechanism   (factor $\times 1.2$)

Get it all right and you may improve your hit rate by a total factor of

$$6 \times 3 \times 2 \times 1.35 \times 1.2 = 58$$

If he was right, we could all do better, much better.

To improve the effectiveness of direct mail

1 **Get a good mailing list**. You are buying an expensive ticket for a lottery if you buy a list directly from the list owner. Keeping the list up to date is a difficult and expensive business. Too many list owners cut corners when it comes to cleaning the list. You can improve your chances by going to a reputable list broker. Brokers want your business. To keep your business they want you to be delighted. Given an accurate brief they will find exactly what you want. They buy in lists every day. They know those who keep their lists up to date and those who do not. But be extra careful when buying lists on the Internet. They may have been collected by dubious means and using them to send unsolicited e-mails can lead to your site being removed by your Internet service provider.

2 **Be clear about your offering**. Differentiation is vital in marketing. You must make it absolutely clear why the customer should buy from you.

3 **Get and hold the reader's attention**. Speak directly to your reader. Identify a problem that is hurting them or make an offer that they would die for.

4 **Use long copy if you're certain that the reader will want to know more**. If they don't want to know more why are you writing?

5 **Use incentives, coupons or free gifts**. People are greedy, but make sure that what you offer is really attractive.

6 **Use telemarketing first and last if you can afford it**. See the telemarketing case study above.

7 **Think carefully about your timing**. Most products are seasonal in some way. You may need an exceptional offer to sell heating oil in July.

8 **Make it easy to respond**. Provide response mechanisms with the customer's convenience in mind, not yours. People like (0)800 phone numbers, but not if they are unmanned or always engaged. Most of us don't like those tin voices that tell us to 'Press 1 for account enquiries, ... press 9 to express despair ...'

9 **Look for creative ways to get your message into the right hands**. It doesn't need to be a rose, though I think roses are nice.

10 **Personalize your letters**. No one likes to think that you can't even be bothered to use their name.

11 **Avoid sexual assumptions**. Not all bosses are men. Not all secretaries are women. And finally:

12 **Learn how to use new concepts such as E-Market Dominance**.

To write letters that sell

1 **Plan**. The great copywriters say they spend 90% of their time planning and 10% writing. Those who plan best and therefore do the most effective writing can charge up to $50,000 for a single letter.

2 **Personalize your letter**. Build a personal relationship with your customer from the first moment. You need to become the friend they rely on. Most of us regard letters which are sent without the courtesy of using our name as the worst of junk mail. To recover from a start like that demands a wonderful offer and a truly creative letter. Worst of all is 'Dear Sir or Madam': if you can't even get the reader's sex right, what chance do you have in accurately predicting his or her needs?

3 **Write your letter from the recipient's point of view**. If you can offer the solution to an important problem which you and I both know that I face, I might bite your hand off. Frankly, the wonderful technology or what have you that your firm has doesn't interest me. I want to know what your widgets will do for me, not how clever you think you are.

4 **Customers buy benefits**. Your biggest benefit is your offer. Tell the reader early and powerfully what your offer is, then build your case until the reader cannot wait to buy. Remember you only have on average eight seconds to grab your reader's attention.

5 **If your product is new to your readers, explain it to them in detail and hammer home what it will do for them**. If it has been around for some time tell the reader what makes it different and better than competitive widgets and emphasize what that difference does for them. The more ferocious competition is, the more you must convince readers you are offering them better value.

6 **Prove you can deliver all you promise, and more**. Include quotes from delighted customers or authorities.

7   Most firms spend most of their time and efforts on trying to attract new customers. Don't. **Delighted existing customers are six to eight times easier to sell**. That means you can get six to eight times the sales simply by keeping in touch. You might even consider saying 'thank you' now and again without pushing for a sale. Happy customers who have a need will come to you to fulfil it.

8   Of course, we all make rational decisions that would delight the economist. It is only others who use emotions when they decide to buy. **Mix emotions and logic in your correspondence**. Logic implies that the reader is logical and that implication appeals to their emotions.

9   **Move the reader to buy now**. So make buying easy.

10 **Emphasize and <u>underline</u> what you want the reader to notice**. But remember that if you emphasize everything, you emphasize nothing.

11 **If your product or service is expensive, your letter needs to be longer**. Long copy sells and there is a proven relationship between the cost of the offer and the length of the letter.

12 **Sign letters**. It may be a chore, but people like to buy from people they like and we don't like impersonal facsimile signatures.

13 **Never forget the old dictum that a letter needs to be 'a salesperson in an envelope'**.

Breaking the eight-second barrier

Copy writing gurus such as Drayton Bird have tested opening sentences of letters and have suggested a number that have been proved to work. The first few words of a letter determine whether your reader will read greedily and sell him or herself on the offer, or consign your work of literature to the bin. Here are some ideas for appropriate openings:

1   **Ask a provocative question**. I sometimes ask prospective clients who are buying training: 'How much have you wasted on training in the last few years?' Most tell me in great detail and with not a little chagrin. Then I tell them how they need never waste another cent. Provocative questions take a little moral fibre, but they arouse, sometimes passionate, interest in what you have to say.

2   **Suggest a vital decision**. 'The decision you will make after reading this letter may make the difference between disaster and prosperity.' Your offer of course must be sufficiently important to the customer to justify such an approach.

3   **As you know ...** People love to be told how knowledgeable they are – that's why those who most enjoy training courses are those who didn't really need the training.

4 **If you're anything like me ...** People like to buy from people that they like and we like best people who are like us.

5 **What if ...** 'If you could wave a magic marketing wand, what would you wish for?' You make an informed guess and show them that they'll get it from you: more profit, higher sales, happier customers, less customer hassle, or the biggest benefit that your offering can deliver.

6 **Congratulations**. 'Your position as an industry opinion leader entitles you to ... Only the other person likes flattery, but it is amazing how much they all love it.

7 **Invitation**. 'You are invited to a secret preview.'

8 **Free gift**. Preferably with no strings attached.

9 **Narrative**. 'A funny thing happened when I took up my pen to write this letter.'

10 **Introduction**. 'We don't know each other, but we should because you and I.'

11 **You did that, so we're doing this**. 'Your generous action has not gone unnoticed.'

12 **You're a rare bird**. 'The American Express Gold Card is not for everyone.' This is the opening of one of the most famous and successful letters ever.

13 **'The experts say ...'** Respect for expert authority is a hardwired part of the human psyche.

14 **'Are you paying too much ...'**

15 **'Why are we doing this?'** Your good reason for doing it must be good for the customer, not you.

16 **Give good news after bad**. 'Competition gets tougher every day, but you have the answer in your hands right now.'

17 **'Have you ever wished ...'**

18 **'Why don't (do) they ...'** (It helps when we all hate 'them'.) The great Peter Drucker was once the main speaker at an international business conference. Another speaker finished and the chair asked for questions. There was silence. Drucker intervened. 'I have a question, sir. Why is it that you always snarl when you mention customers?'

19 **'I've missed you so I ...'** A bit like *Readers Digest* perhaps, but *Readers Digest* does pretty well.

20 **'I've enclosed ...'** Make sure the enclosure is interesting, valuable or useful to the recipient.

21 **Solve a problem**. 'You don't need to lose sleep over rising interest rates ...'

22 **'I'll get straight to the point.'** If you try this you must be brief, even terse, so be sure you can get your offer across in very few words.

23 **Because you're an A you must be a B**. 'Cat lovers like you love ...

24 **'You are important to us so we want you to be the first to know ...'**

25 **Others can't, we can**. 'No one dare promise to get your Web site consistently in the top ten, *no one but us.*'
26 **'When was the last time you ...'**
27 **'Less than an hour ago I realized ...'** The shorter the period of time the more compelling – within reason.
28 **'I love to share great ideas ...'**
29 **'I'm surprised that we haven't heard from you ...'**
30 **'In the less than two minutes that it will take you to read this letter ...'**

Some customer feedback

In some very recent research into the rapidly growing and aggressively marketed telecom, satellite and cable industry, customers were invited to indicate their experience and preferences in respect of direct mail. Here is what they said:

TYPE OF DIRECT MAIL RECEIVED

Information on new products and services	46%
Special offers	41%
Information on existing products and services	26%
Newsletters and magazines	12%
Information on unexpected products and services	12%
Brochures and catalogues	11%
Bills	9%
Offering membership of loyalty schemes	8%
Questionnaires	3%

Source: DMIS

FREQUENCY OF DIRECT MAIL

	Actual	Acceptable
Once a week	3%	5%
Once a month	22%	15%
Once a quarter	49%	45%
Once every six months	14%	13%
Once a year	3%	5%
Less often	1%	1%
Never	7%	14%

Source: DMIS

A little over half of those surveyed indicated that receiving direct mail made them more likely to buy from the sender again. Of these, 58% of men and 44% of women wanted to 'understand the product'.

Drawing conclusions from a single study is a risky business, but this research conforms more general surveys elsewhere in some key points:

- Direct mail is acceptable as long as it carries desired information.
- Mailings should be frequent enough to keep in touch, but not too often.
- The numbers who are actively against receiving direct mail are a significant minority.

E-Market Dominance works in part by only sending information or entertainment that is specifically desired, expected, personal, relevant to the customers' expressed needs, and with a frequency that the customer finds acceptable. It is this sensitivity to the customer that makes the difference.

If the opportunities to use advertising in new ways are exciting, the use of electronic direct mail will blow your mind. E-Market Dominance enables you to attract new customers, keep the best of them for life, and make high and sustainable profits.

RING IN THE NEW, BUT KEEP THE OLD BELL IN TUNE

New marketing methods are wonderfully effective. They are inexpensive and they give you highly profitable business: that is why the old methods are under threat. But old tried and tested methods must often be used to build the basis for the massive growth the new methods can deliver.

E-commerce is not about technology. It is about marketing, sales and profits. This means you must start the journey into the new world of business by being better than the best in using tried and tested tactics. Think of it like a pump. First you prime it. Then you have an unending flow of clean pure water. Add the new methods and that stream will be one of pure gold.

BRIEF MARKETING ASSESSMENT

If you are a television viewer in the UK at the moment, you may have watched with pleasure and even a slight sense of wonder the advertisements of breathe.com.

- Do you know what the company sells?
- Have you visited their website?
- Is their massive investment in an undoubtedly clever series of advertisements likely to be repaid by increased sales?

MINI CASE STUDY Reuters Instinet

Reuters Instinet is an online service that has been conservatively valued at $8 billion dollars. It will probably be floated in 2001 and the flotation will almost certainly be successful. Revenues are rising; the stocks of the parent company are enjoying growth fuelled at least in part by the success of Instinet on line. So why wait? Why not make hay today while the sun is shining?

Peter Job, Reuter's Chief Executive, insists that the flotation will take place when the business is ready and not one minute sooner. And when will the business be ready? According to Job it will be ready when 'it is well-rounded (has the right balance of unique or superior products and the right customers) and it is well-managed'.

Similarly, your online enterprise will have great value when you have the right products properly promoted to the right people at the right price. Not before. A website is not an 'open sesame' to riches, but an online business, properly conducted, may well be.

And finally . . .

Think what these facts mean to your marketing efforts:

- The average consumer sees around one million marketing messages a year, or 2,739 each day, or up to 171 in an average hour.
- There can be up to 300 ads in a single newspaper.
- To cut through background noise like that and make your voice heard you really need to do it right. Since it is expensive you need to do it right first time.

WHAT YOU WILL HAVE LEARNED IN THIS CHAPTER

☞ There is so much marketing taking place today that traditional methods are suffering from diminishing returns.

☞ There are new and more effective methods, but these work most readily when combined effectively with the best traditional approaches, at least at first.

☞ It is possible to do much better than the norm with a little knowledge and determination.

☞ Getting it right is a sound and essential basis for making optimal use of the new ideas.

☞ If you skipped this chapter to get to the new stuff you made a big, possibly fatal, mistake.

☞ Key point: e-business will succeed only if it is well supported by good basic business practice.

CHAPTER THREE

CUSTOMIZE OR DIE

☞ If you and I have no relationship prior to the purchase, and we have no relationship following it, then our entire interaction is centred on a single solitary transaction. And our interests are diametrically opposed. I want to buy the most product at the lowest price and you want to sell me the least product at the highest price.

DON PEPPERS AND MARTHA ROGERS

THE ONE TO ONE MANAGER

WHAT YOU WILL LEARN IN THIS CHAPTER

☞ You will understand why the Internet has enabled us to return to customization.

☞ You will learn about three areas which can benefit from customization.

☞ You will learn some guidelines to help you to identify possible areas of customization in your own Internet business.

☞ You will see how customization can boost your profitability.

CUSTOMIZATION

In the days when every product was made as a one-off, business was seen as a kind of combat. Marketers launched 'campaigns', salespeople 'targeted' their prospective customers, managers vied with each other to 'out-flank' the competition. This combative approach to marketing and selling is still adopted today. All energy is directed into positioning ourselves for the fight. This creates an environment of 'one-size-fits-all' and a resultant lowering in value obtained by each side.

An effective move to product and service customization requires a paradigm shift in our relations with customers and suppliers. A true commitment to 'walk in the other fellow's moccasins' is needed so we understand the needs, wants and desires of the other person, firm or corporation.

The evolutionary trend has been from every product being a one-off, via mass production, followed by a splintering into niche marketing with standardized products then mass personalization and on to one-to-one marketing.

Mass production made standardization of processes and product parts a necessity. Manufacturing plants became larger and larger and more and more specialist. This had the inevitable effect of distancing the manufacturer from their customers. This in turn led to the need for layers of intermediaries, such as dealers, retailers, agents and brokers.

Savings in production, labour and material costs meant many more people than before could afford to buy these goods. For those of you aged enough to remember Montague Burton the Tailor, you will know how they and firms like them changed the face of British tailoring. Up until then, men's clothing was cut and made by hand. Along with Burtons and John Collier (the window to watch), they seemed to be on a street corner of every town in England. They provided excellent quality tailoring to Middle England.

'Off-the-peg' suits were in vogue. Only the rich could afford bespoke tailoring. Many of these early, off-the-peg suits were pretty awful. As the post-war Quartermaster would say whilst issuing a de-mob suit, 'It fits you where it touches'. People believed that such standardization could only lead to this reduction in quality and for a time perhaps it did. Like so many things in life, we were immediately led into the realms of diminishing returns between the cheaper, off-the-peg item, and the better, made-to-measure alternative at many times the price.

But expertise in standardization of manufacturing processes improved beyond all recognition. Before long it was possible to buy a whole range of goods which were of very high quality but were made in large quantities and at reasonable prices. Shoes are a good example of this. Shoe-making machinery is now so sophisticated that very high quality shoes can be made comparatively cheaply. I had the pleasure of meeting Mr John Lobb of Lobbs of St James's, where cobblers still hand-make shoes on wooden lasts to fit the most awkward of well-heeled feet. I met him in his tiny, cosy office above the shop and over-looking St James's Street, where his family has been selling shoes since .... The wall was covered in photocopies of cheques from the rich and famous who have their shoes made on the premises at St James's. Our conversation naturally turned to the comparative qualities and prices of his made-to-measure shoes, versus high-quality off-the-peg shoes like Churches, or one of the other up-market shoe manufacturers. A pair of Lobbs shoes cost over £1300.00, whereas a pair of Church's excellent shoes would be around the £200.00. How on earth can the extra £1100.00 be justified? To his credit, Mr Lobb did not try to justify his prices – he does not need to. He has a full order book and waiting list. No standardization here!

The very term 'off-the-peg' has connotations of goods that are ill-fitting and badly made. In the early moves away from bespoke production, this may have been true. As technology and expertise improved so the gap between hand-made and machine-made closed and, in a way, reversed. That is to say, machines were soon able to exceed the quality of the hand-made. As we know from the motor industry, 'off-the-peg' motorcars are of a far higher standard than their earlier hand-made counterparts. Even Morgan Motors, the sports-car manufacturers, have allowed some standardization to creep into the manufacture of their delightful and somewhat addictive cars. Charles Morgan and his father, joint Managing Directors and direct descendants of the founder H F S Morgan, reasoned that their customers care very much about the fact that the cars are still hand-built. But they would not care whether the shears that cut the metal body-parts before hand-rolling into shape are manual or electric – so they now use electric ones. As with Lobbs, Morgan have a waiting list of people prepared to pay a premium for the cachet of owning the best that British hand-built craftsmanship can make.

So, from the point where everything made is made individually, we have moved to the point where the majority of things are standard and choice is limited to the range of whatever the manufacturers decide. The Internet has brought the wheel of progress around a full turn by making customization affordable by the many rather than just the few. As more and more customers see that they can have a product or service exactly how they want it, so the demand for customization will increase. It is not only the products that benefit from customization. The interactive nature of the Internet means that several layers of intermediaries may no longer be needed.

Issues in customization

Customization brings with it massive benefits to the customer. They can have the exact products they want, because they select the components that go into the final product. For example the website www.activeresearch.com provides buyers with what they call a 'personal shopping expert' who is trained to act on their behalf. The expert asks each visitor to the site their personal needs, preferences and tastes. Armed with the customer's unique shopping profile, the 'expert' enters a virtual store containing the most comprehensive and up-to-date product information available. The expert returns with product recommendations specifically tailored for each individual. The customer then has the option of sorting the list, making side-by-side comparisons, and eventually of linking to the site where they can buy the exact product of their choice.

To introduce customization into your own site you need to consider and address the following issues:

- Privacy.
- Database integration.
- Any legacy systems you might be running.

For you to be able to offer any active research service, your visitor must be prepared to give you a certain amount of personal information. People have very genuine and understandable concerns about the use and distribution of such information. But if you follow these three rules, you should give visitor the confidence to disclose to you the information you need:

1   Only ask for the information you absolutely need.
2   Explain the benefits *to the customer* of giving you the information.
3   Make it clear that they can opt-out of the relationship at any time.

Building an online one-to-one relationship is like building any other. We do not get married before we have dated. The best route forward is to take time and constantly re-assure your customer that you are an ethical company and are acting in their best interest. GuideZone (Figure 3.1) offers help.

STAGES IN CUSTOMIZATION

The route from a basic brochure website through e-commerce to the ultimate of a fully integrated e-business can be tracked by the following stages:

- Establish an effective website.
- Generate traffic to the site.
- Convert site visits into sales.
- Generate return visits.
- Raise the per-visit spend.
- Protect your profitability.

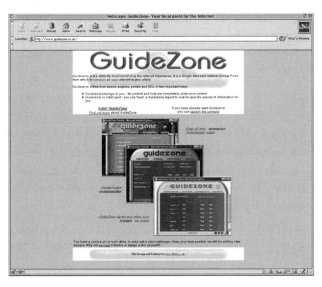

FIGURE 3.1   GuideZone enables visitors to tailor the site appearance. A GuideZone agent can be used to 'push' information on your chosen subject

Establish an effective website

An effective website is one which achieves the objectives of the owners. These might be:

- Selling goods and services.
- Servicing a community of one kind or another.
- Provide an adjunct to a conventional business.
- Servicing an existing user base.

Websites do not need to be colourful and animated to be effective. Most companies building a website for the first time allocate the majority of the Internet marketing funds to the build of the site. Often, this leaves very little over to do anything else with the site, so it languishes in all its animated glory. It remains lonely and unloved even by its creators, who begin to resent the money spent on this much-hyped thing called the Internet. Conversely, if they spend between 10 and 20% of the available funds on the site build and allocate the rest to marketing and promotion, the site will soon begin to pay for itself and will fund the inevitable site re-build as lessons are learned and new requirements are identified.

Generate traffic to the site

An unvisited website is a very sad object. It can be made even sadder by the addition of a hit counter registering a paltry number of hits over a long period of time – most of which hits were probably the owners visiting the site themselves. The Holy Grail of Internet marketing is to generate substantial numbers of visits on a consistent basis.

This will be achieved by adopting the twin approach of both passive and active marketing.

PASSIVE MARKETING

Passive marketing is optimizing your site to register highly on the search engines. Examples are: fixing up your site so that those little spiders can crawl all over your site whilst you sleep, adjusting your web pages so that their crawling results in the collection of all of the needed information in the form of keywords, meta-data, titles and body text without obstacles.

ACTIVE MARKETING

Active marketing is everything else you do to boost your visitor numbers. Apart from making your web address a very prominent part of your corporate identity, active marketing includes

- Online and off-line advertising.
- Direct mail.
- E-mail marketing.
- PR.

Convert site visits into sales

Make it easy for your visitors to complete a sale. It still astounds me how many sites, including some who should know better, make the act of ordering more like an intelligence test. They hide the 'order' button well-nested in a secondary page, often three-quarters of the way down a page, so that it does not sit on the screen at normal resolution. Remember the rule:

'Take every opportunity to expose yourself to the dangers of sale'

Here is a check-list to help you to avoid some of the 'howlers' committed even by Internet companies:

- Make your main navigation bar static, so the order button is always on the screen.
- Check your site every day to ensure that all links are working.
- Ask computer illiterate friends to make test purchases.
- Get them to report their experience to you and make any site adjustments needed.
- Check the order form to ensure that each piece of information asked for is really needed.
- Build in personalization facilities to reduce the effort needed to make purchases.

Generate return visits

Whole books have been written on getting visitors to return to your site regularly. This is because return visits indicate a satisfied customer and can be the start of a long and profitable relationship. Research shows that the visual and design elements of a website are amongst the least important factors causing people to return to the site. Flash animations and swirling logos do not impress regular visitors. Indeed, you can discourage such people if you force them to sit through the routine of your logo compiling itself fancily on the screen, when all they want is to get to your order page to make a replenishment order. The three top causes of return visits are:

- An entertaining site.
- Useful content.
- Tailored to the need of the visitor.

For loyal customers, the ability to interact personally with the site will continue to be a major factor in their ventures into e-commerce.

Raise the per-visit spend

Skilled salespeople in the dirt world know that if a woman buys a pair of blue shoes, she is also a good prospect for a matching top, and perhaps, a contrasting scarf and pair of earrings. This process of cross-selling can double or triple her spend with you. How can this be achieved from your website? Many of the better e-commerce companies, such as Intershop (www.intershop.com)and Openmarket (www.openmarket.com), have cross-selling facilities built in. MarketSwitch (www.marketswitch.com) produce a software suite, they call 'Cross-Selling Optimizer' (see Figure 3.2). This provides a solution for companies whose various divisions may be marketing different products to the same customers. Financial services companies may send offers from their credit card, loan and mortgage divisions to the same person, thereby competing for that person's attention and resources.

Protect your profitability

The ability of visitors to compare prices might lead us to assume that the Internet market will be driven solely by price. This may be true for certain products and for some time, until the market shakes out. In the long run people will still want value for money rather than pure price cutting. Being creative in seeking and displaying the added value in your offering will help differentiate your company from others.

The factors that will protect your long-term profitability will be retaining your customers and continuing to delight them.

COLLECTING CUSTOMER INFORMATION

There are a number of methods you can use to collect and make use of customer information. Marketers must always bear in mind the sensitivities of the people being asked for information. What might seem to be an inoffensive question to us could have sinister connotations for them, causing them to quit your site and try your competitor's, who have not asked so many or such personal questions. Remember you can always supplement the initial

FIGURE 3.2 MarketSwitch produce a 'Cross-Selling Optimizer'

questions later, as the relationship grows. Here are some rules for collecting this type of information:

1   Collect only what you absolutely need.
2   Demonstrate the relevance of the question.
3   Only make vital questions mandatory.
4   Give value in return for the information.
5   For sensitive questions, put the form within a secure server.

Now for some ways of collecting customer details.

Registration form online

Online registration forms and guestbooks are now very commonly used to collect data about customers, their preferences and their needs. The data collected via the guestbook is the basis for providing personalized service to your visitors and turning them into loyal customers. If the information could be perceived by the visitor as sensitive in any way, then you should collect it under a secure server, so that before the visitor begins to enter their data the secure server window will pop up. This helps give visitors confidence that you are treating their information with courtesy and due respect for their privacy. Once captured, this data will need to be stored on a database to make it really useful to the marketer (Figure 3.4).

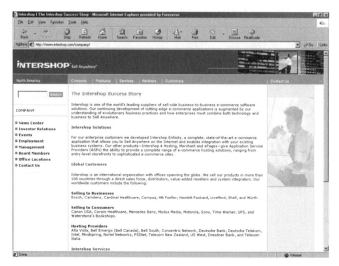

FIGURE 3.3   The Intershop range of e-commerce applications offers many of these customization facilities

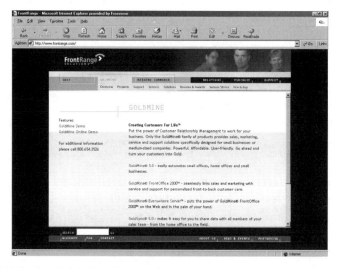

FIGURE 3.4   Goldmine is one of the better-known contact management systems

Visitor database

There have been many advances in the use of database sites in the last year or so. Technologies such as Active Server Pages from Microsoft (ASP) have enabled even small sites to benefit from having a database behind the site. For small applications where the numbers of visitors contemplated will be relatively limited, Access (also from Microsoft) will do a very fine job for you. For larger applications, or where scalability from a small start-up to storing and manipulating very large amounts of data is needed, Oracle or SQL provide an appropriate tool-set.

From the database a range of applications can be driven:

- Cross-selling.
- Targeted e-mail marketing.
- Sales lead generation.

Some of the better proprietary contact management databases, such as Maximiser (www.multiactive.com), Goldmine (www.goldmine.com) (Figure 3.4), and ACT (www.symantic.com) also have some Web enablement.

Cookies

Cookies are tiny programs that can be deposited in visitors' computers so the next time they visit your site they will be recognized by it. Many people are nervous of cookies and use browser tools to prevent them from being deposited. From the marketer's point of view they are very valuable and can enable you to provide a more personal service. They can:

- Greet the returning visitor.
- Trigger cross-selling options.

E-mail polls

Using targeted e-mail you can send out questionnaires to assess customer satisfaction and gain feedback on the service you provide. If this is supported by an incentive programme to encourage customers to respond, you can glean a great deal of information at very low cost.

CUSTOMER RETENTION

Given that it can often cost up to eight time more to find and secure a new customer than it does to sell to an existing customer, it is vital that we focus some attention on this important subject. The Pareto 80/20 rule, that 80% of our profit comes form 20% of our customers, means that giving more attention to the top 20% will pay huge dividends.

We need to categorize our customers so we know how much time and effort to pay to each of them. One way is to categorize them according to their contribution to your net profit. List all customers and look at the revenues derived from each of them in the past twelve months. Then analyse the cost incurred to service each of them. If you find it difficult to find exact details of revenues and costs, a reasonable approximation would do. Then categorize them like this:

- Top 10%:   Diamonds
- Next 50%:   Golds
- Below 40%:   Dogs

You will benefit from some rough rules of thumb – though remember your categorization needs to be regularly reviewed so you do not ignore good customers who are just not spending a lot with you yet:

1   Revere the Diamonds
2   Go for the Gold
3   Kill the Dogs

I do not intend to be offensive with the use of the word 'dogs'. 'Kill the Dogs' means looking hard and long at these customers and deciding 'Are they actually costing me money to do business with them?' If the answer is yes or maybe, you should seriously consider curtailing your effort to win new business from them. The effect of doing this will be to free up time and resources to give greater attention to the Diamond and Gold customers, where 80% of your profits come from.

One way to make your Diamonds and Golds feel special is to give them a private area of your site, which can contain valuable information they will find useful and could encourage them to perceive your site as one of their personal resources. This area can be passworded to make it special, but remember it must provide real value. This need not be costly for you and can include such resources as:

- Industry White Papers produced by your staff.
- Access to their data on your own back-office systems.
- Research material.
- Software downloads.
- Customizable Power Point presentations.

There are a wide range of features that can make your site one people will return to time after time. These include:

- Make it an indispensable resource for customers.
- Reinforcing the benefits of your product rather than its features.
- Show value.
- Make the visit entertaining and enjoyable.
- KIT marketing.
- Integrate with other systems.

Make it an indispensable resource for customers

How you achieve this will very much depend upon your industry and your products and services. This entails frequent up-dates and new content, but the effort and cost involved can prove to be money well spent. Some examples are:

INDUSTRY	SITE	RESOURCE OFFERED
Finance	www.Bloomberg.com	Latest trading prices of stocks
Web design	www.fdd.com	Domain name checking
Car sales	www.toyota.com	Customized car builder

Reinforcing the benefits of your product rather than its features

Most people when describing their product or service tend to list their features raw of any benefits. In reality, you can only describe a benefit if you know your customers' needs and preferences. This is quite possible once you have collected the appropriate data, but on the website we can make educated guesses as to the possible benefits.

FEATURE	POSSIBLE BENEFIT
Waterproof	Safe in all weathers
	Usable in the bath
High resolution screen	Easy on the eyes
	Capable of handling detailed images

If you have difficulty in defining the benefits of your products and services, simply make a full list of all the possible features. Say the feature out loud to yourself and follow it by saying 'which means that ....' Whatever it means is probably a benefit. It is benefits that sell products, not features.

Show value

This is like describing benefits except that it refers directly to the price of your product. What you want to achieve is to alter the thinking of your customers away from 'Ouch! That costs $x' to 'OK that costs $x, but it means that I can do ...'. Value means a lot more that price. Many websites give the impression of being frightened to display prices or fees for the products or services. They hide them away, deep within an impenetrable site. Why not be proud of your prices, but make sure that you demonstrate the value your customer will get from them.

FIGURE 3.5   The Foolish approach to personal financial investment is to make it fun

Make the visit entertaining and enjoyable

Even the most mundane site can be made more enjoyable if you give it some thought. This has been achieved par excellence by The Motley Fools (www.fool.com). They have turned the serious world of finance and investing upside-down. They refer to themselves as Fools and the establishment financiers as The Wise. You can judge for yourself the veracity of these names (see Figure 3.5).

In seeking to make your site more fun and exciting, try very hard to make any changes or enhancements appropriate. Think outside the square by all means and do not be afraid to reverse the traditional methods. But no-one is impressed by a mundane and irrelevant quiz on what is supposed to be a serious business site.

KIT marketing

KIT means 'Keeping In Touch'. We want to be in regular touch with our clients and prospective clients but many times we have difficulty in finding appropriate things to say in our next communication with them. The difficulty arises where a customer, for good business reasons, only needs to deal with us on an infrequent and irregular basis. Their buying cycles are unpredictable, and we want to be sure that we are 'in the frame' next time the cycle turns full circle.

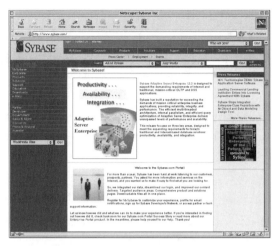

FIGURE 3.6   Database applications will proliferate on the Web. Sybase is one of the more powerful databases available

Integrate with other systems

Integration of other systems onto the website will continue to be a growth area in the Internet market. Over time, all new applications will almost certainly be developed with the Internet foremost in the mind of the developers. Even now, new developments are being built with browser front-ends. This will continue because when a company has massive amounts of data stored on mainframe computers, they will want to provide elements of that data on-line. The major database providers such as Sybase (www.Sybase.com) are providing very powerful web tools to enable integration with the website (Figure 3.6).

WHAT YOU WILL HAVE LEARNED IN THIS CHAPTER

☞ The manufacturing and production of goods has changed from every item being a one-off, tailor-made piece. Mass-marketing and production has made this uneconomic.

☞ We have learned to accept standardization as part of the price we pay to have all types of high-quality, affordable goods. The Internet and other technologies has completed the cycle to enable companies to provide the option of mass-customization.

☞ Identifying possible areas where your own business may profit from customization can lead to many benefits, such as reduced production costs and increased customer satisfaction, which in turn lead to increased bottom-line profits.

CHAPTER FOUR

THE FIRST STEP OF THE REST OF YOUR JOURNEY

☞ You cannot manage change. You can only initiate it.

PETER DRUCKER, at an international conference on managing change, 1999

☞ Before I was a genius I was a drudge.

IGNACE PADEREWSKI

☞ Sell the bloody products. Stop flapping about branding the sites, because it really ****** me off. And you can quote me on that.

MARCUS BICKNELL

WHAT YOU WILL LEARN IN THIS CHAPTER

☞ Understand the first leg of E-Market Dominance.

☞ Develop a detailed E-Market Dominance customer programme.

☞ Understand the few and unnecessary problems that could be associated with E-Market Dominance and avoid them.

☞ Balance today's needs with tomorrow's opportunities.

I know an old fashioned sales trainer. He believes that the world of sales is an on-going war between the good guys (the sales people) and the baddies (the customers). For him it is a conflict in which when foul means fail you need to try ever fouler methods. The idea, as he still proselytizes it, is to paint the customers into a corner and having got them there to 'nail their hats on'. For him the only response to an objection is to say 'If I can satisfy you on that will you buy today?' How the customer feels, what the customer wants, what the customer thinks, are all potential minefields that could cause the salesmen to become concerned with the enemy as people. That would never do. In war we don't kill people, we destroy the enemy. We have to get them before they get us. The important thing, the key concept in his training, is to have the closing technique, like your gun, always at the ready and to be quick to fire from the hip.

He fell into a kind of love with 'Benjamin Franklin's Revenge', the 'Fork' and most of all the insidious blackmail of the 'Puppy Dog Close' some forty years ago and he remains faithful to his first loves. All is fair in love and war so he would teach the 'low ball' (if he knew it) and still trusts in small print which tells the customer 'once hooked and landed it will cost you the earth to wriggle out of this one'. This guy actually employs a lawyer full time to enforce his relatively meagre sales. He believes that sales is a zero-sum game, a matter of 'I can only win if you lose. So you gotta lose'. Sometimes, I suspect, he lies awake at night wondering – for even he must have noticed – why the techniques he believes in with such fervour no longer work as they once did.

Beliefs are important when it comes to building sales, but not the beliefs of sales people or sales trainers. The Internet has changed all that. Today customers are in general better informed, clearer about what interests them, ready and able to compare offerings, and above all, knowledgeable about the unethical tricks that worked so well in the past. Add to this the fact that customers are short of time and attention and it becomes clear we need a different, customer-centred route to making the sale. The concept that works today is not about how to sell but how to make it easy for the customer to buy. If you believe just one thing about doing business in the knowledge age, believe this: *people like to buy from people they like*. Today's customer, particularly the affluent, educated, knowledgeable customer who is keen to buy on the Web wants a relationship with the seller, a relationship of trust.

The Web is a 'pull' medium. People are drawn to it in search of solutions to their problems and satisfactions for their desires. We are pulled in many directions by those who share the antiquated views of my sales-trainer friend. We are frustrated by information overload and failure to find what we really want to know. When an ISP uses pop-up advertising to distract and irritate us, the losers are eventually the ISP and the seller. When someone demands we opt out of buying rather than opt in, albeit with no more than the click of a mouse, we would like to send a ruder message (I would give much for a mouse which, with a single click, sends the message '**** off!') We are looking for, we need, a friend – or rather, more than a friend: a mentor.

A mentor is defined in the dictionary as a 'wise and trusted friend'. If you are wise and determined to make sustainable profits on the Web or elsewhere in the present business environment, you will become that mentor, you will be the wise and trusted friend customers want and need. The first step to E-Market Dominance enables you to become that essential friend. When push looks like coming to shove, it enables you to still gently push the customer in the direction of buying your products and services not once but for a lifetime – because *people like to buy from people they like*.

WHAT OLD-WORLD MARKETING TEACHES US

On average, as a rule of thumb, using traditional methods of marketing (advertising, direct mail, telesales), it takes seven customer contacts to make a sale.

That is why television advertisements drive you mad with their frequency. Of course, some offers are so compelling that, for some people at least, they work first time. Haemorrhoid advertisements are designed to do just that. If one advertisement is all you can afford, you had better tell those in pain that you have the soothing unguent that they need. But even if you do this, and do it convincingly, the numbers you will move to buy will be sub-optimal. After all, you are asking for their cash on a very short acquaintance. One of the reasons I write books is that when I advertise a seminar, those who have read my books, seen me on television or read my name in the press or on those little labels on bookshop shelves, feel that to some degree they know me. Books, you might say, shorten the time it takes to get bums on seats.

But only so many people have read my books or seen my ugly mug on television. For the vast majority my best advertising efforts struggle to overcome the simple questions: 'who is Tom Lambert?' and 'what has he ever done for me?'

In contrast to my mug, however, consider a well-designed, interesting and entertaining website. People find it. They like what they see. They stay a while and – this is vital – they return. The frequency of contact is determined by the customer. With no further effort on your part people get to know you. They begin to have warm feelings for you as they start to build, from very small beginnings, a feeling of trust.

They also leave little things behind. With modern technology it is possible to record where people spend most of their time. You can begin to build a dossier on the great unknown, the marketplace. But with E-Market Dominance you can do much better than this.

May I?

A small, but interesting point of buyer psychology is that once buyers want to know about your offer, they want to know as much as possible. The truly great sales people understand that what you really need to sell to the customer is not your product but what your product can do for them. They want to know that in detail. Once they decide they want to know they will listen with avid interest to what you offer. What is more, they will ask for more information, often by using the very 'objections' that my sales trainer would choke off by trying to force the buying decision. As you feed them information they interpret it in terms of their own needs and desires. In short, they sell themselves on your product or service. You are no longer the sales person. You are the trusted friend and advisor who helped them find what they wanted to know in order to make an informed choice.

E-mail is the one way that you can have this kind of informative, helpful, entertaining, educational conversation with up to millions of customers on a one-to-one basis. E-mail enables you to talk to each of them strictly in terms of what they want to know. And they really do want to know: in a recent survey by PricewaterhouseCoopers, 83% of those questioned said their primary goal in using the Internet was to receive information by e-mail. Millions are joining the Internet each year. What an opportunity!

Does it not make sense for you to join the relatively few (as yet) who have the nous to seek from their potential customers a mandate to keep them educated, informed and entertained? It ought to: it is not just the key to more business, it is the means by which higher profits are made. People like to buy from people that they like (remember?) and they are often prepared to pay a little more for that privilege as long as they still get value.

Research continues to show that two things are identified by customers as reasons to buy on the Web:

1   Detailed knowledge of the offering.
2   Discount pricing.

It is important to understand, however, that discounting is only important where insufficient knowledge is available. People certainly want low prices, but what they want more is to minimize risk. E-Market Dominance minimizes risk by treating customers as adults who want to be in a position to make an informed choice. Given that, many are prepared to pay a premium price.

More general market research has shown consistently year by year since 1936 that the biggest reason for buying, always more important than price, is convenience. In the dirt world convenience comes in many guises. It is convenient to have your car serviced at the garage you pass on your way to work. It is convenient to dine at the restaurant that takes your type of credit card. It is convenient to use the mall where parking is easy. It is convenient shop at the store which gives you credit. It is convenient to drink at a bar where they know your name and your favourite poison. On the Web buying is ultra convenient – so how do you get the vital competitive edge? You give yourself an edge by offering your customers what they want most, the information they need to reduce risk when they want it and without creating sales pressure.

ACTION SUMMARY

To make the first leg of E-Market Dominance work for you and bring you high profits from life-time customers and friends:

- Get expert help to design a website that offers potential customers the appropriate education, information or entertainment that is dictated by their needs and which can be satisfied by your products. Highlight where you can those aspects of your offering which relate to their hobbies and passions or which can effect their lifestyle in significant ways. Consider using relevant online competitions or surveys.

- Establish Double S.M.A.R.T. marketing objectives. Include at the minimum: sales revenues, sales revenue increase, profitability, customer satisfaction measures, life-time customer value, specifics of information capture at each stage of the customer relationship, percentage of referral business. You may start with just the e-mail address and main area of interest and get more detailed from there.
- Identify your target audience: those who buy most, buy frequently, have bought recently. Or you may find it better to use demographics: age, sex, race, disposable income, education, geographic location. Or you may want to use the special characteristics of the Web to identify life styles, hobbies, etc.)
- Tell the customers what they want to know rather than what you want to tell them.
- Create a unique value proposition that delights your customers and is not based solely on price.
- Find out and understand the various motives that drive people to exchange permission for information or entertainment.
- Use that understanding to provide free online information or entertainment.
- Love your customers to death.
- Invite customers gently but persuasively to provide the personal information which will enable you to serve their needs better. You may do this by any of the online media, banner ads, data-collection devices, competitions and special offers. All the important ones are described in detail elsewhere in this book.
- Provide information and entertainment that is desired, personal, timely, and relevant through opt-in e-mail, auto-responders and electronic newsletters.
- Leverage the mandate you have to serve the customer better by collecting and using more customer information.

TEST IS STILL A FOUR-LETTER WORD

It is a well-worn but vital rule of marketing that market testing is more reliable and less expensive than market research. If you have an idea it is always better to test it on a small scale rather than look to research that can be misleading. If people buy you have solid information, if people say only they would buy, that can change as soon as they feel the pressure to spend comes on. From the word 'go' get into the habit of market testing.

HERE ARE THINGS YOU NEED TO TEST FOR:

1   Are you achieving greater and greater conversion of enquiries into sales by better targeting of potential and actual customers?

2   Are you getting better response rates than you did with traditional marketing?

3   Do customers tell you, and confirm through their buying habits, that you are giving them something they value?

4   Are more and more potential customers opting in to your offer of information?

5   Do they want to continue communicating with you?

6   Are you able to leverage the initial mandates to get closer and closer to customers' changing needs?

7   Do you know more about your customers than before?

8   Are you getting more referral business?

9   Is your internal decision-making and product development improving?

10 Are you increasingly better able to concentrate on those customers who give and receive the best value?

11 Are you getting a bigger share of the best customers' buying?

12 Is profitability improving?

13 Are your people more committed and anxious to stay with you?

14 Are growing cost savings becoming evident?

15 Are sales per person employed growing, static or falling?

All these and more will happen with E-Market Dominance. If you are doing it right you should see the signs of improvement surprisingly early.

NOW SOME THINGS TO TEST FOR WHEN YOU HAVE A NEW OFFER IN MIND:

16 The headline. Remember that in a world full of missed communications you have only a few seconds to grab and hold attention.

17 The price. You may find to your surprise that what won't sell for £30 will go like the proverbial hot cakes for £300.

18 The effect of special offers.

19 The use of postscripts or other attention getting devices on any written materials.

Doing it wrong

The first step to E-Market Dominance is designed to enable you and your customers to enjoy mutually beneficial one-to-one relationships. That said, it is hardly necessary to conduct complex research to find out what gets in the way of such relationships. But such research has been carried out. For the sake of completeness, this is what customers say that they hate:

- Pushing too hard for the sale.
- Asking for the sale too early.
- Presenting obvious advertising puff as if it was information.
- Messages that are too loud, too long and too insistent.
- Messages that are not relevant to customer needs.
- Messages that are too frequent.
- Messages that are not relevant to customer desires.
- Deception and fraud.
- Sale of personal information to others, including the hated spam merchants.
- Exaggerated claims.
- Invasion of privacy.
- Irrelevant, impertinent questions.

THINKING THE RIGHT WAY

It is always worth remembering that E-Market Dominance is about a single sale only to the extent that the first sale is the start of a mutually satisfying relationship for life. It is designed to build a loyal and contented customer base, each member of which will stay with you and become the best advertisement your business could ever have. We are realists, however. We understand that without sales that put bread on the table today you may not be around tomorrow to enjoy the fruits of a longer relationship. That is why E-Market Dominance is designed to be a two-pronged approach, a comprehensive concept that will give you sales today and more sales tomorrow. (See Chapter 12 for detailed advice on how to get accelerated sales the E-Market Dominance way.) Before you decide to go all out for jam today, why not consider whether you really do need an immediate sales boost more than you need a steadily growing business?

When I am hired to conduct strategic planning sessions for client companies they very reasonably ask 'We fully understand the value of creating our future, but should we not start by ensuring that the order book for the next few months is full?' They are right of course, but they are not entirely right.

The first step in strategic planning is, or ought to be, to build a superior springboard. The second step is to identify the best ways of using that springboard in an environment in which change is the only certainty. So before embarking on an important strategic decision it is vital to think seriously about the degree to which you are making the most of your time, effort and money today.

Analysis of the here and now

The effective business manager should have the following questions constantly under review, and the review should lead to timely and ongoing action.

1 Are there any activities you are engaging in today which fail to provide profits commensurate with the time, money and effort put into them?

2 Which customers whom you serve today provide a less than adequate return in terms of profit when compared with the cost of looking after them?

3 If you are involved in non-profitable activities or in looking after non-profitable customers as an investment in future business, when precisely do you expect to enjoy the returns you are anticipating?

4 How will the anticipated profit compare with the best you can make today by going all out for quick sales?

5 Which activities you are engaged in today do not give you leverage opportunities in terms of:
- Additional revenues and profits?
- More delighted customers willing to act as advocates of your company?
- Providing you with a flow of referral business?
- Reducing costs?
- Reducing effort?
- Reducing business risk?

6 What could you most easily change about what you are doing today to give you the above benefits?

7 Why are you not already doing it?
- Are your strengths and competences inadequate?
- Are you simply doing what you have always done?
- And getting what you always got?
- Are too many of your people 'fat, dumb and happy'?

At this stage let us pause so I can say again what I said before, for it is vital. Remember there are more profit dollars and pounds to be made from giving customers more of what they like about you than there are from carefully eradicating every tiny fault in your business. But your efforts must be aimed at the right customers for the right reasons. You need to be ceaselessly considering every possibility of increasing the return you enjoy while continuously reducing the cost of giving exceptional service. Successful corporations and companies world-wide put their resources into creating and keeping worthwhile customers. They are also prepared to bite the bullet and fire inactive or unprofitable customers who cost more to service than they provide in profit.

RESEARCH

Recent research by de Montfort University has shown that paying sales commissions can lead to unprofitable customers accumulating as salespeople go for volume before all else. Such customers put your future at risk by draining crucial resources that could be better employed elsewhere.

So, take a cool look at your sales and marketing activities to ensure that you are not rewarding practices that are working against your true interests.

On with the questions:

8   What exactly is the correlation between sales and marketing spend and profit today?

9   What is the average life value, in terms of profit, of your customers?

10   Which specific customers generate profits well above the norm?

11   What characteristics do they have in common?

12   Which customers, by name, generate profits below the norm or cost more to service than they are worth?

13   Why do you continue to deal with them?

14   Are you spending more on attracting new customers than you are on keeping your most profitable present customers?

15   Is this tactic well enough known to your loyal customers that it might antagonize them?

16   Are the new customers you are attracting more profitable than the old?

17   Which customers, by name, are giving you referrals? How do you thank them?

18   What is it that you do that delights them?

19   Is serving them profitable?

20   Do the customers they bring to you generate higher than average profits?

Having answered these questions and thought through their implications, you may wish to consider some more. Here are another seven:

1   What must you do to ensure you retain your most profitable customers?

2   How can you get all your people to concentrate on what works?

3   How can you encourage your most profitable customers to be your most active advocates, sending you more and more customers just like them?

4   How can you get rid of under-performers (customers, suppliers, products, services, employees), without damaging your business or your reputation?

5   How can you be sure you are not throwing away customers of great future potential when you clear out those who are insufficiently profitable today?

6   How can you change the mindset of your people so they maximize life-time customer profits while minimizing costs and improving customer service?

7   How can you remove the barriers to placing the first order in the way of those whom you recognize as the key accounts of the future? Could you:

- Reduce or obviate the perceived risk of first purchase?
- Offer guarantees you can deliver which are enticing to those you wish to attract?
- Effectively relate the cost of winning the business to the probable life-time value of the customer – and go for it?
- Encourage your sales and marketing people to concentrate their efforts on the worthwhile quality customer, rather than unprofitable volume?
- Train your sales and marketing people to focus on the customer rather than on the product or service?
- Fast-track the process of building good relationships with worthwhile new customers?
- Differentiate your corporate behaviour at least as well as you differentiate your product offering?

At the same time you want to keep and extend the life-time value of your best customers. So how will you:

1   Identify those whom you most want to keep. Can you:

- Analyse the value of orders in terms of profit, rather than revenues?
- Establish the number of repeat orders placed each year?
- Work out the projected life-time of your best customers?

- Establish exactly what it is that your best customers like about you, and give them more of it – at lower cost?
2 Find those little touches that make all the difference and multiply them so that they grow exponentially from the customer's point of view?
3 Encourage your most profitable customers to feel they are, in a meaningful sense, an integral part of your business?
4 Having kept them, how can you encourage them to help to increase your profitable customer base, and increase the value and frequency of their own orders?

If you increase the number of more profitable customers, reduce the number of unprofitable customers, increase the unit of sale and the frequency of purchase you will have a massive effect on your business right now. And you can do it, because others have done it before you. If you do all that while reducing costs, you will have created the springboard for a world-class performance, because the effect on your bottom line will be phenomenal. What is more, if you are prepared to do the thinking about what must be done and when to do it, E-Market Dominance and this book will give you the tools and techniques you need for success beyond your dreams.

The key purpose of E-Market Dominance is to build and sustain a mutually profitable relationship between the business and its customers. This is a process that cannot and should not be rushed. E-Market Dominance is unique in that it recognizes the requirement to satisfy today's business needs as well as to build the future prosperity of the company. To understand the proper balance between now and the future demands clear thinking. But no one can do your thinking for you. In this book we do not try to do that, rather, we give you the tools and techniques that will enable you to do it yourself, to decide what you think is necessary.

E-BUSINESS CORPORATE ANALYSIS

☞ The Internet is not about technology. It is about sales and marketing.
Those who insist otherwise really **** me off.
MARCUS BICKNELL, , Chairman and owner of more
than 60 Web businesses, including Alta Vista.

The following survey is designed to enable you to take a fresh look at your e-business strategy, tactics and results as you consider the degree to which you have established and are meeting optimal objectives for your firm. It is not exhaustive, but is sufficiently comprehensive for most businesses practices to enable at least one or two 'eureka!' thought break-throughs.

I. What are the key strategic or tactical benefits you are seeking from your e-business initiative? Why have you chosen to go to the expense and trouble of having a website? Please tick each item you are seeking from an online presence and give the others some thought. Should you widen your thinking about what the Internet might deliver for you? Have you set your sights on the right outcomes for today and, more importantly, tomorrow?

Sale of online advertising   ___
Building brands – existing products/services   ___
Opt-in e-mail marketing   ___
Customer/market information   ___
Access to world markets   ___
Affinity (host/beneficiary) marketing   ___
Direct B2B sales   ___
Direct B2C sales   ___
Global presence/visibility   ___
Knowledge sharing   ___
Online training and development   ___
Sale of lists to e-mailers   ___
Cost reductions   ___
New advertising channel   ___
Attracting new customers   ___
Improved buying terms   ___
Recruitment and retention of staff   ___
Shorten supply chain (reduce intermediaries)   ___
Personalized customer service   ___
Reduced time-to-market   ___
24×7 availability to customers   ___
Global business platform   ___
Identify new suppliers   ___
Enhanced responsiveness to market   ___
Online distribution   ___
Faster decision making   ___
Low-cost entry into new markets   ___

II. To what degree have you been successful in enjoying the benefits of your e-business strategy? Has the Web delivered what you planned for? Has it delivered the unexpected? Do you need to revisit your strategy and beef it up a little – or a lot? Please circle the appropriate number using the following guidelines:

0 = No success as yet
1 = First glimmerings of results
2 = Some clear early benefits experienced
3 = Considerable benefits
4 = A major success

Access to world markets	0	1	2	3	4
Sale of online advertising	0	1	2	3	4
Building brands – existing products/services	0	1	2	3	4
Opt-in e-mail marketing	0	1	2	3	4
Customer/market information	0	1	2	3	4
Customer retention	0	1	2	3	4
Affinity (host/beneficiary) marketing	0	1	2	3	4
Direct B2B sales	0	1	2	3	4
Direct B2C sales	0	1	2	3	4
Global presence/visibility	0	1	2	3	4
Knowledge sharing	0	1	2	3	4
Online training and development	0	1	2	3	4
Sale of lists to e-mailers	0	1	2	3	4
Cost reductions	0	1	2	3	4
New advertising channel	0	1	2	3	4
Attracting new customers	0	1	2	3	4
Improved buying terms	0	1	2	3	4
Recruitment and retention of staff	0	1	2	3	4
Shorten supply chain (reduce intermediaries)	0	1	2	3	4
Personalized customer service	0	1	2	3	4
Reduced time-to-market	0	1	2	3	4
24×7 availability to customers	0	1	2	3	4
Global business platform	0	1	2	3	4
Identify new suppliers	0	1	2	3	4
Enhanced responsiveness to market	0	1	2	3	4
Online distribution	0	1	2	3	4
Faster decision making	0	1	2	3	4
Low-cost entry into new markets	0	1	2	3	4

III. What are the key performance indicators of your e-business? Please tick the appropriate items. What are the signposts that will tell you that it is working for you? What are the warning signs that should scream at you 'do something different and do it now'?

Increased sales revenues in existing markets   ——

Increased share of revenues from new markets   ——

Increased profitability   ——

Enhanced return on capital employed   ——

Investment funds attracted   ——

Enhanced market value of company   ——

Competencies developed   ——

Information flow   ——

Cost per transaction   ——

Information distribution cost   ——

Increased stock turnover   ——

Customer retention   ——

Customer satisfaction   ——

Market share   ——

Share of customer   ——

Overall cost reduction   ——

Staff reductions   ——

Sales per staff member   ——

Overall productivity   ——

Speed to market   ——

Number of customers   ——

Just in time deliveries   ——

Number of website visits   ——

Number of website transactions   ——

Trends recognized   ——

Sales per website visitor   ——

Number of customer opt-ins   ——

Speed of response   ——

Service quality   ——

Staff retention   ——

Customer churn   ——

Staff churn   ——

Website down-time   ——

Brand recognition   ——

Transaction security failures   ——

IV. Having assessed your objectives, the status of your business to date and the key indicators of your online business success, you may well want to re-assess or reconsider your initial strategic and tactical considerations. If this small survey has helped you to think again it has achieved its purpose. Here are some things to review:

- Are we attracting enough visitors?
- Do they stay?
- Do they welcome the offer of further information?
- Are we treating our customers as individuals with different needs?
- Do visitors buy online?
- Do they come back to visit again?
- Do we know with certainty what the emerging needs of our customers are?
- How do we compare with our competition when it comes to delighting the customer?
- Do we know who are our online competition by name and understand each one's unique marketing proposition?
- Does our site add transactional value for buyers?
- Does it give us added value as sellers?
- Does it make it easier than ever to do business with us?
- Is our unique selling proposition emphasized effectively?
- Could we use online activities to sell and make rather than make and sell?
- Is our site properly integrated with the rest of the business?
- Is our site too clever to be useful to visitors?
- Does our site help build our service standards?
- Are we attracting enough prospects of the right kind to our site?
- Have we entered into the right online strategic alliances?
- Do we make it easy to do business online?
- Is our offline distribution up to the job?
- Should we find ways to deliver more online?
- Do we really understand how to keep in touch with the ever-changing search engine algorithms?
- Are we treating our site as a technology break-through rather than a marketing and sales operation?
- Have we been persuaded by those with an axe to grind that a website is merely an electronic brand-building exercise?
- Have we a comprehensive strategy in place or was our web presence cobbled together by junior 'techies' after the chairman returned from the golf course full of web enthusiasm?
- Does our offline marketing support success online?
- Has our web presence enabled us to cut costs?

- Have we passed some of the advantages we have gained to our customers in the exceptional value and quality of our offering?

If you have not yet established a web presence there is much merit in considering the above before you invest time, cash and effort in doing so.

CASE STUDY   WWW.EXPORT.COM 22 JULY 2000

The Internet provides many different opportunities for business to co-operate for mutual prosperity. Consider this report:

As of the above date 6,019 Dutch companies had opened a shop window that enables buyers and agents in overseas countries across the globe to identify eager suppliers of goods and services from A (424 companies)–Z (40 companies). The attractive website encourages visitors by offering a range of pages including a tie-in between countries overseas and companies ready and able to do more business there, an alphabetical list of products, services and suppliers – all in English, the international language of trade, of course.

WHAT YOU WILL HAVE LEARNED IN THIS CHAPTER

☞ Business is business. The advent of the Internet does nothing to change that.

☞ Unless you have a plan of where you're going you have no way of knowing when, if ever, you get there.

☞ The vision and the mission are tools of the business and must be designed to fulfil this function.

☞ **Strengths** win business.

☞ Resolving weaknesses is far from being the name of the game. **Strengths** win business.

☞ Customers are not all equal. Some deliver pain, others provide profit.

☞ Investing in those who provide profit is eight times more valuable than rectifying the causes of pain.

CHAPTER FIVE

THE LOYAL CUSTOMER

☞ Weapons are inauspicious instruments, not the tools of the enlightened. When there is no choice but to use them it is better to be calm and free from greed.

SUN TSE

☞ When superiors and subordinates are of like mind, will and energy work together.

THE MASTERS OF HUAINAN

☞ The stretch organization is ready to build bridges – below the waterline.

TOM PETERS

WHAT YOU WILL LEARN **IN THIS CHAPTER**

☞ Understand in greater detail the value of the loyal customer.

☞ Place a dollar/pound value on loyalty.

☞ Accurately identify the customer needs and desires.

☞ Strategically establish in detail those customers that you wish to attract from competition.

☞ Develop a vision and mission to be achieved through E-Market Dominance.

LOYALTY IS DEAD, LONG LIVE LOYALTY

Few things remind me so chillingly of the onset of old age as the recurrent feeling that things ain't like they used to be. 'I can remember a time', I tell all who will listen, 'when things were different. When you could count on people. When there was loyalty and decency, when people gave their word and kept it ....' I stop with something of a jolt. I am reminding myself of the Jonahs I occasionally stand behind in the post office queue as they wait to draw their pensions. Yet there is much truth in what I, and they, are saying. Consider a few facts.

In the US today corporations, on average, lose half their customers every five years, half their employees (without dumb-sizing) every four years, and half their investors fly from one quick-buck bubble to another in less than one year. Customers, employees and investors are in a state of flux that verges on the frantic. The combined effect is dramatic. The old business cycle used to amble gently along at a rate which meant that the mature company could, on average, expect a life span of more than sixty years. Today that average life span is reduced to about twelve years and is falling. The economic and social costs of lack of loyalty are immense and rising.

Customers, given few other satisfactions, enter increasingly into one-off transactions based on price and price alone. Job-surfers flip from job to job almost as readily as they change television channels, bringing a wondrous level of ignorance in their wake. The workforce is increasingly called 'our most important asset' but is treated as disposable. Investors follow the instincts of herd animals, putting your pension savings and mine into high-risk stocks for short-term gain with no thought for tomorrow beyond the value of this year's bonus.

No wonder I'm getting cranky. We have created a world in which nothing has value beyond the quick buck that today may bring. The cost to business itself is enormous. Research by Reichheld and others shows that corporate performance is currently stunted by between 25% and 50%, and household names go belly-up or disappear with depressing regularity.

THERE IS A CYCLE OF DISLOYALTY

Customers intent on shopping only on price still expect high-quality service and give the company that fails to provide it as much hassle as they can prior to moving on. Uncommitted employees regard customers as trouble and do no more than is absolutely necessary to provide a meagre level of 'satisficing' (not enough to satisfy, just enough to avoid too much trouble) before they experience the high levels of stress which encourage them to move on to new employers, new customers and the same old hassle. Corporations with little going for them but a strategy of 'pile 'em high, sell 'em cheap' surf the globe to establish ever-lower production costs. And investors, their earnings threatened by under-performing corporations, search out the latest equivalent of seventeenth-century tulip bulbs. So corporations cut costs and heads; employees feel unsafe and uncommitted; customer service goes from bad to worse; customers demand low prices; and ... So it goes on.

But not for all. Arie de Geus has researched the winners in business: those corporations that had prospered for three hundred years or more. He discovered that they were:

- Frugal with resources.
- Committed to learning.
- Flexible in processes and products.
- Highly sensitive to the market's real, often hidden, aspirations.

While others cut prices and service to screech 'me too, me too' at an uncaring customer, those companies that are building secure prosperity for today and tomorrow are following the de Geus model. They are using new technology shrewdly so they can do more for the customer using fewer resources. They are more productive, more pro-active in providing customer service, and more profitable. They learn everything relevant to giving exemplary customer service, whether it concerns delivering higher quality at lower cost, meeting changing customer needs, expectations and desires, or leading in global best-practice. And they share learning throughout the business on the basis of life long learning – just in time. They are flexible, ever ready to adopt new ideas, but they use their accumulated knowledge to avoid becoming change junkies pursuing change for its own sake. And finally they use market intelligence intelligently to build customer loyalty, use customer loyalty to further build knowledge, and seek customer agreement to exchange information with each on a one-to-one basis in a way made only possible because of today's technology.

Just as there is a vicious cycle resulting from ignoring customer fidelity, so too there is a virtuous cycle of loyalty. We shall look at this in the next chapter. For now, let us concentrate on avoiding the vicious cycle.

Because e-commerce delivers a unique opportunity to focus on customers one by one, it provides a unique opportunity to create customer loyalty and everything that comes with it. In an ever faster spinning business cycle, when competition is increasingly global and in which costs can be reduced to provide higher customer value, a loyalty strategy is not an optional extra. So try this self-assessment exercise:

SELF ASSESSMENT
. . . .
Are you under threat? Could your most valued customers defect?

Do you know, with certainty, where in a global market   Yes   No
the major competitive threats to your revenues and profits
will come from?

Have you analysed what your key customers want now and   Yes   No
are likely to want in the future, in sufficient detail for you to
be able to write it down and get their unqualified agreement?

Have you clearly identified threats to your business that are   Yes   No
avoidable and put in place strategies to ensure that you will
not be caught off-guard?

Have you identified specific threats to your revenues and   Yes   No
profits that cannot be avoided by any action you take now,

and developed contingency plans based on key indicators
will warm if you are in actual or potential danger?

Do you know specifically – from your customers' points of view – where competition could offer satisfactions which you don't offer at present, or cannot offer in the near (very near), future?	Yes	No
Do you know precisely what your key customers' most important needs are now?	Yes	No
Do you know what your key customers might like, but do not expect at present?	Yes	No
Can you satisfy their most important needs better than your competition can?	Yes	No
Have you planned how you might build on your present strengths to give your customers what they might dream about tomorrow – today?	Yes	No
Have you considered how you could make any competitor decide that the cost of entry into your chosen markets is too high?	Yes	No
Are you completely clear about your Web strategy?	Yes	No
Have you thought through why it is in your customers' interests for you to have a Web presence?	Yes	No
Are you prepared to test and go on testing your website design, effectiveness, ease to use, and customer friendliness?	Yes	No

Unless your answer to every question is 'yes' you are vulnerable where you could be most hurt. Instead of being on the defensive, it is well worth considering how you might move toward the offensive. That is what E-Market Dominance is about: it provides the strategic framework and tactical action to build and leverage your strengths.

WHERE DO YOUR VITAL STRENGTHS LIE?

There is an enormous body of research which shows that a corporation which is introspective only in regard to its weaknesses and by diligent action removes them all, makes relatively little additional profit but often incurs a high level of cost. Those who look with care at their key strengths and find ways to leverage those things they do best will delight their customers and build new and far greater profit levels at minimum or falling cost. E-Market Dominance provides a wonderful opportunity to leverage your strengths. But to take full advantage of anything, first you need to understand it.

Analysing your strengths

1   Where is your company better than average in terms of operational excellence, service to customers and keeping costs down?
2   Where does your company have superior knowledge of customers and their emergent needs and desires?
3   Will your customers mandate you to increase that knowledge?
4   Do you find it easy to attract and keep above-average staff?
    - Do they enjoy their work?
    - Do they feel personally committed to the company?
    - Do they take a real pride in communicating with, understanding and serving the customer?
5   What specifically and concretely are you particularly good at doing, in the eyes of your customers, which enables you to make your highest profits and create the greatest customer delight?
6   Where do you already have the greatest ability to communicate on a one-to-one basis with your delighted customers?

Now think a little about what actions you might start to take. Again, you will return to this in detail soon. Remember to control the instinctive belief that the priority is to correct your weaknesses. Rather, the priority is always to give the profit-producing customer more of what they already like about doing business with you.

Preparing for action

1   What are the strengths and competencies you have now which will enable you to win more profitable business in those parts of today's markets which you currently serve?
2   What are the strengths and competences you need to build quickly in order to exploit more fully the most profitable markets today?
3   What are the strengths and competences you have which will enable you to prosper in the most exciting and profitable markets of the foreseeable future?
4   What strengths and competences must you build to thrive in the most profitable markets of the future?
5   What strengths and competences must you build to set the standards for your industry in the most exciting markets of the future?

E-MARKET DOMINANCE – ACTION SUMMARY

1 Survey your customers to identify what they like about doing business with you, if you are to the slightest degree doubtful about your strengths from the customer's point of view.

2 Survey your customers to establish their emergent needs or wants. Ask them to place no limits on their expectations: 'In a perfect world where anything is possible, what would you wish for?'

3 Solicit from your customers a mandate to keep them individually informed on matters which interest them.

4 Set up, if you don't already have one, a database capable of recording customer interests.

5 Put in place mechanisms for frequent contact with the customer on a one-to-one basis.

6 Identify *all* your key strengths and competences.

7 Build your areas of strength in accordance with customer desires. Take what is already good and turn 'good' into 'world-beating' in the eyes of the customer.

8 Focus on segments, markets, products and services that play to your current strengths and competences.

9 Assess the way the market is going and identify the competences you need to develop into a leading player in the most exciting markets of the future.

10 Put in place the processes which will enable you to create those strengths and competences on a 'just in time' basis.

11 Benchmark, but not just to catch up. Know your competition's best shots so you can leapfrog them in areas where you can easily develop a competitive edge.

12 Consistently review other industries to see what they are doing that you might adopt and adapt to create superior customer service with superior profits.

13 Challenge every employee at every level to make their maximum contribution to offering better service and products faster and at lower cost.

14 Look for ways to get your ideas, products or services first to market, but having taken number one position, work hard to increase your lead.

15 If you suspect or know that you have a 'me too' product or service, find ways to make it different and better in the eyes of your most profitable current and future customers.

16 Consistently analyse your competition's most profitable customers to identify changing needs and selling opportunities.

17   Ensure that everybody in your business has the knowledge to be able to identify customer needs and desires. Relate your strengths to them, not as features but as customer-centred benefits.

18   As soon as you can, involve all your committed people in thinking strategically.

19   Put in place, if you don't already have them, systems for moving thoughts around your organization. (Not old-fashioned suggestion schemes, but vital information, knowledge and idea-sharing systems using the same technology that you use to communicate with your customer.)

20   Create a learning organization that values sharing and life-long learning – just in time.

E-MARKET DOMINANCE – STRATEGIC ACTION PLAN

1   Decide clearly where you want to be in the future.

2   Write a short inspirational vision statement that tells others where you are going and makes them want to come with you.

3   Write a mission statement that tells all stakeholders how they will be treated by you, what you offer, what makes your offering different and better, what values and beliefs are central to your business and drive your decision making. Above all identify what challenges you to be better than the best.

4   Identify your strengths and competences according to the customer needs that they enable you to satisfy.

5   Complete a competitive/comparative analysis and amend your offering and its promotion if necessary to attract your competition's most valued customers.

6   Communicate with all valid enquirers and seek their permission to provide them with useful information or worthwhile entertainment or both.

7   Look for potential allies and offer them a host/beneficiary deal. (You scratch my back and I'll scratch yours.)

8   Constantly identify the emerging needs of your customers and build your capacity to delight them.

LIFE-TIME VALUE

A key part of the concept of E-Market Dominance is that you keep the profitable customer for life while avoiding becoming involved with time wasters. Those who welcome and act on the information you send them are very profitable for you. Over a life-time they become more profitable as you understand their needs better and the costs of consistently delighting them fall. At the same time as they are making a major contribution to your profits, they are acting as advocates for your business, telling others with similar desires where they will get exemplary service.

Working out the life-time value could not be more simple. Take a sample of your better customers. Work out on average how many years each continues to buy from you, and multiply the annual purchases by the number of years. However, this is liable to be an underestimate for four reasons:

1   If you market effectively and study your customers' wants each will buy more from you with every year that passes as well as sending you other worthwhile customers.
2   With E-Market Dominance the customer life cycle will be extended, so there will be additional years of business for you and they to enjoy.
3   You will aim at keeping 95% of your customers for a minimum of ten years because this has been shown to maximize your profitability. You will therefore devote your energies to keeping your key customers happy over the long term.
4   Your employees will become more closely aligned to your customers' changing needs and their growing knowledge will enable you to develop the flexibility relied upon by those firms, researched by Arie de Geus, that have prospered for up to 300 years.

Now let us turn from strategy to business-winning tactics.

WHAT YOU WILL HAVE LEARNED IN THIS CHAPTER

☞   Develop a meaningful vision which will appeal to all and bring the best customers and employees beating a path to your door.

☞   Write a mission statement that is a working tool, not just a collection of fine sounding words.

☞   Identify and leverage those strengths and competences that will delight your customers now and in the future.

☞   Assess your standing against competition, identify where you have a competitive edge and where you can most readily apply your advantage to win sales and loyal customers.

☞   Complete an effective strategic plan for 'clicks', 'bricks' or both.

☞   Establish the case for concentrating on building loyalty among customers, employees and investors.

CHAPTER SIX

THE LOYALTY SPIRAL

☞ The business world seems to have given up on loyalty: many
major corporations now lose – and have to replace – half their customers
in five years, half their employees in four, and half their investors in
less than one.

FRED REICHHELD, *The Loyalty Effect*

☞ The meek shall inherit the earth, but they'll never increase
market share.

WILLIAM McGOWAN

WHAT YOU WILL LEARN IN THIS CHAPTER

☞ Understand that loyalty is an essential, not an option.

☞ Build customer loyalty through employee loyalty and investor
loyalty through both.

Would you believe it? In today's world of rush, the ever-quicker quick buck
and 'pile 'em high sell 'em cheap' marketing, loyalty is going out of style.
Major corporations are treating customers as if they were buses: 'if we lose
this one there will be another one along in a minute'. Companies spend
almost all their marketing budget attracting new customers and by their
very actions irritate and often lose the old. Salespeople, driven by commissions, sign up customers they should know are simply not worth serving whilst
they ignore those who might be more discerning but who would provide a
lifetime of loyal business if they were treated well – as customers should be.
Companies invest heavily in so-called customer service departments instead of
training every employee at every level how to delight the customer. The
convenience of the company comes first. We are constantly being told that
'it's against company policy'. Just think about it for a second and you will
realize that many companies, satisfying (never mind delighting) the customer
is against company policy. Try to talk to the managing director of a company
from which you bought when you have a problem that no one else seems
willing or able to solve. Senior management refuse to speak or write to
customers who have exhausted every other avenue of justified complaint. It
is widely discussed in the automotive industry how the head of one major
manufacturer on receiving a report that a dangerous fault built into a vehicle

would kill approximately one customer in a thousand, responded: 'Lose the report. We lose more than half our customers when they choose to buy another make of auto so what the hell does it matter'. Churn has become a way of life. It is seen as inevitable. That is a mistake. It is increasingly a fatal mistake that is killing ever faster a growing number of companies.

In the 'good old days' when customers were cherished, the average lifetime of a business that survived the rocks and shallows of its early years was around 60 further prosperous years. Now that average lifetime is approximately 12 years and by no means all of those years are prosperous. Conversely there is a club in the UK limited to those companies that can celebrate more than 300 years in business. The most careful research proves that companies that pro-actively build customer loyalty build their own prosperity. But there is so much more to it than that.

GROW YOUR BUSINESS

If your customers are loyal they want you to succeed. Enlightened self-interest alone would be enough to ensure they want you to be there when they need you. But there is more to it: loyal customers are treated as friends, friendship is a two-way street, and friends are people for whom you are anxious to do favours. In a business friends quickly become advocates. What is more, when customers refer to you they are likely to talk to those who are most like them. In short, referrals by loyal, profitable customers bring you more customers who will be loyal and profitable. By building loyalty you attract the best kind of customer and avoiding getting mired by the other kind.

You need to build a referral system. It is not enough to ask for referrals on the odd occasions when the idea pops into the mind. A system does not need to be complicated: on the contrary, it should be designed to be as simple as possible. All you need to do is to ensure that once the customer is close to you and has been delighted by your products and services, you tell them how important referrals are to you and ask them politely to act on your behalf by telling their friends and associates. Fortunately e-mail can take the memory factor out of this. You need only to work out how often it is appropriate to delight a customer before asking them to reciprocate by helping you. Remember that the need to reciprocate has been hard wired into us by evolution. We really do believe that one good turn deserves another. Our only problem is that often we simply are never told what we can do to help. Get your timing right. Don't be greedy or in too much of a rush and you can't go wrong. The people you delight are anxious to help you.

Be very careful not to offer money to those who have a strong desire to help. Psychological research shows that you demean an unselfish good turn by offering money. Cash inducements for what would have been done out of friendship ensure that the good turn is unlikely to be repeated. Of course, it is nice to show your appreciation in return, but be careful to do so with taste and subtlety. Cherish your good customers and build your business by literally making it your business to deliver customer delight. Remember that in today's world of rush and hurry most people welcome privileged and easy access to relevant information as much as they value cash. Back up the information with supreme service and you will keep your customers happy and your happy customers for life.

A few short years ago global research into the characteristics of firms which enjoyed the highest reputation for meaningful customer care showed that, regardless of their sector or national base, they had this in common: they designed the whole company to deliver consistent customer delight.

The following is a self-assessment questionnaire developed by Tom Lambert and used by the British Institute of Practical Psychology as part of the Investors in Customers Programme. I strongly suggest you complete it and compare your assessment with someone else's, preferably a valued but critical customer.

CUSTOMER DELIGHT QUESTIONNAIRE

For each characteristic rate the extent to which the statement is true of your business today. Use the following scale:

1   Not at all true
2   True to a small extent
3   Fairly true
4   True to a great extent
5   True all the time without reservation

I. VISION AND COMMITMENT

1 Every employee is totally committed to the idea of creating delighted customers at the end of every transaction   ____

2 We all seek consistently to do things right first time every time and to do them faster, better and cheaper   ____

3 Executives always demonstrate by their actions their personal commitment to customer delight during every transaction   ____

4 Our driving intention is always to exceed the customer expectations in those things which are most important to them   ____

5 We promote and reward employees on the basis of their demonstrated commitment to delighting customers   ____

6   Everybody in this business has confirmed their personal
    commitment to total quality in everything that we do by signing
    our mission statement and living it every day   ____

7   Delighting the customer always takes precedence over satisfying
    our own internal needs   ____

8   We systematically reward with praise or tangible benefits every
    example of exceptional customer service   ____

9   When rare mistakes occur we focus on problem solving and not
    the apportionment of blame   ____

10 We communicate fully to customers, distributors and suppliers
    our intention to consistently provide superior service   ____

                                            Your total score   ____

            Multiply your total score by two for your percentage score   ____

II. CUSTOMER RELATIONSHIPS

1   When it comes to selling we treat the customer as our partner in
    problem solving and we see our salesperson as a true consultant
    acting in our mutual interest   ____

2   In advertising, selling and promotional activities we are totally
    scrupulous in never promising more than we can deliver   ____

3   We fully understand our customer's changing needs and the
    attributes of our offering that they value most   ____

4   Our customers provide key information which is fully utilized in the
    development of our service and product offering   ____

5   We strive consistently to be the leader in our industry in terms of
    customer retention   ____

                                            Your total score   ____

            Multiply your total score by four for your percentage   ____

III. CUSTOMER PROBLEMS

1   We record and monitor all customer complaints   ____
2   We regularly ask customers to give us feedback on our performance ____

3   Customer concerns are analysed to identify and resolve product
    quality or service quality problems   ____

4   We ruthlessly identify and eliminate any internal procedures which
    cause customer problems   ____

5   We refuse to live with convenient internal policies or procedures
    which fail to give added value to our customers   ____

                                               Your total score   ____

          Multiply your total score by four for your percentage score ____

IV.   CUSTOMER UNDERSTANDING

1   We know in detail the changing way in which our customers
    define 'quality'   ____

2   We provide opportunities for all employees at some time to be in
    contact with our customers   ____

3   We fully understand what our customers require of us no matter
    how their expectations change   ____

4   Our management team at every level studies our customers'
    requirements and builds our market strategy on the accumulated
    knowledge of all   ____

5   Our top management has frequent contact with customers   ____

                                               Your total score   ____

          Multiply your total score by four for your percentage score ____

V.   MAKING IT EASY TO DO BUSINESS WITH US

1   We keep our customers and prospects informed of our superior
    customer value proposition in a way which is anticipated, relevant,
    personal and timely   ____

2   We make customer convenience a key factor in the design of all
    our processes and procedures   ____

3   Our employees are told as clearly as we know how what they are
    free to do on their own authority to delight customers   ____

4   We make it easy for our customers to speak to us at the highest
     level if they believe that they have cause for complaint   ____

5   We do everything reasonable to resolve customer problems quickly   ____

                                                    Your total score   ____

          Multiply your total score by four for your percentage score   ____

VI.   EMPOWERMENT

1   We treat all employees with respect at all times and make it clear
     to all that we have a zero tolerance attitude to bullying or
     harassment of any kind by any person under any circumstances   ____

2   Employees at all levels are actively encouraged to have a good
     understanding of all our products, services and solutions to
     customer problems   ____

3   Employees are supported by resources which ensure that they can
     operate effectively in the interest of the customer   ____

4   At all levels of the business employees are empowered to make
     things right for the customer   ____

5   Employees genuinely feel that they are part of an exciting
     enterprise   ____

                                                    Your total score   ____

          Multiply your total score by four for your percentage score   ____

VII.   TRAINING AND DEVELOPMENT

1   Decisions are pushed down the organization to those who are
     capable, qualified and closest to the customer   ____

2   No lower-level employee is expected to make a decision for which
     they lack the training, skills or knowledge necessary for a good
     outcome   ____

3   Managers are fully trained in the complexities of empowering
     the workforce. The politically-correct approach of 'let my people
     go' is not tolerated. Empowerment is driven by customer needs
     and employee capability and commitment   ____

4   All formal training is backed by a programme of peer coaching
     which is supported by the appropriate tools   _____

5   Employees are cross-trained so that they can support each other
     when necessary   _____

                                        Your total score   _____

         Multiply your total score by four for your percentage score _____

VIII. BUSINESS GROWTH

1   Everyone in this business knows our goals and values and as far as
     is possible shares them   _____

2   We study the best practices of other businesses in order that we
     may do better than the best when it comes to serving our
     customers   _____

3   We ally ourselves with other businesses to provide better value to
     their customers and ours   _____

4   When a new product or service would better meet customer needs
     we bust a gut to make it available to them   _____

5   We seek the permission of all customers to keep them informed of
     all improvements and additions to our range   _____

6   We respect the needs of the internal customer to make things
     quicker and better for the external customer   _____

7   Every employee understands that 'quality' means we must
     consistently delight the customer at lowest possible cost   _____

8   Our employees consistently use their creativity to increase
     productivity and build profitability while delivering exceptional
     service   _____

9   We invest in the development of innovative ideas   _____

10   We know who are the best customers for our products and services
     and we know how to target them   _____

                                        Your total score   _____

         Multiply your total score by two for your percentage score _____

IX. EMPLOYEE ATTITUDE

1   Every employee is fully committed to our goals and proves it by
    cutting costs so that we can continuously invest in superior
    customer services   ____

2   Every employee recognizes they have a personal role in delighting
    the customer and actively seeks to create, identify and satisfy
    customer desires at a profit   ____

                                                    Your total score   ____

            Multiply your total score by ten for your percentage score ____

What it all means

The future prosperity of your business is a function of your ability to delight
and go on delighting your customers. The 'have a nice day' school of customer
satisfaction will not cut it in today's increasingly crowded and knowledgeable
marketplace. If you score less than 100% in any section you are in danger of
losing customers to those who have designed their business for the specific
purpose of attracting and keeping the best, most loyal customers. If, however,
you manage to score an honest 100% across the board, that is great – for now.
The right kind of customer will flock to you once they are aware of what you
offer. That is where e-Market Dominance demonstrates its superiority.
Customers are invited to enter into personal communication with you,
through numerous channels including other reputable people's databases
(see Chapter 11). Once with you they stay and that brings with it a range of
further benefits.

PRODUCTIVITY SOARS

One of the grossest stupidities resulting from the combination of the 'fads and
fallacies' school of authorship and consulting and the pure greed of the latter-
day buccaneer has been the 'dumbsizing' of organizations that needed no such
precipitate and grasping action. Downsizing has put large sums of money into
a very few rapacious back pockets (sometimes aided by a little judicious false
accounting – allegedly) and has needlessly damaged some otherwise excellent
organizations. The evidence shows that in spite of the short-term rise in stock
values which enable a financial killing, the long-term victim is invariably the
company, which has been shorn of expertise and commitment. Accordingly,
two new names for company diseases have entered the lexicon of company
doctors.

The Auschwitz Syndrome strikes a firm when those who survive the cull begin to realize that they have unwittingly played a part in the downfall of their erstwhile colleagues by taking on more than one person's responsibilities for a great deal less than two people's pay. Sooner or later they hit back at the company that put them into this invidious position and when they hit back it is hard enough to wreak havoc with the bottom line.

Just as fatal a malady is the dread Corporate Alzheimer's Disease. This strikes as hard as the non-corporate kind, but it strikes immediately. There is no incubation period. When seasoned employees leave a company all the accumulated knowledge they have gathered and which is not recorded goes with them. For example, a salesperson may know the foibles of an important customer and never record them. As a light-hearted but meaningful example, consider this:

A THOUGHT EXPERIMENT

Joe Bloggs is the chief buyer for one of your major customers. It is not generally known that Joe hates spending time with his irritating family. After a weekend spent with his nagging wife and noisy spoilt brats, Joe always starts the week in a foul temper. Monday sees him as the ultimate bear with a pain between his ears. Joe's mood on Mondays is so foul that if a salesperson calls they will get short shrift and no order. Indeed any salesperson who makes the slightest effort to sell to Joe will occasion such a rage that any outstanding order will be cancelled and the salesperson will be ordered off the premises and told never to return. You lose or fire a salesperson who may not understand the reason for Joe's Monday mood but has learned to avoid calling on Monday. Does such a salesperson think they must record Joe's eccentricity for the future good of the firm? Unlikely. If they think at all they probably think that everybody knows that you don't visit Joe on Mondays.

So one Monday, bright and early, the new salesperson visits Joe, who as my Amercian friends say, is full of **** and vinegar and ....

You need loyal employees just as surely as you need loyal customers – and the two are intimately connected. The costs of employee churn are astronomic. Clearly there are recruitment costs but don't imagine you only pay on a one-for-one basis. If a good employee leaves you may find you have to try two or three replacements before you land on one who has the potential to do the job as well as the original. Then you have the unavoidable learning curve. If the newcomer can immediately perform as well or better than the predecessor you are neither lucky nor clever. You were employing the wrong person before and they fired the company, not vice versa.

In the US those who employ consultants are generally more loyal buyers of the service than their counterparts in Europe, but occasionally in spite of a widespread feeling of satisfaction a client may suggest they fancy trying a change. As a working consultant I find that an easy way to keep the client is to ask whether they care to have someone else go through the learning curve I had to go through before I was truly useful to their company. International research shows that economies which for cultural or other reasons have loyal employees and are loyal to their employees in return do better in GDP growth. 'Sit by Nellie' (peer coaching) is often the cheapest and best form of training, but only if Nellie has been around for long enough to really know the ropes and the knots that can be tied with them.

One of the excuses for labour churn is that it brings in new ideas. The trouble with that is that if new ideas, even from bright people, are based on ignorance they are often bad ideas, or ideas which have been tried before and which failed – expensively. With the right training and encouragement, creativity among seasoned employees can be kept high without arousing any desire to initiate change for its own sake. If you want good ideas from outside you have plenty of alternatives. You can hire a consultant. (We will do anything for money. Howard Shenson used to say that being offered money for advice was an insult and 'if you're going to insult me, do it big time'.) You can share experiences with your strategic allies. You can send your brightest people on part-time MBA courses or other reasonably extended external training (preferably based on Action Learning), where they will have myriad opportunities to pick other people's brains and develop solutions to difficult and expensive company problems. You can attend Idea Share Fairs and swap ideas with your peers. You can conduct Idea Hypermarkets or Open Wall sessions in-house. If you are truly desperate you can even read books – godammit.

Loyal employees can provide almost all you need by way of innovation, and they can do much more. Loyal employees are in constant touch with loyal customers. They learn about emerging customer needs before the customers are fully aware of what's happening. The relationship can keep you ahead of the game. But as always, that's not all. When your customers and employees are friends, customers automatically become part of your intelligence-gathering network – if you encourage them. Clients often call me simply to tell me what the competition offered them or to send me copies of recent direct-mail letters. Loyal employees are committed employees. Committed employees are anxious not only to meet company goals, but also to do so at lowest possible cost if only so that the best possible customer value proposition is affordable. They can and will cut the costs of doing high-quality, high-return business at every opportunity.

But what is the tie-in between customer loyalty and employee loyalty? Why do loyal customers enable you to attract and retain the best employees? On the one hand:

- Loyal customers are hassle-free customers. Employees work in a less-stressful, friendlier atmosphere.
- Loyal customers enhance the image of the firm. People like to work for the top company in its market(s).
- Loyal customers bring in more customers. They make life easy for employees.
- Power flows to s/he who knows. Loyal customers deliver information.
- Loyal customers provide job security.
- Loyal customers enable higher profits and better salaries and bonuses.
- Loyal customers' needs grow, offering more interesting work, greater challenges and real job satisfaction.
- Loyal customers' business pays for better training and development opportunities, and loyal employees make them work.

On the other hand:

- Loyal employees are happy employees. They are a pleasure to do business with.
- Loyal employees are knowledgeable employees. They know the systems and the products and have the smarts to help solve customers' problems.
- Loyal employees are the customers' friends. That relationship will bring in referrals and repeat business.
- Loyal employees take a pride in their work and in their workplace. They strive to do things better, faster and at lower cost, so customer value is on a constant upward spiral.
- Loyal employees learn from each other. They create a genuine learning community that cuts the cost and increases the effectiveness of training and development.
- Loyal employees are flexible. They understand the whole business and they happily do whatever it takes wherever it is needed to make the business thrive.

So loyal customers beget loyal employees, and vice versa. Just how this works may be called the loyalty spiral.

RESEARCH ON THE LOYALTY SPIRAL

Research, mainly in the US, indicates that creating high customer value starts and sustains a cycle of increasing profitability. In outline what happens is this:

1   As the most desirable customers are attracted to the business stay and give a greater part of their spending power, revenues, market share and profits grow. Because the perceived value is strong, the company is able to

become increasingly selective in new customer acquisition, concentrating on customers who offer the highest profitability with the least hassle.

2　The high reputation of the company and its elite customer base enables it to attract and retain the best employees. The satisfactions of being part of the best company and serving the best customers build commitment, motivation and loyalty among employees, who then get to know the customers better and are delighted to provide better service at lower cost, thus reinforcing customer loyalty and further improving profitability.

3　As productivity and quality improve, costs diminish and the ever-improving customer value attracts more ever-better quality customers. Higher satisfaction influences those customers who have been more hassle than they are worth to change their behaviour, they begin to deliver their full profit potential or are encouraged to go elsewhere. Profits climb and the company is able to invest in training and development of the highest order on the basis of life-long learning – just in time – enabling the levels of customer service to continue spiralling upwards. Personal growth of employees both individually and in teams enables major improvements in process and productivity.

4　Ongoing productivity growth and the relative ease of dealing with loyal customers generates cost and service advantages that force competition into a 'me too' strategy which enhances the whole business sector. The firm is creating the standard for their industry. Competition finds that 'me too' is an expensive strategy, and market leaders are able to increase their lead, building profits and securing stability. This is attractive to investors and makes the company 'darling of the markets'.

5　The market value of the business grows, enabling increased investment in processes and products to build customer delight, which enhances the company's value-producing potential and so further revenue and profit improvements.

Source: Bains Research

E-Market Dominance is a process by which you can attract and retain loyal customers. Let me remind you, if I may, of a remark by a far better writer than I shall ever be. Peter Drucker said that innovation and marketing are the value-adding parts of a business, all the rest merely add cost. E-Market Dominance delivers the added value most efficiently at lowest possible cost. But you will only know this if you measure it.

MEASUREMENT

Building on the Juran–Deming concept that what is not being measured is not being managed, world-class operations look to measure internally while benchmarking externally against competition in order to overtake them. Measurement is not the recording of data so much as a process of activating improvements. If you want to be sure you are getting the improvements loyal customers and employees deliver, you should consider measuring results. The normal areas of measurement are:

1   Quality
2   Cost
3   Flexibility
4   Reliability
5   Innovation

To which I believe you should always add:

6   Productivity.

Let us now spell out what you need to measure in each of these areas.

1   Quality

- The percentage reduction in the total cost of quality
- Percentage reduction in defects
- Percentage of suppliers certified in terms of the quality of their materials
- Percentage reduction in the size of the supplier base
- Percentage reduction in the time between defect occurrence, detection and correction.

2   Cost

- Percentage increase in inventory turnover (progressing toward J(ust) I(n)T(ime) component deliveries.)
- Percentage reduction in data transactions
- Percentage reduction in floor space utilized per major unit of production
- Percentage increase in size of initial orders
- Percentage increase in the size and frequency of repeat orders
- Percentage decrease in customer complaints
- Percentage decrease in mis-shipments.

3   Flexibility

- Percentage reduction in cycle time
- Percentage reduction in set-up time

- Percentage increase in number of jobs mastered per employee
- Percentage increase in common materials used per product.

4 Reliability

- Percentage increase in equipment effectiveness
- Percentage decrease in equipment downtime
- Percentage decrease in warranty costs, material returns, etc ...
- Percentage reduction in engineering changes
- Percentage increase in on-time delivery.

5 Innovation

- Percentage reduction in new product introduction lead time
- Percentage increase in new product sales revenues in relation to the total
- Percentage increase in new, highly profitable customers
- Customer perception of company as leader in innovation in the industry as measured by customer e-mail surveys
- Percentage of management time spent on thinking strategically as opposed to fire-fighting.

6 Productivity

- Percentage increase pounds/dollars of output/sales per employee
- Percentage increase in number of suggestions for process improvements per employee
- Percentage increase in number of product/marketing improvement suggestions per employee
- Percentage increase in profitable new accounts gained by sales
- Percentage increase in demands for relevant, job-related training and education from employees, suppliers and customers.

All of the above will not be relevant to all readers of this book, but we urge you to measure the benefits you achieve where it is important to you and to set specific, measurable, achievable, realistic goals for improvement. Keep the challenge in the business. Always be looking for ways to do more with less. That will keep competition awake at night.

THE LOYALTY MERRY-GO-ROUND

Once you know what to measure, you are ready to ride the Loyalty Merry-go-Round. But, before you step on board, read *The Loyalty Effect* by Frederick H. Reichheld (Harvard Business School Press 1996). The full effects of the loyalty cycle on your business will astound and delight you. That done, follow these steps:

1   Identify the sectors, segments or niches where your best customers lie.

2   Analyse and go on analysing customer desires, needs and expectations. (Chapter 2)

3   Test your ability to create and satisfy emergent customer desires at a profit against competition and develop a strategy to leapfrog rather than play catch up. Never risk a 'me too' marketing strategy. Aim for market leadership in those segments, sectors and niches where your most profitable customers lie.

4   Build a superior customer value proposition that will bind your best customers to you.

5   Find the right customers by using technology, desired information and, strategic alliances. Constantly acquire more worthwhile customers by actively and systematically seeking referrals and sponsors.

6   From the first contact, invite your customers and prospects to mandate you to keep them informed, entertained and involved in your business.

7   Make customer loyalty a key objective and measure your progress regularly. Aim for a customer life of at least ten years and a customer retention rate of 95 %. It can be achieved and will increase your profits massively.

8   Attract the right employees and encourage the sharing of knowledge and information.

9   Be frugal with resources. Build cash or credit that you can use when you most need them and remember that frugal does not mean penny-pinching. It means investing resources only after proper assessment of risk, return and the speed of pay-back.

10 Invest in training and development. Make your training customer-centred and support it with structured peer coaching on the job.

11 Build and keep building a cost advantage through greater productivity. Empower your people, but only when they are ready for it. They are ready when:

   ● They share the goals, vision and values of the business
   ● They are fully trained and sufficiently experienced to make decisions
   ● They are close to the customer.

12 Think carefully about investors. If and when you seek a capital injection be careful to get it from sources you can live with and which are likely to be loyal to you.

WHAT ABOUT THAT OTHER MARKET?

The interaction of loyal customers and loyal employees delivers higher profits and lower costs. Loyal employees in particular provide highly valuable business assets in the form of growing intellectual capital. When committed people study and learn from their rare failures, while at the same time use their creativity to build on their frequent successes, the value of this intellectual capital in the knowledge age is an immense attraction to forward-looking investors. Investment today is directed toward knowledge – thus the Gadarene rush to invest in loss-making dot.coms that may never make a dollar in profit. But companies that work the loyalty spiral offer something more: they combine intellectual assets with profits that grow year by year, and long-term security for investors, customers and employees. No wonder that having this unique stockholder value, companies that have actively created loyal customers and loyal employees attract and retain their investors. This contrasts with the average American corporation which according to research by Bains Inc. loses half its investors and much of its market value in less than twelve months.

WHAT YOU WILL HAVE LEARNED IN THIS CHAPTER

Once you have implemented the E-Market Dominance programme you will:

☞ Have a clear and detailed framework for building and sustaining loyal customers.

☞ Implement customer-centred plans for balanced continuous improvement of all parts of the business.

☞ Meet or exceed the changing expectations of customers at lowest practical cost.

☞ Promote the company effectively as fully customer-centred.

☞ Enable employees at every level to get closer to the customer.

☞ Create an 'unfair' global competitive advantage through a deepened understanding of rapidly changing customer desires.

☞ Attract, delight and retain the most profitable customers in your sector.

☞ Have a means of turning delighted customers into company advocates.

☞ Enhance the company image.

☞ Build new levels of job satisfaction.

☞ Meaningfully empower the workforce to delight the customer.

☞ Implement customer-centred development and training throughout the business.

☞ Build a customer-centred learning community.

☞ Attract and retain the highest quality staff at every level.

☞ Use internal dynamics to build employee loyalty, superior productivity, increased cost advantages, higher profits, and increased investor loyalty through superior customer value.

CHAPTER SEVEN

HOW TO USE E-MAIL TO DEVELOP SALES AND PROFITS

☞ Understand the power of e-mail.

☞ Develop an e-mail strategy appropriate to your business and personal needs.

☞ Identify a comprehensive source of electronic communications services.

☞ Be ready to start to use e-mail to build profitable business.

☞ Be aware of the possible effects of new Data Protection legislation.

On the face of it, e-mail is not the friendliest way of communicating. It arrives with a stream of meaningless titles, acronyms, routeing instructions and other bewildering codes. How can we possibly think this is a good way, never mind the best way to build one-to-one relations with millions of people we may not know? It is about as impersonal as you can get: less personal than a letter penned or typed on good, clean, white, pristine and pleasantly tactile paper, and colder and less friendly than a telephone conversation. We are so comfortable with the telephone today that we almost replace face-to-face contact with it. Deals worth billions of dollars, pounds, yen and deutschmarks are routinely transacted over the telephone without any major concerns about the medium. Sales are made, deals are clinched, hearts are poured out, even hirings and firings are performed by telephone. But e-mail? Why, you can't hear, see or touch this new communications medium, yet it has superseded the others to an astounding degree. What makes it so powerful? The answer, like e-mail itself, is simple yet deep. Many features, which presently seem like disadvantages, will soon be generally perceived as huge benefits.

When we write a letter we are very careful in our choice of words. We pay attention to the layout of the page, even the weight and texture of the paper we use. In the recipient's hands all these speak volumes for or against us. We need to sign our letter for it not to seem impersonal and, if we know a little psychology, we make our signature large, flowing and strong to show our health is blooming and our mood is positive. The standard business letter signed on another's behalf by a secretary is rarely as well received as one signed by the writer. Less welcome still are those pseudo-signatures produced on a computer and, in some cases scribing a fictitious but impressive sounding name. With e-mail all these rules, conventions and prejudices are shown scant respect. A one-line message, electronically signed or not, providing it conveys the intended meaning, is totally acceptable. Layout, typeface, and sadly for old-fashioned pedants such as me, even spelling and grammar seem to have little importance when sending a message by e-mail. The dictum that the medium is the message appears no longer to apply. It is the clarity and brevity of the message that is important.

THE AGE OF INFORMATION ... AND THEN SOME

We have never had such an array of working technology. In the past we had to compromise between our wishes and needs and how well the technology was able to meet them. Different types of computers refused to communicate with each other. The speed of telephone lines made data transfer excruciatingly slow; text, even worse pictures, images and graphics, took forever to download and such was the complexity of the process that the very slowness increased the chances of corruption and loss of material. Now, thanks to Tim Berners-Lee and his merry band of geniuses, we take speed entirely for granted. Indeed we often complain about the way masses of information, both textual and graphical, can reach our PCs in a matter of seconds. I have been known to click onto a site that arrives so quickly that I question myself whether I really have the right site and not the cached version sitting locally on my hard disk. To those grumblers who are always complaining about the slowness of the Internet, I suggest you cast your mind back only five years and say hallelujah. And it's getting faster. *We ain't seen nuthin' yet.*

Here is a comparison of the various communication media:

	Speed	Ease of use	Cost	Personal
Letters	4	4	4	8
Telephone	7	8	3	8
Fax	8	6	4	5
e-mail	9	8	9	9

1 = awful and 10 = awesome

This table deserves some explanation.

LETTERS

We all like to receive letters. This is why direct mail was once so massively successful, despite the moans and complaints of those who purport to hate 'junk mail'. Even the extreme Jonahs, when closely questioned, will admit to a range of exceptions where they bought as a result of direct unsolicited mail. But letters are slow – slow to write and slow to arrive. It can take as much time to gather together the paraphernalia required – paper, pen, envelope, stamp – as it does to write a brief note.

Even the briefest personal letter needs some thought to compose (some think the briefer the letter the greater the thought), and we need to pay attention to readability, neatness and spelling. So letters are not only slow, they are far from easy to produce. The cost of writing a letter is high when all is considered, and this cost escalates in business when we include the need for a word-processor and a secretary or personal assistant. (Downsizing has forced many executives to read and write their own mail, not necessarily leading to an increase in the standard of grammar or style of letter writing. In a way the advent of e-mail has got most of us off the stylistic hook.) And even then the letter may still fail to deliver the goods, which is why one British consultant is able to charge between £3000 and £30,000 for designing and writing a 'simple' sales letter. But letters remain personal and unless they come from the IRS or Inland Revenue we still love getting them.

TELEPHONE

Most of us have a love affair with the telephone. Some of us even remember conducting a love affair over the telephone. Glenn Miller immortalized a telephone number in a number of a different sort. For many of us the telephone is like a drug. The mobile phone is becoming the heroin of the office as home phones are the cannabis. We don't always admit to this – but can you show me any practising addict who will admit that they are hooked? My co-author, when he set up in business many years ago, ran up a colossal telephone bill but brought in very few clients because he spent his days telephoning his friends for no better reason than to hear another human voice. Thrusting young executives and executreens in their BMWs and Porsches have their mobile phone permanently attached to one ear or another or to talk incessantly into what appears to be a length of liquorice. They give no thought to scattering pedestrians and other drivers who get in the way of their communicating. 'Look at me mummy, no hands' is all too often the rallying cry of today's bright, young (and getting ever younger) business thing. The UK government has found it necessary to advise parents to keep their offspring's use of the mobile telephone to a minimum lest the instrument fry their brains. One might be forgiven for thinking that the price of making a call in the UK would be enough to urge restraint.

Why do we love our telephones with such all-consuming ardour? The psychologists and anthropologists would say that it is the unique combination of the personal with lack of intrusiveness that makes the telephone such a fascinating toy. The removal of all sensory input apart from the voice can have an extraordinary effect on the speaker and listener. Why else are sex chat-lines such a booming business? Would it be worth a buck a minute to listen to a disembodied voice talking dirty if you could see the bored housewife at the other end of the line surrounded by knitting and half-eaten junk food? Researchers think that the advent of the videophone will surely detract from this 'innocent pleasure'. When video is the norm the chat-line ladies will have to live up to the photographs in the advertisements or the whole business will sink without trace.

When we can see who we are talking to we will have to revert to the normal conventions of body language, visual cues and facial expression, but, as those of us who use video conferencing in our business know, it will still be a somewhat restricted medium. Ironically, the more like face-to-face communication the telephone becomes, the more the real thing is preferred. But surely the quick, concise telephone call has brevity very firmly on its side?

Not unless you limit your conversations with answerphones. Talking to real people tends to be extended. Because we still adhere to the normal conventions of politeness on the telephone, calls are usually longer than they need to be. We engage in redundant intimacies. Do we really care if the unknown person on the other end is having a nice day or enjoyed their recent vacation? Some years ago a famous British broadcaster was on a visit to the US. He found the ritual of being urged to 'have a nice day' quite delightful, especially when spoken by a charming and attractive young lady. He felt he should reciprocate. The ensuing conversation went like this:

'Thank you sir. Have a nice day.'

'Thank you, and I hope you too have a nice day dear.'

'How do you expect me to have a nice day working in a goddam dump like this serving cretins (in the Mid West pronounced 'creetans') like you?'

It is very easy to make telephone calls, but it is rarely cheap. Telephones are everywhere, in our pockets and purses, on the street corner, in the hotel room, in almost every room in our homes, and in clusters on every desk in every office. Despite the pressure on BT, ATT & T, Big and Baby Bells, and others around the world to reduce charges, and in spite of cut-price call vendors peddling greater and greater savings, the telephone is still a relatively expensive way to communicate.

So we have a popular communications medium that relies, to a major degree, on its shortcomings for its popularity. I will say nothing more of the odd suggestion that mobile phones scramble our brains.

FAX

Few people realize that the technology of the fax is very old. We could have had faxes when Wellington and Napoleon were slugging it out at Waterloo had we the national grid, the telephone and the lines to relay the messages. Like the telephone and e-mail, the fax machine only began to grow in popularity when enough people owned one. The little boy with his empty bean can and string is on his own and uncommunicative until he finds another little boy with another empty can to talk to. E-mail was until recently like the fax machine was twenty years ago. We had the technology but the other fellow lacked it, so it was no use to either of us.

A fax suffers from some of the constraints of the letter, in that we need to compose it, lay it out, write, type, and print it. And after all that trouble some or all of it may be received looking like a badly printed bar code. The main differences between fax and letter are that the cost of transmitting is in the telephone call and not the stamp, and it is quick. The time taken to send a fax wins hands down over a voice call because of the lack of redundant intimacies and verbal diversions. In spite of the past success of the fax and the bypassing of separate machines by incorporating a fax capability into our computers, most communications gurus predict the total demise of the fax machine within ten years as e-mail increasingly becomes the dominant means of communication.

E-MAIL

With e-mail we are happily set free of the need to create formal conventions about layout and verbal padding. These protocols are left to the system to sort out where needed. We feel that as long as we impart our news, request, announcement or other communication, that is all that is required. And we are right, aren't we? Does it really matter if we sign off as yours sincerely, truly, faithfully or whatever? Soon these niceties will be as dead as the 'ultimo' and 'instantum' beloved of letter writers in the early years of the last century. What counts is that we impart what we want to say accurately, to the right person, at the right time, and as cost-effectively as possible. But, I can almost hear you asking yourself, how can this electronic shorthand be described as a personal form of communications?

Frankly the first part of the answer is that an unadorned, unwanted e-mail is a pretty impersonal medium. This chapter will show you how to build on the mind-blowing attributes of e-mail that enable you to make it personal to a degree limited only by your intentions and creativity. Making all communication personal, desired, relevant, and timely lies at the heart of E-Market Dominance and strange as it may seem, this apparently impersonal medium has the capability to make it happen for you, and make it happen at minimum cost.

E-mail is usually the first application of the Internet that organizations put to use. They start with individual e-mail accounts, where each 'owner' manages their own incoming and outgoing e-mails. Before long, the powers that be notice the inordinate amount of time being spent on creating, reading, deleting and generally messing about in e-mail boxes. This is to leave aside the dubious uses to which many people put their business e-mail accounts, about which the less said the better.

But despite the downside, e-mail is the best way to get people started on the road of full electronic communicating. You only have to install one of the proprietary packages – Outlook Express, Eudora, Netscape Messenger – to get you started. These are excellent to get you going, but if you want to get serious about communicating effectively with your clients, customers and prospects you should look at a more powerful set of tools to build an electronic communications strategy.

One of the disadvantages of individual e-mail boxes is that each message is an entity in itself and no history of any value is recorded. Certainly, the message can be archived, relayed and broadcast, but this is not enough. Your e-mail systems' productivity will rocket if you use a package or service from one of the specialist e-mail marketing companies, such as Maildrive Limited (http://www.maildrive.com) or, in the US, Accucast Inc (www. accucast.com) (Figure 7.1).

These and a growing number of others can create for you a corporate e-mail system that is scaleable from the smallest start-up to something capable of handling very large e-mail campaigns. They can also provide the tools for

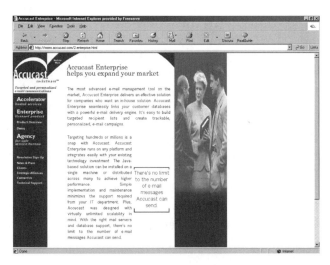

FIGURE 7.1   Accucast is one of the growing band of specialist companies providing e-mail marketing software. They offer a fully scalable system from the smallest up to the very largest e-mail campaigns

establishing a systematized process of communication that can send automatic scheduled interactions of various kinds. These include:

- Newsletters
- Press releases
- Pricing offers
- Membership offers
- Build-up promotions
- Links to specific parts of your web site
- Auto responders.

Let us look at what each can do for you.

Newsletters

Everyone who has tried it knows what a pain it can be to take on the task of establishing and sustaining a corporate or club newsletter. At first it seems easy. The first edition is eight packed sides of A4 and several contributors willingly provide excellent copy. There are lots of pictures that are readily made available. Someone even draws an appropriate and funny cartoon of the Chairman in a compromising position. This begins to look like a really great idea.

Issue number two is a little harder to produce. The article providers seem a lot busier, the picture sources dry up, the newsletter may run to four sides of A4, and, guess what, it is weeks late. Issue three shows every sign of becoming one of publishing's endangered species. If it appears at all, it becomes questionable whether it should have.

With a system like Accucast (www.accucast.com), you can have your editorial meeting in January and create twelve skeleton newsletters. In total, these probably contain little more material that the first paper-based newsletter. New material can be added during the year if needed but if not you simply decide which day of each month you want the letter to be transmitted. It is scheduled once and you can just sit back and let it happen. The result will be that your name will appear every month as an expected and valued communication to all of your customers. It gets you over the problem of 'I need to keep in touch but I have nothing specific to say right now'.

Press releases

Your e-mail database can be segmented into as many different categories as you need. You can even segment your PR database to reflect the key media – newspaper journalists, magazine writers, television and radio presenters – and the really important people – customers and prospects. This means that you can send targeted press releases that will dramatically increase the chances your release will get used. It is more and more important to send press releases by e-mail because journalists, like all writers, are essentially lazy and you need to make life as easy as possible for them. If you send a paper-based release they have to re-type it or have typed the parts they want. This is a major disincentive to anyone who is busy. If you need, in effect, to start from scratch you might just as well start from the beginning with something that you care about with passion. An e-mail release, on the other hand, can be cut and pasted or just lifted as a whole and used by journalists in their own original work.

Pricing offers

If you want another excuse to contact your database you need only create a time-limited pricing offer for your special customers and prospects. This can take many forms. You can link it to volume. You can raise the chances of initial orders by combining an offer with copper-bottomed guarantees. You can use special offers to increase the frequency of ordering. You can use them to gain 'a greater share of the customer'. You can send them only to those customers who have bought one of your products and use it as a personal 'thank you' for their business – especially to those you are confident could make good use of something else you sell. Make each of your communications relevant, personal and desired. In short, use e-mail technology as part of your E-Market Dominance tactics. But, and it's a very important but, use it to identify things your customers want to know and seek their permission to keep in touch. Have them opt-in rather than force them to opt out of your information or entertainment messages. How to do all of this is explained in this book.

Membership offers

Why not turn your customers into members? For those customers who elect to be members, make buying cheaper, easier, faster, better. Save them time and trouble. Give them a good reason to keep returning to your website. Give them a password to enable them to get into a valuable part of it. If the information there is valuable they will love to be part of the in-crowd. This is you opportunity to do what every good service and sales organizations should do: make your valuable customers feel important. After all they are vital to your prosperity.

Build-up promotions

Here is your chance to generate some anticipation in your customers and prospects. The first e-mail can set the scene and subsequently you can add more and more information. Suppose you are selling seminars. You could follow this sequence:

Mail 1	Tell them the subject but not much more
Mail 2	Tell them the speakers (and repeat the subject)
Mail 3	Tell them the venue and dates (and repeat the above)
Mail 4	Tell them the price and invite them to buy.

Links to specific parts of your website

Sending large amounts of data by e-mail takes time for your recipient to download. If you do this unsolicited you will inspire some rude comments at the very least and will risk losing customers' goodwill. One alternative is to put the information on a page of your website and simply tell your recipient about the content of the information with a hyper-link that takes them directly to that particular page of your site. Do not take them to the Home Page or the fancy Flash Movie that precedes it. Here is how to do it:

1. Go into your browser and find the page of your site that you want people to visit.
2. Note the full domain name in the Address box at the top of your browser.
3. Swipe your mouse over the address to highlight it and click on copy.
4. Open your e-mailer and place the cursor where you want the address to be in the text of your message.
5. Click on the 'paste' icon and the address will appear where you want it.

Auto-responders

An auto-responder is an automatic e-mail which is sent from you but is generated by the visitor to your site or the recipient of your e-mail. They can be a very valuable means to transmit information without any human intervention. Auto-responders can be used for a range of applications, including:

- To answer Frequently Asked Questions.
- To send more detailed information following a short e-mail.
- To enable people to subscribe and un-subscribe to your newsletters, e-zines or other regular communications.

Auto-responders can be set up by your ISP. One short word of caution: although they are very useful auto-responders should be used with discretion in building one-to-one relations via e-mail. This is because they can have the effect of de-personalizing the service you are so carefully building.

Making it personal

To understand how e-mail can be transformed into a medium that can help you create and maintain a one-to-one relationship with hundreds and later thousands of customers, prospects suppliers, and other contacts, we need to look not at the medium but at the content of the message. As I mentioned earlier, the days are almost gone when we need concern ourselves with the format and social niceties of letter writing for purely business communications. I feel sympathy for those accomplished people who write business letters that are honed and polished with precision. Have no fear, there will always be a place for such letters, but they are not vital to the day-to-day communications for which e-mail is usually so much more appropriate and effective. Of course, we need to ensure that what we send conveys our meaning with as much clarity and punch as a letter, but with e-mail we can say it quickly and efficiently without risk of offending our recipient.

E-Market Dominance demands that, having won our customer's permission, we communicate what is important to that customer when they want to know it. E-mail can make such communication easy. Use it to build profits with communication that is wanted, personal relevant and timely and you have made a good start. But as the man in the wellington boots used to say, 'there's more'.

CASE STUDY: Delta Airlines

THE TASK

In 1998 Delta went looking for an efficient and cost-effective way to build stronger relationships by marketing discount airfares to its best customers, who are members of the SkyMiles frequent-flyer programme. Delta viewed e-mail as an attractive alternative to traditional direct mail because it costs less (pennies vs. pounds per message), has a higher response rate (10% or more vs. 2%) and speeds time to market for new promotions.

However, Delta did not want to alienate their best customers with unsolicited, un-personalized e-mail. They opted for the Accucast system from Socketware Inc (www.accucast.com). 'E-mail can be much more personal than something you get in your mail box, but you have to be able to customize it', explained Kevin Dunn, Delta's manager for e-commerce sales and marketing. 'More importantly, you have to allow your customers to opt-in for the information they want to receive and then deliver it as promised'. Delta's challenge was clear: to find an in-house solution that would deliver customized, personalized e-mail messages containing only the information that customers request, at a fraction of the cost of traditional direct mail.

THE RESULTS

Delta established an area within its corporate website where SkyMiles® members could view their account information, opt-in to specify which promotions they wanted to receive information about, and list up to five preferred departure points. 'If we were going to encourage our customers to select their opt-in preferences, then we had to hold up our end of the deal by responding with *totally* customized e-mail', said Dunn. Delta is currently experiencing an average click-through ratio of 10% on the Delta Web Fares and Delta Fan. This is significant considering that traditional direct mail campaigns usually solicit a 1–2% response rate. Delta expects to increase their Delta Web Fares and Delta Fan Fares ticket sales by 400% in the next year.

Currently Delta distributes over one million messages a month. Because of the Accucast's scalability, Delta is comfortable they will be able to handle the increased numbers of e-mail messages as their SkyMiles membership grows. 'Accucast allowed us to leapfrog our competition and emerge as a pioneer in the execution of permission-based e-mail marketing programs', said Dunn. 'Since the installation of the system and the launch of Delta Web Fares and Delta Fan Fares, Delta has significantly reduced marketing costs, increased sales and improved customer service.'

DATA PROTECTION

The dust has yet to settle on what will eventually be the law on Internet Data Protection. In the UK the government has just passed the Data Protection Act 1998 (http://www.dataprotection.gov.uk/eurotalk.htm), which replaces and reinforces the Data Protection Act 1984. This legislation reflects the European Union stance on data protection. Laws in the US are not so stringent and neither the US government nor the European Parliament have done anything to make the situation for the Internet marketer any clearer than it was before. The UK act brings in possible fines of up to £5000 but the legislation has yet to be tested in either the UK or the European courts. Although this is a highly unsatisfactory position for marketers, my advice is to err on the side of caution and structure your campaigns, databases and procedures to comply with the Act. The legislation fails to make clear how and when a data-subject can or has consented. Opt-in and opt-out principles have not been made any clearer by this hybrid legislation. Despite this uncertainty in Europe, the power of ethical e-mail marketing is so great that it is probably unstoppable. Eventually US and European governments will have to agree on a clearer set of guide-lines to protect both data-subjects and innocent marketers trying to do a good job for their clients or companies, yet stay within the law. If you are in any doubt about whether your next campaign will infringe the regulations I suggest you join and consult the Direct Marketing Association (www.dma.org.uk) – see Figure 7.2. below. There is a US–EU accord called the 'Safe Harbors' agreement. This allows US companies to process data from the EU providing they have signed and complied with the rules set out in the EU Directive on Data Protection 1995. Elizabeth France, the UK Data Protection Commissioner, said in an interview in August 2000 when asked what the impact of the legislation would be on e-commerce and e-mail marketing, she replied that:

> The Data Protection Act does not present a barrier to the development of e-commerce or e-marketing; rather it provides a framework of law which will help to gain and retain customer confidence.

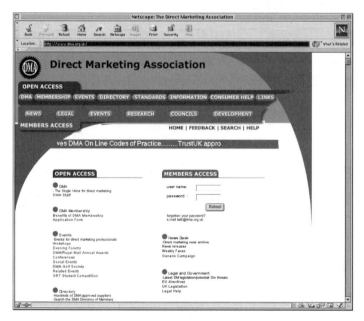

FIGURE 7.2 Every organization involved, or planning to become involved, in e-mail marketing should consider joining the Direct Marketing Association

WHAT YOU WILL HAVE LEARNED IN THIS CHAPTER

☞ Communication, both personal and business, has been revolutionized by e-mail.

☞ E-mail appears to be impersonal, but this too has changed.

☞ What counts now is not the medium but the message, which must be concise, accurate and clear.

☞ E-mail offers efficient, inexpensive, personal, relevant, timely, and desirable communications.

☞ Systems exist to extend electronic communications far beyond simple box-to-box e-mail to include vital business data capture.

☞ Data protection legislation is becoming more stringent, particularly in the US. Marketers must stay vigilant to remain within the law.

CHAPTER EIGHT

DESIGNING AN EFFECTIVE MARKETING WEBSITE

☞ Just because you can does not necessarily mean you should

ANON.

WHAT YOU WILL LEARN IN THIS CHAPTER

☞ Critique your own website and advise on improvements.

☞ Assess the marketing impact on certain aspects of web design.

☞ Know which features of your site impair your marketing effort.

☞ Specify a re-build of a marketing-friendly website.

Because of the nature of the Internet as a medium, the design of the website has a major impact on the effectiveness of the site from a marketing perspective. The medium is new and we are learning on the hoof, making all kinds of horrific mistakes along the way. As more and more site contaminate the Web with needless animations and vibrant or inappropriate colours, it makes sense for us to be sure our own website meets exacting standards in all areas. Design is a fundamental one.

Many sites are established as 'flag-flying' exercises and no attempt is made to sell any product online. Examples of this type of site include the new VW site, a beautifully designed site (Figure 8.1) launched to promote the new Beetle (www.newbeetle.com). Most sites, however, need first to gain a high search-engine presence and then maximize the rewards from every visitor to the site. The aspects of design we will cover here are:

- Appearance
- Build
- Compatibility
- Performance
- Search-engine friendliness
- Links.

Again, let's see what you need to do about each in turn.

FIGURE 8.1   The New Beetle site is a great example of a clean functional and very attractive site.

APPEARANCE

A well-designed site will have a clean and uncluttered feel to it. Despite the fact that most of the main portal sites such as MSN and AltaVista have a very heavily loaded front page, it is far better to aim for the clean and uncluttered. Such portals need to carry links to hundreds of different subject areas of the site and this leaves little alternative but to cram everything onto the front page. This will not generally be the case with a commercial website. With judicious use of the navigation system it is wholly possible to create a clean appearance to your site. Here are some of the design factors that contribute to creating such an appearance.

Use of colour

Just because designers have millions of colours available to them, and modern monitors have very good resolution giving high picture quality, does not mean you need your front page to look like the inside of an Italian ice cream shop. Choose two or three main colours and use them throughout the site. Create consistency, not only within the site but also with the look and feel of your corporate image. Dark backgrounds can make the text hard to read, so be sure to test out the results on a low-resolution screen. That should put you off dark-coloured backgrounds for life.

Animations

Modern animation tools such as Flash from Macromedia (www.macromedia. com) are miracles of modern programming. They have put massive computing power in the hands of every designer at a very reasonable cost. To see some of the possible uses of their tools Macromedia have a gallery of sites: try looking at the CCA Galleries site at (www.ccagalleries.com). Make use of these tools by all means, but do try to confine their use to areas where they add value (Figure 8.2). It is very tempting to give designers free rein – but you may end up with your logo flying in from all parts of the globe before spinning wildly and disappearing up some fundament or other. Resist this at all costs.

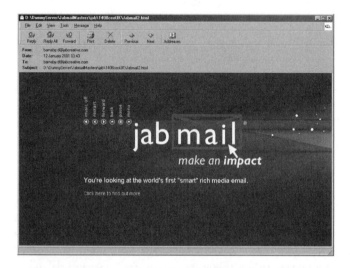

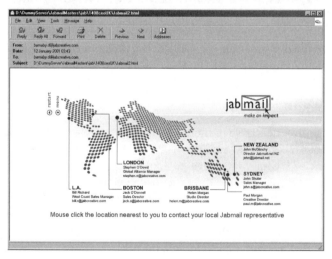

FIGURE 8.2 JabCreative are innovators in e-mail technology. They have devised a way to send a media-rich animated 'mini-website' encapsulated within an e-mail. This means that it will pass through corporate fire walls, and because they Verisign each JabMail, the recipient can be sure that the JabMail is virus free.

Long pages

Many websites use the tactic of having fewer pages but making them very long, with hypertext links to take you from the contents list to the particular part of the long string of text you need. This does work in practice, and it can be quite helpful if you think the visitor might want to print-off the whole of the text. But from a neatness point-of-view it is not the most effective method. It is usually better to split the text into reasonable lengths and put them onto separate pages linked from a navigation button or to a secondary link.

BUILD

The seven Ps apply here: **P**roper **P**reparation and **P**lanning **P**revents **P**athetically **P**oor **P**erformance.

When planning your new website bear in mind the following aspects:

- Navigation
- Frames
- Content
- Java.

Navigation

Stick to the KISS principle when designing your navigation system: Keep It Simple Sweetie (or Stupid). Complicated navigating will result in lost visitors.

Remember:

> ❝If they get lost in your site
> you will lose them from your site,
> probably for ever. ❞

There are a few very simple rules to follow when designing the routeing through the site. These include

Depth not width

This means that the main navigation buttons need to be kept to a minimum number and subsidiary subjects should be nested, to appear only when you are in the appropriate area. A good ratio is something like this:

People   >   Sales   >   Sales Director
                                  Sales Manager
                                  Personal sales
                                  Corporate sales
                                  Key Accounts

Admin	>	Finance
		Purchase
		Sales
		Company Secretarial
Technical	>	PCs
		Servers
		Networks

Do not rely on the browser back-button

Now that the main browsers have effective back-buttons, it is tempting to rely on them. Remember there are occasions when they will not operate, and there are people who do not use AOL, IE or Netscape. Do not leave this to chance: always put a back- and next-button somewhere obvious on *every* page. Avoid cyber cul-de-sacs.

Frames

Designers love frames because they make it easier to construct the page. But remember the restrictions and rules about frames:

● Some old browsers will not read frames
● Many search engines will not index the text within a frame
● If you must use frames offer a non-framed version of the site
● Keep frames off the front page.

Content

This is what your site is all about: content, content, content. If your content is fascinating, enough people will return to your site time after time, even if it looks like an old train timetable. Try to make it new and interesting. If you have unique content, so much the better. If it is unique, say so AND SAY IT LOUDLY. It is the very thing that will differentiate you from the millions of other sites that have concentrated on looks and not content.

Java

I have nothing against Java or JavaScript (these are different – see the Glossary at the end of this book) per se. They can do great things for your website, such as animations. JavaScripts can give you clever little gimmicks such as clocks or pop-up windows. Almost undoubtedly your designer will tempt you with tales of great things they can do, if only you will let them use Java. Remember

Nancy Reagan and 'just say no!' It is not worth the hassle. The nice chaps from the *Sun* newspaper will hate me for saying this but:

> 66 Java slows down your site
> Java can crash your browser
> How necessary is Java? Not very! 99

COMPATIBILITY

If we are lucky enough to have a reasonably new computer, with a 17 or 19 inch monitor screen, it can be very easy for us to forget those who are less lucky, or less computer-aware. When building our site we must bear in mind the variety of possible users and design so that we give the optimum number of people access to the benefits we offer in our site. We must build the site to have the following features:

- Compatibility with the major browsers:
  AOL and Compuserve
  Internet Explorer version 3 and upwards
  Netscape version 4 and upwards
- Screen resolution 800 × 600
- 28,000 bps modem
- Mac and PC platforms
- Offers site option without animations or text only
- Accessibility to people with disabilities.

The only sure way to know that you have such compatibility is to test the site to see if it does indeed have of the above features. Remember we are trying to exclude the few and attract the many.

There is a site which has been set up to help you do this: www.anybrowser. com (Figure 8.3). It will check out your site for screen size, design, HTML validation, and search engine readiness.

To analyse your site for accessibility see www.cast.org/bobby. Bobby is a web-based tool that analyses web pages for their accessibility to people with disabilities. CAST offers Bobby as a free public service in order to further its mission to expand opportunities for people with disabilities through the innovative uses of computer technology. Enter the URL of the page you want Bobby to examine and click Submit. Bobby will display a report indicating any accessibility and browser compatibility errors found on the page. This dialogue will only test one page at a time. If you wish to test an entire site as a batch, use the *downloadable version of Bobby*. Once all the pages of your site receive a Bobby Approved rating, you are entitled to display a Bobby Approved icon.

FIGURE 8.3   An AnyBrowser test will highlight any possible areas of your site that require attention

PERFORMANCE

Though the Internet has kept pace with the millions of new sites that are posted every day, it is still slow. Site builders need to be aware of steps they can take to improve the performance of their site, even on old hardware and slow modems. There are a number of sites on the Web that will help you find out how well you are doing in the Web performance league. Check out www.web sitegarage.com for example (Figure 8.4). They provide a range of critical diagnostic checks:

- Browser Compatibility: verifies that your website will display in different browsers
- Register-It! Readiness: makes sure your site is ready to be indexed and submitted to the top search engines and directories
- Load Time Check: reports load time from 14.4K to T1
- Dead Link Check: detects hard-to-find dead links
- Link Popularity Check: finds out how many sites are linking to you
- Spell Check: catches misspelled words
- HTML Check: sees how your design compares with the best.

www.siteowner.com also offers a range of services to help you tune-up this valuable and growing asset – your website.

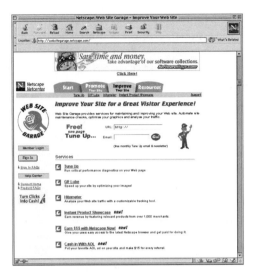

FIGURE 8.4   The Web Site Garage provides a range of site maintenance routines

SEARCH ENGINE FRIENDLINESS

We cover this aspect of managing your website in Chapters 8 and 9 but it is such an important topic to the online marketer that we will remind you here of the most important elements of this. The keys here are:

- Good keyword selection
- Relevant titles
- Link pages
- Keyword-rich domain names.

Good keyword selection

To select the most effective keywords for your page, you need to think like a marketer. What are your customers looking for when they use a search engine? Which keywords do you think someone might enter when looking for a product or service like yours? For example, which would be more effective to use as a keyword phrase: 'wide-leg, four-pocket, denim overalls', or 'clothing for kids'? Ask yourself how your target audience thinks in order to develop a list of effective keywords, then follow these guidelines in selecting keywords for your site:

- Be specific, not general: 'e-mail software' is better than 'software'.
- Use two- or three-word phrases, instead of one word: 'large screen TV' is better than 'TV'.

- Avoid the use of highly competitive words: Think of creating specific niches for your website through the use of your keywords. While you may want to rank highly for 'children's clothing', there may be overwhelming competition for that keyword phrase. Think also about including more targeted phrases such as 'children's outerwear' or 'flame retardant sleepwear'.

- Think like a customer: How do your customers describe your products or services? Is it a 'cellular phone' or a 'cell phone'? A 'desktop computer' or a 'PC'? Be sure to integrate commonly used words into your keyword phrases, as well as commonly misspelled words!

- Consider adding a regional aspect to your product or service: If you run a Bed and Breakfast in Suffolk, 'Bed and Breakfasts-Suffolk' or 'Bed and Breakfasts-England' will deliver more qualified leads than 'Bed and Breakfasts'.

- Use words directly related to your website: While the words 'Cindy Crawford' may attract a lot of traffic to your site, it is likely to be the wrong kind of traffic. Following up poor-quality leads is expensive for your sales force. Also, search engines can ban a site for supplying keywords that are unrelated to the site's content.

- Make each word count: Avoid using 'throwaway' words such as 'the', 'and', 'or'.

Relevant titles

Make sure that you give every page a title and take this opportunity to make each title relevant to the page. The search engine spiders will index the titles and varying your titles will enhance your position on the engines.

Link pages

Links to other non-competing sites will give you an improved visitor rate. Judicious selection of your link partners will make sure that these visitors are the type of prospect you want. For help, see www.linkexchange.com.

Keyword-rich domain names

Now you can register domain names with up to 63 characters, you have the opportunity to register domain names. This will probably never be noticed by your visitors but will lift your position on the search engines. If you are selling theatre tickets in New York, what about registering a few keyword-rich domains and pointing them to appropriate pages of your site – such as:

www.newyorkcheaptheatretickets.com
www.broadwaytheatretickets.com
www.cutpricebroadwaytickets.com

ADDING FACILITIES TO YOUR SITE

By adding useful features to your site you will find that people will linger – perhaps stay through to purchase. It can also serve to make your site more professional, more international and, best of all, more profitable.

Currency converters

Because you will receive orders from all over the world, it is important to enable your visitors to see your prices in their currency. Even if you have a rough idea of the relative values of the major currencies, it is more compelling to be given the correct amount in your own familiar currency. A number of companies offer currency converters. Here are two possible options for you:

Oanda	www.oanda.com/converter/classic
Xenon	www.xe.net/currency

Shopping carts

Adding a shopping cart to your site will make the process of buying much easier and quicker. Undoubtedly, this will increase your sales. There are hundreds of sites on the Web offering shopping carts of varying degrees of effectiveness. Following these guidelines will help you to separate the good ones out from the bad.

- Minimal number of clicks to make a purchase.
- Enable buyers to review the cart contents.
- Show buyers that there is a distinction between putting items into the cart and making an order.
- There should be a reasonable range of delivery options.
- Confirmation of the purchase is vital and optionally, you may want the cart to store buyers information for their next visit.

You can get a full review of the latest shopping cart and other e-commerce software by subscribing to Dr Ralph Wilson's Research Room at www. wilson web.com. – see figure 8.5 over the page.

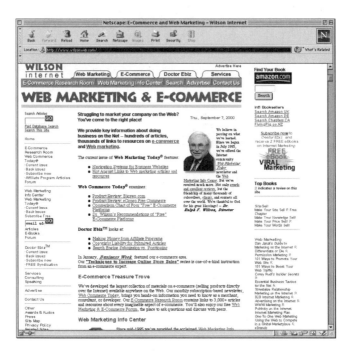

FIGURE 8.5   Regular visits to Wilson Web wil keep you abreast of the latest Internet trends

☞ Make an educated critique of your own website, and those of your suppliers and competitors.

☞ See how aspects of the design and build of a website can have a positive or negative impact on the ability to market the site effectively.

☞ Without becoming a techie, to give clear instructions to a Web designer on the exact requirements of your site from a marketing perspective.

CHAPTER NINE

WEBSITE POSITIONING

☞ Position: the state of being advantageously placed.
Place where troops are posted for strategical purposes
Concise Oxford Dictionary

☞ I could never make out what those damned dots meant.
LORD RANDOLPH CHURCHILL, speaking about decimal currency

WHAT YOU WILL LEARN **IN THIS CHAPTER**

☞ Why the major search engines are so vital in e-marketing.

☞ What they look for.

☞ How to select an effective set of keywords.

☞ Definitions of some important web-positioning terms.

When our shop-keeping forefathers went forth to expand their businesses, they looked for premises with the heaviest passing pedestrian traffic and the most appropriate type of passer-by. For them it was easy. All they had to do was wander around town and when they found an empty shop that took their fancy, stand nearby for a while and see what happened. After a few minutes watching the shop, they could get an idea of whether this location would be good for their type of business. Tobacconists needed lots of factory and office workers rushing past on their way to and from work. Sweet shops needed a local school or schools with the kids ready to squander their pocket money on damaging their teeth. A grocery shop needed to be near transport, buses, trams, and trains so heavily laden shoppers could get home.

Such observations by prospective shopkeepers could take several days. They wanted to know how the pattern of traffic differed over the days of the week, times of the day and even with the seasons. These cautious preparations often made the difference between a shop which filled with busy buyers and one which, although more expensively fitted-out and with more exciting goods on sale, remained empty and unprofitable.

As these early shopkeepers became more sophisticated, they employed others to do this 'people counting' for them. They counted the total numbers passing, they counted the split between male and female, children and adults, working-aged people and senior citizens. Somehow they tried to categorize what type of people comprised the throng or trickle, depending upon which shop you were talking about. Were they waged or unwaged? Were they gentry or aristocracy? These 'counters' all took what my Granny would call 'grand-pills' and became consultants, pollsters or statisticians, and took on such titles as Retail Planning Strategists. The huge fees they are able to charge show the massive difference the best position can make to the success or failure of a retail shop. The values of each shop depended less on the condition of the property and much more on where it was sited – position, position, position!

As we said in Chapter 2, research consistently shows that what still makes the crucial difference is convenience. The key to success was and is a matter of making it easy to buy. *Always expose your business to the dangers of sale.* When it comes to ease of purchase, positioning remains the first step on the road to prosperity.

FACTORS TO CONSIDER IN POSITIONING YOUR BUSINESS

Retail position selection in the dirt world has changed considerably, mainly because of the motor car. The car has changed pedestrian traffic patterns in our towns and cities. Shops in more secluded positions but near the car park will score better than shops in more prominent positions a mile from the nearest parking. Position is no less important than it has ever been – but the factors which make one position 'good' and another 'bad' have changed out of all recognition and probably will continue to do so. In the cyber-world, the lack of 'passing traffic' makes positioning of your business even more important.

Local shop	Supermarket	Cyber business
Pedestrian traffic	Catchment area 10–15 miles	Hit rates
Window frontage	Malleability of planners	Source of visitors
Type of goods on sale	Size of car park	Fulfilment of sale

The major retailers and supermarkets of today wield such heavy clout in the market that they have been able to change our habits. Not for them the passive acceptance that the corner of high street and market place is *the* spot in town. The combination of their financial ability to sway planning authorities and the convenience for us to be able to plonk trolley-loads of goodies directly into the boot of the car has reduced the importance of the old established premier positions of only a few years ago.

All this has happened in the past fifteen years. The effect of good positioning on the Internet will be a sea-change just as big as that caused by the financial muscle of Tesco, Sainsbury's, Safeway, *et al.* but at a fraction of the cost.

Such comparisons between the positioning of the Victorian haberdashery, supermarkets and today's dot.com business can help show how the same meticulous planning by our forefathers can be just as profitable for us when we plan our cyber business. As important as ever they were are decisions about how to:

- Conceive your ideal visitor
- Increase numbers of customer visits
- Optimize customer spend levels
- Raise customer loyalty and rate of return visits
- Maintain profitability over costs
- Raise marketing profile
- Build customer loyalty
- Optimize customer life-time buying.

Your ideal visitor

When I was a little boy at a Catholic primary school, my English teacher, Sister Mary Annunciata, would advise us that if we wanted to be sure to marry a nice Catholic girl, all we had to do was arrange our lives so the only girls we met were Catholic. The simplistic beauty of this sage advice has stayed with me to this very day: following Mr Punch's advice to those considering marriage, I remain a carefree bachelor, unmarried to this day. But Sister Mary had a point. Why get myself into redundant intimacies with girls who might have that fatal flaw – unCatholic! If I can arrange my personal relationships that easily why can I not arrange my business affairs so that the majority of people I met are the kind of people who meet my 'ideal customer' criteria? That way I would not waste my hard-won marketing investment on no-hopers, tyre-kickers and got-no-money's. Sister Mary, thank you!

I can almost hear you say 'OK Brian, we all know we should be spending more effort on getting to our ideal customers – but how do we do it?' How do we decide which of our prospective customers we should be aiming for?

Picture this rural scene. It is a bright, sunny, crisp autumn day on a moor in northern Scotland. The guns are in place, the ghillies (Scottish gamekeepers) are out of sight, the dogs have been silenced. Far away to the front, a shrill whistle blasts – the old-fashioned kind without a pea. Nothing happens for several minutes. Despite the refreshing coolness of the air and the warmth of the watery sun, the tension mounts. A quiet rustle suddenly turns into a flurry. There, out in front like a fleeing army, come the enemy. How many are there: five, ten, – more? Blimey, which one to fire at? This one? No? That one? Oh, for heaven's sake, pick one of them! Bang, whoosh, whizzz. The bang is the firing of a borrowed 12-bore spraying lead and smoke at all twenty of the advancing winged entrées. And, yes, you've guessed it, the whoosh and whizz is every one of them whooshing and whizzing overhead and flying directly into the cover of a convenient wood behind. 'I see you favour burrrrd conservation', mutters the ghillie.

Shooting grouse, whatever your political views on the matter, and selecting your ideal customer have many things in common. From the above imaginative exercise come the 'Laws of Customer Selection'. These insightful and erudite rules are designed to help you to identify your best possible customer. Only after you have learned them can you decide at which of the multitude of prospects should you be aiming your own 12-bore.

Laws of Customer Selection

From the list of possible criteria given below, you can decide the level of importance each criterion has for your particular business. Check each of the boxes 1 (unimportant) to 10 (vital) and fill in the total on the right. List the selected criteria in order of importance, putting the highest-scoring criterion first. This should give you a much better idea of your 'target' customer than you had before. In turn this will help you avoid the troublesome and potentially unprofitable customer. How often have we wished we had not taken on that particular customer? The Pareto Rule that 80% of our profit comes from 20% of our customers should encourage us to identify clearly what those 20% look like and where can we get more just like them. Luckily, I am not just going to tell you what information you need, I am also going to tell you what to do with this valuable information. Just be patient with an old man. The rules first, then the game!

For each attribute, score for importance on a scale of 1 to 10, 1 being of little or no importance and 10 being absolutely critical to your business success. Here are the seven attributes:

- Wealth
- Business or consumer
- Location
- Industry
- Size
- Corporate compatibility with us
- Technological compatibility with us.

1   Wealth

How important is the relative wealth of the customer? Can they afford your products or services?

2 Business or consumer

Thank God for the Americans and their gift for acronyms: they gave us the now ubiquitous terms B2B and B2C. These have nothing to do with Blackpool landladies or the Old Testament, but if you use B2B marketing in a B2C campaign, or vice-versa, do not expect any sympathy from me. We will speak later about this serious matter.

3 Location

How important is the location of the customer? This factor can be very important if you need physical contact with your customer. If you can find a way of minimizing the importance of the location criterion you will increase the benefits of being an e-business. In e-businesses where location of the customer has a score of 4 to 10, the amount of benefit they can glean from the global and scalable nature of the Internet is severely curtailed. This could be because of delivery of the purchased goods, the need for your staff to visit the customer, laws of a particular country, or the type of good being sold. On the other hand, if you can find ways to reduce this to a score of 3 or less you will be able to make fuller mileage out of the ability to take orders and fulfil them electronically. You will also benefit from being able to serve customers around the world without any need for physical contact.

4 Industry

Does the industry of your customers matter to you? The more vertical (specific) your market, the more important – and in many ways easier – it is to target your audience. Internet marketing has given you the ability to target your audience in a way which was only available to large companies with heavy marketing and research budgets.

5 Size

All great marketers know the importance of relative size. If you have ever sailed a little boat into a crowded harbour on a hot bank-holiday weekend and the harbourmaster allocates you a berth alongside a gin palace four times your size, you will be more aware than ever that size matters. This is not to imply that as a small company, you should only be looking to deal with companies of your own size. After all, the Internet is one of the world's great levellers. A good, well-planned website can make a small company look substantial. Niche products and services are needed by companies of all sizes and it is often small companies that provide them. Knowledge of your prospect's relative size is therefore important so you will have a better idea how to approach them with the best chance of winning their business. How do we define company size? The simple answer to this is 'badly'. We refer to most UK businesses as SMEs. This is not because the definition is in anyway helpful. It is simply because that is what the EU wants us to call any business with between 10 and 250 employees. More helpfully, you can set your own criteria for deciding what is the most appropriate size of customer for your particular product or service.

6 Corporate compatibility with us

What is he talking about? We have to be compatible with the customer, not the other way round. Don't we? Of course we do! We are a customer-focused company. We do everything in our power to meet customer needs. Our product development comes from customer demand. We have regular dialogue with our customers to make sure we remain aware of present and future needs. So what are you on about when you talk of compatibility? Of course we are compatible – otherwise they wouldn't be our customers, would they? True, but just HOW compatible are you? If you are only prospecting with the sort of company likely to be compatible with you then you are more likely to win that sort of company as customers. Remember Sister Mary Annunciata?

Bob Miller and Stephen Heiman, in their excellent book *Strategic Selling*, say we should consider these factors in deciding compatibility:

- The importance they place on their own reputation
- Their standard of ethics
- Attitudes towards people, including customers, suppliers and employees
- Openness to innovation
- Relative importance placed on quality rather than quantity (or price).

7 Technological compatibility with us

If we are a high-tech company trying to sell state-of-the-art equipment to a tired old company with out-dated skills and equipment it could be seen as a great opportunity. Just be sure that it not only the machinery that is tired and old. It could be that the management is that way too. Potentially the customer from hell?

HOW TO INCREASE THE NUMBERS OF CUSTOMER VISITS

What the Victorian tobacconist wanted was more people to enter his shop. To achieve this he created an attractive window-display and perhaps placed small ads in his local paper. The amount he needed to spend on advertising depended largely on his shop's position. The more peripheral his position the less he could rely on the natural bonus of passing trade. With the Internet no one has the benefit of choosing a central position. Every website, of a large multi-national corporation or the smallest Internet start-up, has exactly the same amount of natural exposure on the Internet – none!

Despite this apparently egalitarian starting point, there the fairness ends. How much prominence your site gets from then on depends totally on the amount of directed publicity you commit to it. Such publicity includes:

- Corporate literature
- Offline advertising
- PR
- Direct mail
- Online advertising
- Search engine positioning.

It is the last of these which concerns us here. It is also the one where the 'small guy' can benefit most from the unique nature of the Internet. The only thing preventing the smallest site from getting top 10 rankings is knowledge and hard work. Where else can you search for 'flights' and get British Airways, American and KLM, as well as a one-man travel firm in Croydon, all on the same listing? There is every chance that the one-man agency will get the business and the giants, for all their marketing skills and big budgets, get side-lined because Mr Croydon offered a better (not necessarily cheaper) deal.

THE IMPORTANCE OF THE SEARCH ENGINES

The Internet search engines became a necessity as the Internet and then the Web grew larger and faster than any of its founders ever imagined. Yahoo, for example, started with some guys at Stanford University recognizing the problem of finding sites amongst the vast numbers out there, even then back in the dark ages of last century.

Software spiders

There are two types of search facility on the Internet today. One is the true search engine. These employ small remote programs often called 'spiders', though sometimes also called 'robots' or 'bots'. These hard-working little fellows spend their lives visiting sites and indexing the text. In theory they will find your site even if you do not bother to submit it to the engine. In reality they are much more likely to index you if you visit the engines at the 'Add URL' or 'Submit' page. The spider actually records the words from your site, indexes them in its database and sorts them according to its own rules for later retrieval. Because of the size of the Internet many search engines are beginning to truncate their indexing at a given number of pages. We understand that Alta Vista stops at 400. If you have a very large site you might do well to consider submitting each of the more important pages of your site.

Directories

The other type of search facility is the Internet directory. These rely upon site owners to submit the details of their site before the directory will index them. Generally they link only to your home page, rather than indexing all the text on each page. The best-known of the directories is Yahoo. It was one of the first search facilities on the Web, as opposed to the Internet, and is still one of the best-used services, handling over 40 % of all searches. This may be due to change since Google have become very active and now claim to be the biggest engine on the net. Getting listed on Yahoo means visiting their site and the 'Add URL' page. Submit only one page, because an editor will visit and rank your site for relevance in your selected category. We understand that only around 10 % of sites submitted to Yahoo actually get listed. To assist you to get listed, Yahoo have introduced a 'Listing Support' telephone number. We cover getting listed on Yahoo later in this chapter.

Hybrid search engines

Some directories are of a hybrid nature, in that they also have a search engine crawling about to give their editors fodder for indexing, as if they were short of work. Yahoo is an example of a hybrid. They recently severed their arrangement with Inktomi so this may also be due for a change.

THE MAJOR SEARCH ENGINES

Over 90 % of all Internet searches are carried out through the 12 largest search engines. The other 1488 or so are so small or simply too specialized to be of any interest to us. Because of this we are able to learn the requirements of each of the important engines and tailor our site to make it more attractive to the spiders – to be a bit fly, you might say! These engines change from time to time: some bold newcomers enter this very competitive arena, others fade away for whatever reason. The current top 10 in order of size seems to be:

1 Google
2 Alta Vista
3 Excite
4 Lycos
5 Web Crawler
6 Northern Light
7 Go2
8 Infoseek
9 Inktomi
10 Yahoo.

Competition between the main engines is so intense that they keep up a constant battle for supremacy. This means that they are forever changing the way they work. They try all sorts of clever tactics to improve their service to their users, which means improving the relevance of the result a searcher will get with any particular keyword. Many of us have had the dispiriting experience of submitting a search and getting only four or five unique sites in a list of ten. The reason for this is that some clever webmaster has manipulated their site and has overdone some of the techniques we describe in this book. He may also have tried some of the less ethical methods and has spammed the engines by bombarding them with keywords. Unscrupulous people will use words such as 'sex', 'porn', 'chat' and other words that bear absolutely no relevance to their site whatever. This benefits them temporarily but not for long. It annoys searchers because they do not get what they thought they had asked for. It annoys the Search Engine boys because such a scam costs them credibility in the eyes of their clients. And it annoys the owners of more relevant sites that are unfairly deposed onto later pages and end up not being found by the very people who are looking for them.

People are creatures of habit: they tend to find a search engine they like and stick to it. But after a few experiences where they see the results are not very fruitful for them, many searchers will be tempted to try other engines and may be lost forever to their former favourite. Can you blame the search engine policemen for de-listing sites that spam the engines? Frankly they deserve to be de-listed and a few de-other things too. Good riddance to them. Do bear this in mind when you are fighting for your rightful place on the top of the engines. Do it by ethical means and try to make sure all your keywords and texts are relevant to your site. All the techniques described in this book are ethical and by following our guidelines you will not go too far wrong. In any case, why would you want to attract the Internet's all too obvious dirty-mac brigade? They are not going to benefit your online business.

Search engines need to protect themselves from the spammers whose greed and thoughtlessness are jeopardizing the reputation of search engines generally. In most cases the search engines do a really amazing job. It behoves us all to respect the achievement by which we are able to type in esoteric words such as 'slavonic mythology' or 'cactus growing' or 'moldovite collecting' and be presented, *within seconds*, with hundreds of sites about these subjects. Familiarity with the Internet raises our expectations and may make us blasé about this achievement. From time to time we should stop to remind ourselves how fabulous this ability really is.

Search engines have a range of tactics they employ to counter the wily ways of the search engine guerrilla. These include:

- Changing indexing algorithms
- Charging for top 10 positions
- Spam filters to reduce site duplication on the index
- Adding search filters to help searchers refine their search
- Changing their rules about:
  keyword repetition
  relevancy
  categories
- Adding a database to sit 'above' the engine
- Adding geographic sub-sets of the main engine.

Any Internet business that spends money on creating an attractive, professional website and does not allocate funds to position this site high on the engines may as well buy a car and not spend any money on petrol. Almost every website designer will offer, as part of the build process, to submit the site to the search engines. Invariably this involves sending off a set of single-word keywords to a submission service. Mostly this uses a software tool which can send details of your site to varying numbers of search engines; the more they offer the less seriously you should take them. Because of the ever-changing requirements of each engine, you will find they are never in 'sync' with each other. This means that if you want your site to be high over a range of the main engines, you need to submit differently to each of them. This cannot be done properly by an automatic software submission.

To demonstrate these differences we list below the preferences of some of the main engines. Do not take this list as comprehensive or up to date. Engines change their requirements so frequently that we have not tried to keep up. The only way to be sure you are up to date is to check on each site as you manually submit your site.

Whilst this book is not intended to be a technical description of how to optimize your site for the search engines, we do want to give marketers full knowledge of what needs to be done and where to find the most complete information saying exactly how it should be done. We do not suggest you should be able to carry out the work yourself, but rather that you can instruct technical staff with authority and knowledge. We also want you to be aware of what works and what does not. So what follows is a description of a few of the main engines. It is not comprehensive since the details are subject to weekly if not daily change. But it will give you some ideas about the various differences in each engine.

THE MAIN SEARCH ENGINES COMPARED

Alta Vista

Very hot on spamming

Likes longer pages

Has several international versions

Indexes from four sources: Own index

Ask Jeeves

RealNames

Look Smart.

Excite

Provides results for Netscape and AOL

Cannot manage image maps

Keyword stuffing, repetition and irrelevancy will be penalized as spam

Keywords in body text add to relevance

Recognizes synonyms.

MSN Search

Will accept only one URL per day

Has discretionary directory

Keywords in titles, metatags and body text add to site relevance

Powered by Inktomi.

Getting listed on Yahoo

Because of its importance – over 40% of searches are carried out through it – we should spend a bit of time looking at Yahoo (Figure 9.1). It is a directory and therefore is manned and indexed by human editors who review and categorize every site submitted to them. Yahoo do not allow you to submit multiple doorway pages. Do not try to fool your Yahoo editor: they have seen all the tricks before. They will not blacklist or refuse to list your site, but if you mess them around it is up to them how long it takes to get round to you. Your site will not be visited by a Yahoo spider so meta-tags are not required for this submission. Bearing that in mind, this is how you get listed on this invaluable Internet portal:

1   Make sure that your site is fully finished and looking as good as it ever will. 'Under construction' signs can devastate your chances.
2   Visit the site at www.yahoo.com.
3   Enter your URL into the search box (not the browser address box) to see if you are already listed. If you are, check that you are in the most appropriate category. If your site is in the wrong category, click on the 'change details' link.
4   If your site is not listed go ahead and submit. Do this manually. Never expect a submissions package to do this job effectively. Yahoo is too important to leave this to chance.
5   At the bottom of the Home Page click on the link 'How to suggest a site'.
6   Select an appropriate category from the fourteen suggested:

Arts & Humanities	News & Media
Business & Economy	Recreation & Sports
Computers & Internet	Reference
Education	Regional
Entertainment	Science
Government	Social Science
Health	Society & Culture

Yahoo give guidelines about selecting your category. They suggest you need to keep the following in mind to find the most relevant category:

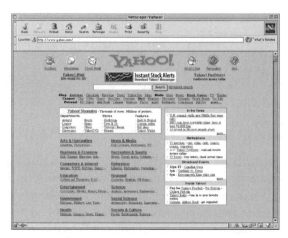

FIGURE 9.1   Yahoo! is one of the most popular search facilities on the Web

- Is your site commercial or non-commercial?
- Do you need to be regionally specific?
- Personal sites go into the Society & Culture category.
- Look for categories which display sites 'like yours'.

Devise a good descriptive title for your site. Follow these guidelines:

- Include keywords near the beginning.
- Use your actual business name within the title.
- Do not exceed 40 characters.
- Start the title with a letter early in the alphabet: 'All legal work family tax Barrett and Jones'.
- Write and then re-write a good description of your product or service and the contents of your site. The maximum length is 200 characters or 25 words, so make every word count. Try to make it keyword-rich and avoid 'stop' words such as 'the', 'and', 'or'.

   Make the description accurate. Yahoo editors have absolute discretion whether or not to list your site. If you mis-describe your business, they have the option of re-categorizing your site or not listing it at all. Be honest. Say precisely what you do.
- If, after about two weeks, you are not listed try the whole process again, making any changes you think might have affected the editor's decision. You can also telephone Yahoo's help line and ask for their assistance.

If you have control over your company or business name remember the earlier the name comes alphabetically the better your chances of being clicked. But do not make a name change just to better your chances in the engines

LET'S GET TO THE BOTTOM OF THESE WEB PAGES

Internet website pages are not all used for the same purpose. Also, they get called a whole host of different names. These names are often ambiguous and misleading. Since everyone calls each type of page something different let's try to make some sense out of the jargon.

Home page

The Home page is usually the first page activated by your browser when you access a site. Many designers, not aware of the importance of this access page, turn it into the Corporate History page, or the Site Map. That misses a valuable positioning opportunity. By all means have a corporate history, but put it on a secondary page. If you learn nothing else from this book chapter, learn this: treat every engine individually and give them what they want. Get away from the idea that your Home page should be full of flash animations, or have a table of contents. The single purpose of your Home page is to attract the visitations of the search engine's spiders. A 'real' Home Page is designed with a particular engine in mind. Start with Inktomi, because this engine is the default engine for several major engines and directories, including Yahoo until recently. Start by visiting each engine in turn and go to the 'Submit' or the 'Add URL' page and follow the instructions to the letter. Proceed to build a single Home page for every engine. Link this page to your site and you will find this alone will increase traffic to your site. These pages become one-way valves into your site: you will only ever see them on your way to the site from the engine. There should be no back-button allowing you to return to these Home pages.

Index page

This is the page with the HTML coding. It is one of the pages not normally seen by site visitors. If you want to see the index page of any site, float the pointer over any clear area of the page and right-click with your mouse.

Doorway pages

Doorway pages are so called because they create a doorway into the site for the search-engine spiders. They are very basic and often hold very little in the way of text but their job is very important to your position on the engines. Doorway pages can be created automatically using an excellent package called Web Position Gold (www.webposition.com) (Figure 9.2).

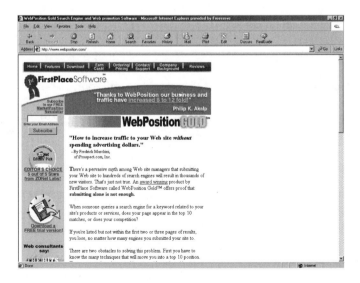

FIGURE 9.2   Web Position Gold is the submission tool of choice for professionals like Coastal Sites

FIGURE 9.3 Quadrant Internet can carry out UK search engine submissions

Focussed Content page

Focussed Content pages have the advantage over normal doorway pages in that they hold relevant content to meet the more recent needs of some of the engines, which changed the way they regard a body of text (Figure 9.3).

Archway pages

An Archway page allows the site owner or their staff to enter the site and make changes to anything on the Archway page, but allows no access to other parts of the site. This ensures that untrained staff cannot accidentally damage the site.

KEYWORDS

If you have been around the Internet industry for any length of time you will have heard people talk *ad nauseam* about keywords, meta-tags, hit-rates, and a range of other esoteric mysteries. The sad fact of the matter is that the vast majority of people using these phrases have no real idea of what they are talking about. Keywords today are as vital to the e-business person as a corner shop position was for the Victorian haberdasher. These little chaps can make the difference between fame and oblivion. They can hold your hand and dance you all the way through the pearly gates of e-heaven, or drop you like the IP Address from Hell.

Let's first dispel some daft myths talked about keywords. The facts are that:

- They do not need to be single words.
- They can be multi-word phrases.

- You can have as many as you like.
- They should be what the searcher would use – not what you'd like to be called. So:

Real estate agent	not	Andrews Realtors
Detroit bagel bakers	not	Smith's Best Bagels
Antique furniture auction	not	Carruther's Fine Art

Change your shoes

The first thing to do when choosing these vital parts of your site is to change your shoes. Am I mad? No, not really. All I want you to do is to place yourself in the position of a person browsing the Internet. As the American Indians say, 'walk in the other fellow's moccasins'. Think about when you are looking for a quick-print shop on a strange road. You do not look round for their name sign sticking out into the road. You may not even know their name. All you care about is that they are print-shop and not a kebab shop. So you look out for 'Copy-shop' or 'Instant Printing'. Why think it is any different on the Web? But we seem to, judging from the way people use the engines. So the normal generic names for describing our site are important. Using 'Part-worn vehicles' as a keyword instead of 'Used cars' will get you to the top of the engines for part-worn vehicles, but the fact is that most people will type 'used cars' when they want to buy a part-worn vehicle

Don't take my word for it!

Your ISP will almost certainly be able to provide you with statistics from your website. You simply need to ask them for the Referer Logs for the dates you need. In selecting your keywords and keyword phrases you can use your statistics to find out which keywords were used to find you. This is such an important source of vital information that if your ISP cannot, for whatever reason, give you these statistics do not waste time: change ISP at once! Alternatively you could buy your own stats package and ask your ISP to provide you with the raw log files. This can give you greater control over the data. Remember, these stats only tell you where you have been successful, not where you have not! They can help you to eliminate keywords that are not producing any visits, but you could do with more help in finding keywords that people are using to look for sites like yours.

Why not select your keywords by finding out what people are actually searching for? There is a company in Kansas called Word Spot (www.word-spot.com) which produces reports about keyword popularity (Figure 9.4). One of their bigger reports is so big that they claim it regularly burns out hard drives when running it. Less dramatic is their weekly Top 1000 Keyword/ Keyphrase report. For a fee of around $9.00 per week they will send you a listing of the most used keywords in your 'keyword universe'. This means you can select from the words actually being used to find your kind of site. Suppose you are in the new MP3 market (downloadable music from the Web).The range of keywords used by people to find MP3 sites can be quite surprising. By using the WordSpot report you could discover that 837 people searched for MP3 but if you added the word 'music' you stand a 39 times better chance of being ranked highly than for the basic single-word search.

Here is an excerpt from a WordSpot report on top MP3 phrases:

Top mp3 phrases

Overall		
Rank	Quantity	Text of query
4	837	mp3
68	208	mp3 midi
347	66	mp3z
429	57	mp3 s
4483	11	mp3 and download

Searches done in June 2000	
Count	Search term
599982	mp3
47877	free mp3
33587	mp3 download
25881	mp3 player

FIGURE 9.4 WordSpot will help you to build an effective set of keywords and keyword phrases

How to increase your site relevance

In this context, the word *relevant* refers to relevance to a particular search engine. It follows, therefore, that you need to make the words on that particular doorway page of that engine relevant according to that specific engine's rules.

Meta-tags

Meta-tags are the text, which is typed into the <HEAD> section of your site. This part of your site does not appear in the browser so is not normally seen by your site visitors. They should contain the following information:

- The name of your site
- A description of your site's content
- Your keyword and keyword phrases.

If you fail to enter these, and it is amazing how many sites don't have them, then if and when a spider finds your site it will probably index the first 25 words of the text that are not in a frame. For an excellent and very detailed instruction manual on how to enter meta-tags see the Web Position site at www.webposition.com

Use the <ALT> tag to include keywords

The <ALT> tag is usually only used to give a description to a graphic on your page. You can use this section to include some keywords since some search engines will give points to keywords in this tag.

Use the Heading tags to include keywords

Just as with the <ALT> tag, you can add some keywords within this tag. Make sure that you check the search engine rules to see if you might be penalized by this.

Include keywords in links

Because some engines score the text in links very highly this is an excellent place to put your keywords.

TITLES

It is quite astounding how many sites are created with poor or non-existent titles. If you make your page titles descriptive of what you do then the description will be picked up by both the search engine spiders and visitors who see what they are looking for simply from your title. Unless your company is a well-known brand and therefore a 'pull' in itself, then make your title say what you do. You have plenty of chances to say who you are once you have lured them into the site. For the technically interested the HTML looks like this:

```
<HTML>
<HEAD>
<TITLE>Budget Hotel Accommodation New York and Boston<TITLE>
```

The vital importance of links

The value of linking to other sites, as many sites as possible, almost any site, has not yet been recognized by the vast majority of Web marketers. I am not suggesting you agree a link with just anyone. I do suggest you should err on the side of linking rather than refusing a link. Also, you must be pro-active in finding sites to link with. Don't eschew the link-sites, which are sprouting up these days. Think about linking with your competitors.

What? Are you mad? Link with my competitors? OK! OK! I only said think about it. Just consider why there is often a proliferation of similar businesses in a particular part of a city. We often speak of the 'antiques area' or the 'clock-makers area' or the 'financial district'. I predict that very soon competing business will be allowing links between them and all parties will benefit – the linkers, the linkees and most importantly, the site visitors and prospects who will be able to compare services, prices, terms and then make contact with a range of possible suppliers.

READY, STEADY ...!

In order to get your site properly positioned you need to assemble all the information needed to give your site the best possible chance of being very high on the search engines. Here is a summary list of items you need to get together before starting out on the positioning work:

- A set of keywords and keywords phrases
- A number of titles of varying lengths (3–4)
- A site description for use with the directories
- Consider registering one or two 'keyword-rich' domain names.

BEWARE PAGEJACKING

The US Federal Trade Commission announced a new type of Internet scam called pagejacking. Read and take note.

According to the complaint, in a practice called 'pagejacking', the defendants made exact copies of Web pages posted by unrelated parties, including the imbedded text that informs search engines about the subject matter of the site. Then they made one change that was hidden from view: they inserted a command to 'redirect' any surfer coming to the site to another Web site that contained sexually-explicit, adult-oriented material. Internet surfers searching for subjects as innocuous as 'Oklahoma tornadoes' or 'child car seats' would type those terms into a search engine and the search results would list a variety of related sites, including the bogus, copycat site of the defendants. Surfers assumed from the listings that the defendants' sites contained the information they were seeking and clicked on the listing. The 'redirect' command imbedded in the copycat site immediately rerouted the consumer to an adult site hosted by the defendants.

Source: www.ftc.gov/opa/1999/9909/atariz.htm

WHAT YOU WILL HAVE LEARNED IN THIS CHAPTER

☞ The search engines are vital tools in getting benefit from the World-Wide-Web. This chapter should have given you a detailed insight into their importance, what they look for and how to arrange your site in such a way that will improve your rankings on any searches on that engine.

☞ The selection of keywords should be seen from the visitor's viewpoint and not from that of the site owner.

☞ Effective keywords are those which bring not only greater visitor traffic, but also more relevant, appropriate and interested visitors.

CHAPTER TEN

MONITOR YOUR PROGRESS

☞ Everything that is measured tends to improve

ANON.

WHAT YOU WILL LEARN IN THIS CHAPTER

☞ The value of monitor and tracking your visitor results.

☞ The facilities available to you to track and monitor.

☞ The terminology to do with tracking and monitoring.

This is the area of Internet marketing that is most often ignored. It is the least glamorous side of this fast-moving world. People tend to turn to monitoring when things are not going as well as they had hoped. This cyber navel-watching is often a knee-jerk reaction to try to boost a lagging response rate. There is no doubt that reviewing the monitoring facilities available to you will show you some ways of improving matters, but this should be something you should be attending to even in the good times – then you can make them even better. You do not need to be a mathematician or statistician to benefit from the knowledge of your website statistics.

TERMINOLOGY

There is much confusion over the terminology relating to website traffic. To set the record straight(ish) we have tried to define as clearly as possible all of the most important terms. These include:

- Hits
- Page impressions
- Visits
- Log files.

Let us deal with each in turn.

Hits

This is one of the most commonly misused terms in web-stats. It has been ironically referred to as How Idiots Track Success. The term 'hit' refers to a single request from a web browser for a single item from a web server. Thus, if a page of your site has one frame and six images, then visitors to that page will register as seven hits on your log-files. This is great stuff to brag about in the bar; but will not be sufficient for marketing purposes and some other form of measurement is therefore needed.

Page impressions

This counts the number of single web-page visits. It is usually the number of HTML pages that have been accessed and excludes the extra numbers relating to images. This is therefore a much more meaningful measurement of traffic onto your website. There are a number of benefits of tracking your visitors.

- Checking how page impressions change every five minutes for a day, will tell you when people are accessing your site. You can also determine whether people visit your site before, during or after working hours.
- Checking what percentage of your page impressions come from registered visitors can help you determine whether encouraging people to log in is worthwhile. You can also get some indication of how your site might perform if you required visitors to log in.
- When your visitors come to one of your pages via a link or banner, this information can help you determine the visitors' interests. This will also help you decide whether your advertising spend is paying for itself, or whether it would do so if you were to advertise.

Visits

This is also sometimes called a 'session' because it records each page visited by the same IP address at any one time. This might seem to be the Holy Grail but remember it relates only to the specific computer from which the visitor accessed your site. So, if ten people used the same Internet café computer, this would look like ten sessions from the same person instead of just the same machine. But it gets worse. Many ISPs, as well as ASPs like AOL, assign IP addresses dynamically as visitors log on. This could mean that a visitor in the morning gets assigned the same IP address as someone in the afternoon. Simply counting the unique IP addresses would give you a very inaccurate view of your traffic. That IP address might be in use by yet another person that evening. If you were to use this resulting data, you would count all three visitors as one.

Log files

These are files generated by the ISP web server in a pre-ordained format created by the National Center for Supercomputing Applications (NCSA). There are three main types of Log-files:

- Access log
- Referrer log
- Error log.

Access log
This will give you a set of standardized information such as IP address, date and time, filename and size of file.

Referrer log
This is a very valuable source of stats since it tells you how people found your website. This means you can tell if the visitor came from a search engine and therefore which one. It will also let you have information about the keywords that were used to find you. Over time, you can build up a list of the keywords used and put that data to good use by:

- Identifying which keywords are actually pulling in visits.
- Enabling you to search on those keywords to find out who else is being successful with that keyword or keyword phrase.
- Deciding for those keywords which are not attracting visits, can be dropped or rc-optimized to see if you get an improved response.
- Where visitors enter the site on a page which has graphics but the visitor does not allow these graphics to download, this might lead you to decide that the graphics need to be re-optimized. Two good tips here are:
  (i) Display a JPEG first, which downloads fast, and then replace it with a GIF to give you the required quality.
  (ii) Make the JPEG black and white and the GIF coloured.

Error log
Error logs are very helpful in finding problems with accessing your site. They will give you information on such things as lost connections, time-outs where the process took too long, networking errors, invalid URLs, and password mismatches.

TRACKING SOFTWARE

There are a growing number of web statistics analysis tools, which come in a wide range of scope and cost. The options include everything from basic freeware to expensive monitoring and audience analysis services. Remember

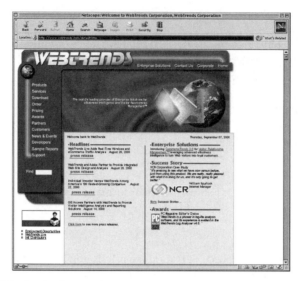

FIGURE 10.1   Web Trends is a popular statistics package

that what you choose should be based not just on your budget but on what statistics you want to see and how you'll use them.

WebTrends (www.webtrend.com)

WebTrends produces a range of products for analysis of Web traffic and performance, and for website security (Figure 10.1). Log Analyzer is the basic product, which packs in a lot of useful and valuable features for its low cost. Reports generated by the WebTrends Log Analyzer give the Web manager clear, easy-to-read tables and colourful graphs showing trends, bandwidth usage, market share, and more. You can produce and view reports in Microsoft Word and Excel and in HTML, ASCII text, and comma-delimited formats. Log Analyzer tracks user sessions for page requests, file downloads, scripts executed, locations, and other data, giving you access to critical data points for analysis.

wwwstat (www-ccs.cs.umass.edu/stats/gwstat.html)

Originally developed as part of the Acadia and WebSoft projects at the University of California at Irvine, this Perl-based log analysis tool works in the Unix and Linux environments. It provides basic statistics with a minimum of display and reporting frills. On the upside, you can get at the source code and modify the software to fit your specific needs. A companion program, gwstat, takes the output from wwwstat and translates it into graphs illustrating your traffic.

Hitometer (www.websitegarage.netscape.com/products/ netanalysis/index.shtml)

The Hitometer report provides an analysis of how many people visited your site, who they were, when the visitors came and search engine data. You can also drill down on a particular month or day to view more detailed data. The statistics provided include: Visitors to date/Visitors this week/Visitors this month; site type and country; top domains visiting your site; top referring pages; user browser/platform selection; daily/hourly breakdown; unique visitors; along with the top search engines used to find your site and keywords your visitors are searching for.

net.Analysis 4 (www.netgen.com)

Depending on operating system and support/training options, net.Analysis provides 150 types of complete graphical reports on your website. net.Analysis can automate the analysis process from Web data handling to report production and distribution. A scheduling feature lets you automatically retrieve, import, and store Web data on a daily, weekly or monthly basis. Providing both historical and real-time reporting capabilities, net.Analysis lets you track user behaviour and interaction on your site.

Aria (www.macromedia.com/software/aria/)

Aria was chosen as the best traffic analysis tool in 1998. The latest version improves on an already impressive suite of tools. Available in three different suites, they provide tools for single hosts (Aria), geographically dispersed multi-server sites (Aria Enterprise), and e-commerce sites running third-party e-commerce platforms (Aria eCommerce). Three components – the Monitor, a server API plug-in; the Recorder, which receives, processes and stores data in real time; and the Reporter, which produces hourly or on-demand reports – work to give you access to vital performance and monitoring data.

Accrue Insight (www.accrue.com)

Accrue Insight monitors live network transactions and log files, providing specific data on your website and its visitors. Insight can tell you the number of pages actually delivered, not just how many are sent to the visitor. It also reports on how many users stop a page download, a visitor's connection speed, and other metrics. Accrue Insight is a powerful product, designed to operate effectively across websites receiving 50 million hits per day and hundreds of web servers supporting more than 2,000 websites.

WHAT YOU WILL HAVE LEARNED IN THIS CHAPTER

☞ Monitoring your site traffic in an educated way will enable you to decide on an Internet strategy devised from known visitor behaviours.

☞ There are many facilities on the Web to enable you to be effective in monitoring your visitors traffic on your website, several of which are given in this chapter.

CHAPTER ELEVEN

STRONG ALLIES

☞ Plan for what is difficult while it is easy, do what is great while it is small.

SUN TSE

☞ Seeing what others do not see is brilliance, knowing what others do not know is to sustain greatness.

THE MASTERS OF HUAINAN

☞ If allies are strong with power to protect us
Might they not protect us out of all we own?

OSCAR HAMMERSTEIN II, *The King and I*

WHAT YOU WILL LEARN IN THIS CHAPTER

☞ Fully understand how to implement the second leg of E-Market Dominance.

☞ Build your Web- and bricks-and-mortar business the no-cost way.

☞ Build customer awareness of what you offer.

☞ Enhance the image of your company.

☞ Prosper in an increasingly competitive market.

THE SECOND LEG OF E-MARKET DOMINANCE

No one who has an interest in strategy underestimates the value of strategic alliances. Working with others in pursuit of your mutual interests creates genuine synergy that is able to increase business and productivity, avoid duplication of effort and decrease costs. But that is by no means all.

Today we filter out much advertising as a result of excess. Although there is more effort, expense and imagination devoted to it and we encounter more ads every day of our lives, we have seen it all before and crave novelty. Only the extremes of shock or groovy entertainment catch our attention. Even where advertising grabs our interest with its slick appeal experience has taught us to respond along with Mandy Rice Davis 'They would say that wouldn't they?' It is all a matter of trust and there is not a lot of trust about.

Each of the two legs of E-Market Dominance works to bring trust back into the market place. Warren Bennis used to rage at 'moronic' trainers who, back in the 1970s, wrote T-R-U-S-T in enormous letters on a white board as if the act of writing would make it happen. 'Trust only flourishes', he would say, 'when two or more people do something together and it works for all of them'. But if a product or service is so new that you have had no opportunity to try it and no parade of enticing advertisements have been busily building awareness, how do you come to trust either the product or those who supply it?

Hoary marketing theories promote 'risk reversal' and branding, both of which are fine. But what if you mistrust the value of the guarantee or recognize that branding is a pure function of the cash outlay on the frequency of advertising, as most sophisticated buyers do today? Then you need something better. Fortunately trust is transferable. If you have faith in me and I suggest you can trust someone you haven't met before, you accept my recommendation as if it were an article of faith. 'Any friend of Tom's is a friend of mine', you say and happily lay yourself wide open. Most times your trust is justified and you have a genuine new friend. Trust and synergy, these are the simple thoughts that lie behind this second leg of E-Market Dominance.

In the relatively recent past much has been written on the importance of relationships in selling. My own book, *The Power of Influence*, tries to explain in simple, practical terms the psychological findings that show that it is more effective and more ethical to help the customer to buy rather than to sell to them. The concept is simple. The 'sales persons', whether selling goods, services or ideas, align themselves with the buyer as mutual problem-solvers seeking the best source of satisfaction for the buyer's needs. Putting it very simply, they form a relationship. But why stop at the customer? Why not form relationships with others that will enable you to build an immediate rapport with their customers? Why not be like the bridal wear seller, the hairdresser and the florist, only more so? Or, to coin another law,

> 66 The greater the degree to which technology plays a role in the market place the greater the need for personal relationships. 99

Barbra Streisand sang most beautifully of people needing people, and at the level of survival our primeval ancestors learned that they needed each other. Our evolutionary and genetic past combines to remind us that the route to survival is through co-operation, and co-operation demands trust and long-term relationships. Without relationships your website is just another sales letter with fancy additions. The wonderful thing about the new technology is that it provides greater opportunities than ever before to enter into meaningful, business-building relationships. In the UK, as I write, the major clearing banks are ditching employees and customer service in a short-sighted pursuit of mere technology. Meanwhile newcomers to the banking sector are making inroads into their customer base by using the Internet intelligently. The two legs of E-Market Dominance enable you to make ever more sensible use of the opportunities that technology offers. It is a process that is proven and infinitely expandable.

SUMMARY STRATEGIC PLAN

1   Find suppliers of non-competing products that appeal to customers with the same wants and needs as yours.

2   Show them that your product or service is something that will genuinely benefit and delight many of their customers.

3   Offer them a deal whereby they endorse your products or services. There can be mutual endorsements or commission on sales according to circumstances.

4   Monitor sales and track orders.

5   Build an E-Market Dominance relationship with each of your new customers.

6   Develop a new group of loyal customers for life.

7   Delight these new customers with your communications, products and service.

8   Create many more advocates for your business.

9   Watch your business flourish.

WHY THIS LEG OF E-MARKET DOMINANCE WORKS

1 No cash outlay

If you pay anything at all you only pay commission on sales. If you can honestly endorse and promote your partners' offerings to your loyal customers, you pay nothing more than a little of your time spent saying something nice about someone else to your customers. And if you do it honestly you delight your own customers further in the process. This is a very proper use of your time not least because it enables you to spend a little time to make a great deal of money.

2 The response rate is up to four times that of 'permission' marketing

Tests show that those who promote their own products, in a permission marketing role, can often get a superior response rate through honest third-party endorsement of another firm's products or services. There is no Mandy Rice Davis effect: no 'They would say that, wouldn't they?'

3 The approach combines and creates a synergy between your E-Market Dominance and that of similar, responsible others

Nowhere does synergy mean that two plus two equals a great deal more than five than when used as part of an E-Market Dominance strategy.

4 Costs are low and controllable

You buy no mailing list, printing or stamps. You provide a communicator with something more (and new) to communicate. Even at that level it is a win/win situation as any busy journalist will tell you. All that you must be sure to do is to back up your strategic partner by offering a superior product and top-quality service to his or her customers.

5 There are no better ways to target buyers

By definition these prospects are interested in the products, services and information you can deliver. They want a relationship with you. The only problem is that, up to now, they probably didn't know you existed.

6 It's a genuine third-party endorsement

Given there is no Mandy effect, you and your partners must only endorse offerings that will genuinely satisfy the customers' needs in such a way as to delight, and go on delighting them.

7 Your 'sponsor' delights his customers further through providing easy access to your ability to serve

Surfing the net can be a laborious kind of fun. Many key words lead to literally millions of sites. If you have what it takes to delight another firm's customers those customers will be eternally grateful that their time has been saved. In the affluent world of the Northern Hemisphere most of us are fortunate enough to have money to spend. The two things we lack are time and attention. Anyone who can save us time or make our attention worthwhile has, and deserves, a little of our money and our thanks.

8 Neither loses customers, but you both gain

As long as one offering does not replace the other and you both play straight down the line, you each gain new, profitable customers for life. If either partner tries to be over-smart you may be sure that he will be seen for what he is, and the Web has ways of dealing with scam artists.

9 These are customers for life

These customers have chosen to opt in. Times may change. So might their needs and wants. But if you stay in touch, you will change your offering to meet their emergent desires. They will be with you for life and they will become advocates for your business.

10 The Internet is all about information

People love news and newsletters. They always have. My one-time personal guru Howard Shenson attracted around a quarter of a million people world-wide to subscribe to a 'post and paper' newsletter many years ago. A newsletter was highly profitable but it was labour-intensive. So much so that Shenson spawned a range of enterprises that sold newsletter content. The Internet has made it easy to provide information and entertainment related directly to the reader's interests. What people want to know they read avidly. Information is the biggest seller on the Internet. There are no gatekeepers to stop your information reaching the decision maker, as there are with direct mail. The dragons went into the dungeons years ago.

FINDING STRATEGIC PARTNERS

1 Newsletter publishers

Visit MediaFinder.com today. With almost 100,000 newsletters listed, there will be a number that appeal to people to whom your products and services would be a welcome addition. Click on to a few newsletters, read them and identify those who could help you to become the Web millionaire about whom we are always reading. With a first-rate product or service, great information or entertainment, and life-long relationships with delighted customers you deserve everything that is coming to you. If you prosper the ethical way you will continue to prosper.

2 Mailing lists

I am never truly happy with mailing lists. Too often they are put together by means of which I disapprove, they are often far from well maintained and their sale on the Internet far too often leads to spamming. In the world of stamps and envelopes I recommend that you always use a reputable professional list broker who knows how to navigate through the minefield, or the list that you use will have only one response: 'PLEASE TAKE MY NAME OFF YOUR

LIST'. If, however, you know better, MediaFinder.com lists owners of lists as well and good luck to you.

3 Business directories

If a firm is likely to have a sizeable customer base which shares the interests of your customers you can find them in the various directories on line from Yellow Pages onwards. Before you approach any as a strategic ally try being a customer. Check out their Web site, opt in to any e-mail contact or newsletter and see for yourself whether their communications are of a type with which you want to be associated.

4 E-zine directories

Many e-zines have thousands of subscribers who, in general, share interests. They could endorse your products or services to great effect. Subscribe for an issue or two to those that appear interesting before approaching them as a potential strategic ally. The directories are many. Try some of the following for information and ideas:

- Our List of Hundreds of E-zines
- e-Zines Database
- John Labovitz's E-Zine List
- Electronic Journal Access
- Zine Rack.

5 Website directories

When it comes down to it you can't beat a strategic ally who is already doing something very similar to what you are doing, only possibly better at present. A list of Web marketers, listed by category is worth more than gold dust. Try:

- Yahoo (probably the biggest and best directory of them all)
- Click Trade
- Web Side Story.

6 Surfing the Web

The Web often responds kindly to those who play with it. The right keywords and phrases open a treasure trove of information. If someone who looks appropriate comes close to the top of the list for a given keyword, that is a real treasure. Work with them and the world will come to know your name. I am told that the professionals use WebFerret to enable them to search seven search engines all at the same time. Wow! It sounds complicated to me, but look at webferret.com. Not every one is a technophobe like me.

7 Bulletin boards, forums and discussion groups

Most chatrooms and the like bring together like minded people to share their interests and knowledge. Most fight shy of promoting products or services directly, but none stop you from asking 'does anyone know a good source for …?' To find forums that are appropriate to you, you may wish to try:

- Yahoo message boards
- ForumOne
- Lycos Search: Message Boards.

Some forums exist solely to promote online business. Why not look at:

- E-zine Publishers Business Exchange
- LinkUp Discussion Group
- Expose.

8 Networking

If you know people who know people they might very well be able to recommend a possible strategic ally. Internet discussion groups can help to quickly build the extent of your personal network. But beware of multi-level marketers. Although I am sure many are ethical and hard working, I have personally met a sufficient number of those who are neither to be wary of the whole tribe. The desire to build 'down-lines' makes these people ace net-workers, but I suspect that few benefit from the relationship, not even those who build it.

9 Frequently seen banner advertisements

If you see an advertisement over and over again it is probably doing some good. If it's appropriate, take a closer look as above – you have nothing to lose from intelligent checking.

10 Authors and other strange people

These days people who write about the field in which you operate almost certainly have websites and those sites are there for a commercial purpose. With the exception of business bodice-rippers, royalty payments would seldom keep a very small monkey in peanuts. Conversely any human that writes about anything has a sort of specious authority that gives power to any endorsement they make, at least to their loyal readers. Add to this the fact that they almost certainly keep in touch with their readers through a news-letter or something similar and you may have a prime case for a strategic alliance.

SO YOU WANT TO BENEFIT?

Step One: Get your offering right

If you expect someone to recommend your product or service to their valued and valuable customers you have to offer something which will enhance, not threaten, the relationship they may well have built up over years. You must ensure that your offer and the service that backs it is capable of consistently delivering delight. This is why Comparative Analysis is so important (see Chapter 4).

Step Two: Finding the right partners

The vital word here is 'right'. Your prospective partners must:

1 Have built a strong relationship with their customers based on trust. These customers must have similar interests to your own.
2 Contact their customers regularly delivering information or entertain-ment which is desired, personal, timely, and relevant.
3 Have a large enough database of prospects to make the partnership worthwhile for you both.

Step Three: Making contact

Most websites offer a range of ways to make contact. Identify the most personal and use that: after all this relationship is among the most important you will make. Where it is possible, a telephone call is good, so is a fax or a letter. The thing to avoid is a bulk e-mail sprayed out to hundreds of potential partners. Whatever you call it, spam remains an unwanted intrusion and people who trade online are probably more sensitive to it than most.

THE INITIAL CONTACT

Here is an outline of the kind of things that you might say.

1 I loved your Web site.
2 Your customers and mine have much in common.
3 Could we help each other?
4 I can see how you treat your customers. I treat mine the same caring way.

5 An alliance with me could enhance your relationship with your customers and make you money.

6 May I send you a sample of my product (description of my service – with testimonials) for you to consider?

7 If you are happy to recommend my product/service I would be delighted to offer a special deal to your customers. (Be careful here that the deal you offer is not one that would upset your current customers. Where possible make your own loyal customers a good deal at the same time. Some will be on both databases.)

8 Since my customers tend to become customers for life I would be glad to pay you most of the profit on the initial deals I make with your customers. I will make my money from the recurrent repeat sales ... or ....

9 I will happily give a similar endorsement of your products if appropriate.

10 I believe absolutely that for both of us our relationships with our customers can be enhanced if we work together.

Risk reversal

Offer credible and worthwhile guarantees for your partner and the new customers. Make sure that your 'host' has the choice of selling direct if preferred. You have no wish to take customers or business away. If they wants to, agree to the endorsement being tested with a small subset of their customers. Write the endorsement yourself if you can, but make it clear that nothing goes out to their customers unless the host feels totally comfortable with it.

Step Four: The agreement

No one but lawyers like lengthy and legalistic contracts, but in business clear agreements in writing are essential. This is not an invitation to an open season on distributing writs. A contract is simply a clear, unambiguous statement of what has been agreed between you and another businessperson. The contract is there to establish clarity and to avoid misunderstandings. Going to law is a distraction that most reputable business people avoid, but some very disreputable ones use as a smoke screen.

In most countries today the simplest of contracts is thought of as binding on both parties. A nice clear letter stating what you agree to do, what your strategic partner will do, who will pay how much to whom and when is all you are likely to need. It is pleasant if you each sign two copies. That shows a degree of commitment and even enthusiasm for the deal, though in many countries even this is unnecessary. As long as one party sends a copy to the other and can show it was received and not amended, it normally stands as a contract binding on both.

HOSTING

The above has been written mainly for those who wish to enter into strategic alliances where another endorses their product or where each is happy to promote the other to their loyal and delighted customers. You may wish to consider the possibility of building a one-way street where you are the host and others benefit from your endorsements.

As a consultant, author, broadcaster and conference speaker I may, from time to time, identify opportunities for other consultants and trainers whom I trust. Conversely there are those who virtually stumble over work opportunities for me. Since some are better at finding than doing, and since I definitely prefer the doing to the finding, we can sometimes enter into ideal host beneficiary relationships – with them as the almost full-time host. Having others find assignments for me is perfect from my point of view. I am kept busy doing what I do best. And it is great for those who find me the work too. Since I can command a higher fee than most and am happy to pay my 'agent' a large proportion of it for saving me the trouble of going out and crying my wares in the streets, they can make more than they might from selling their own, slightly less well-known, skills. Those who represent not just me but a small stable of people like me can easily make much more than any single member of their team of highly paid 'stars'.

Similarly, if you have a strong database of delighted customers it may be very much in your financial interest to actively seek out those who would pay generously to have you promote their products or services. The usual rules apply. They must have an excellent product, provide superior service, look after and communicate with all customers in such a way as to keep them delighted and loyal, and they must be realistic about how much they are prepared to spend on effortless extra sales.

In my business independent consultants occasionally cluster together in networks in which each (in theory at least) attempts to sell the services of the others. Frequently they decide, for what reasons God alone may know, to pay a finder's fee of a meagre 10 % for work passed their way. They then all sit at home waiting for the work to roll in and wonder in their more lucid moments why nothing happens. If the labourer is worthy of his hire, no labourer is more worthy than the good salesperson. The commission must be generous (25 %–40 %) or nothing works. So if you see yourself in the role of host, I advise you to limit your efforts to supporting realistic beneficiaries who appreciate and will pay for your efforts.

Remember that in strategic alliances the response rates are likely to be very much higher than those created by any other means. You can make a massive income without the need either to develop, make or distribute the product. Your income will be increased and your effort minimized if you endorse suitable high-ticket products or services. In general it is easier to have 100 people send you £250 each than it is to persuade 1000 to part with £20, a fact that most pile 'em high, sell 'em cheap sales outfits forget.

SUMMARY ACTION PLAN FOR HOSTS

1   Contact the owner of the business whose products or services you believe you can ethically and effectively endorse.

2   Explain how your customer base could provide profitable extra sales.

3   Outline your terms of business, especially your expectations in terms of sales commissions: perhaps 55%–65% of initial sales and 10% of repeat business.

4   Suggest a clear contract that gives you your fair share of repeat sales.

5   Indicate how you expect orders to be tracked.

6   Point out that the real money is in back-end sales and that you are only prepared to do business with those who treat their customers in such a way as to generate such sales.

7   Remind them that they have no advertising or marketing costs for this additional, life-long business, if they work with you ... and ....

8   If they reject your offer simply move on. It is their loss and you have plenty of other fish to fry.

THE WORDS IF NOT THE MUSIC

Host or beneficiary, someone must write the endorsement. The secret is to make it clear to all potential customers that the individual providing the endorsement does so convinced that, in so doing, the true beneficiary will be the customer. Unless the endorsement will truly help customers to achieve something they want, it is a waste of space. If you have spent time and money building a strong relationship with your customers, the last thing you want is to write an endorsement which, fairly or otherwise, gives the impression that you are now suddenly after the quickest buck you can lay your hands on.

I am amazed when I train sales people to understand buyer psychology that there are still some who are so enamoured of a so-called closing technique that they use it and thereby destroy the relationship they have built up so carefully. An endorsement must not give the slightest impression of pressure of any kind. It is a service to the reader advising them of a product or service that may give them great satisfaction. Above all the endorsement must be genuine and genuinely offered to help the reader. Often the endorsement is embedded in other information. For example I might, in my newsletter, write a brief article on 'The E-Commerce Revolution' in which I say something along these lines:

> One way many businesses are flourishing on the Web is by working together in joint ventures or strategic alliances. There is much excellent information available online from the top marketing gurus, including Greg Schleismann, a leading authority on affinity marketing.
>
> Yesterday I looked in detail at www.jvmarketing.com. His free news-letters are full of useful information and their membership fee of less than £2 a day seemed . . . .

A BRIEF SUMMARY OF E-MARKET DOMINANCE

E-Market Dominance is designed to maximize profitable sales by bringing together the best low-cost ways to use technology in the market place. It has two legs, each of which works very well alone, but both of which are essential for optimal success.

First you must have a comprehensive strategy to attract prospects, turn prospects into customers, customers into friends, and friends into life-long advocates of your business. You achieve this by:

- Using state-of-the-art marketing processes to attract high-quality prospects.
- Developing a mandate to build a relationship through keeping in touch with information which is desired, personal, timely, and relevant to each individual customer.
- Providing products and services which consistently delight your customers.
- Keeping your eye firmly on emerging customer desires and making sure you are ready and able to satisfy them.
- Building customer and employee loyalty so your understanding increases as customers and employees become friends and friends become advocates.

Second, you then grow your business further and more profitably by:

- Adding customers by entering into strategic alliances only with those who have customers who will want your offering.
- Ensuring your allies are people who treat their customers as well as you treat yours.
- Gaining genuine third-party endorsements for what you sell and what you do.

● Seeking opportunities to endorse suitable products and services in your frequent communications to your loyal customers.

WHAT YOU WILL HAVE LEARNED IN THIS CHAPTER

☞ Why you need to build strategic alliances and third-party endorsements.

☞ How to find suitable partners.

☞ How to approach such partners.

☞ How to write the agreement.

☞ How to write endorsements that don't read like advertising fluff.

☞ How to reward your strategic allies.

☞ How to build new customers for life.

CHAPTER TWELVE

PRICING STRATEGIES FOR SUCCESS

☞ She knows the price of everything and the value of nothing

OSCAR WILDE

☞ Affluence means influence

JACK LONDON

☞ If you would wish to know the value of money, go and try to borrow some

BENJAMIN FRANKLIN

WHAT YOU WILL LEARN IN THIS CHAPTER

☞ Understand that pricing is a key strategic issue.

☞ Develop a profitable strategic and tactical approach to pricing.

☞ Clear your mind of any belief that the Internet has to be a 'pile 'em high, sell 'em cheap' operation.

THE MORE THINGS CHANGE, THE MORE THEY REMAIN THE SAME

The year that I was born – yes, as long ago as that – a research programme began in Chicago into purchasing. Not surprisingly, 'price' was close to the top of the list. People like to get a bargain. Though price was close to the top, it was not, as I have mentioned elsewhere, the number one reason for buying. For the last 60 or so years, 'convenience' has held the top spot on the buyer's wish list. Now the Internet has made it really easy to compare prices. Surely that is enough to push price into the number one position.

The answer is a definite maybe. If you are offering a 'me too' product identical to what your competitor offers and you give an identical level of service, then price is likely to be the single differentiating factor. You better be wary of anyone who has better buying terms or more efficient service than yours because they can price you right out of business and still make a profit.

If, on the other hand:

- You have a unique product or service.
- You can present your product or service as distinctive and customers believe you.
- You are truly nice people to do business with so that your customers come to you in droves and stay with you for life.
- You provide more personal, accurate, relevant, and timely information than your competitors.
- Your customers ask for the information you provide and enjoy receiving it.
- You are recommended as the cat's pyjamas by someone customers trust so they have faith in you from the word go.
- You deliver even more than customers expect.

If you are and do all of these things, price is less of an issue to your customers. It should remain, however, a key issue to you.

People will pay a premium for convenience. How much will they pay and how will you give real value *from the customers' point of view?* How can you be both fair to the customer, again from their point of view, and optimize the profit potential of your business? If the economists are right in their belief that there is a clear and automatic relationship between price and demand, how do you maximize both? (It is a given of much economic theory that we are rational automatons acting exclusively in our immediate financial interests. Happily, economists are rarely right, as our inability to manage the macro-economy testifies. It is their misfortune that neither value nor values can be easily graphed.) Should you even be thinking of maximizing profit and revenues? Is there a better way? These are strategic questions all businesses should consider and review again and again.

MINI CASE STUDY ONE

Twenty-five years ago European and US television manufacturers were hit by cheap sets imported from Asia. Some attempted to survive by cutting prices and (possibly) cutting corners. The smart money in both continents, however, went into improving style and quality and increasing prices so that buyers were satisfying their need for status. For a while the few remaining manufacturers prospered. Scandinavian, German or US televisions became a status symbol on both sides of the Atlantic. To a small but loyal band of consumers price was not an issue, perceived value was the vital factor.

Meanwhile the Japanese in particular used new technology to improve quality and reduce prices in real terms. Subsequently competition became even tougher, but quality continued to ensure prosperity. Survival of an American or European television and audio has often been on a knife-edge, but one thing is certain. Had there been a price war, there would soon have been no Europe- or US-based companies to survive after the first few, heartbreaking years.

Let me not mislead you into thinking that high-price strategies are the only way to go. Undercutting your competition can create market dominance in the long term, where all else is equal. It is like a game of poker where you can bluff with a poor hand simply because you have enough money on the table to keep going while those with better hands fold either through lack of funds or funk. But if you are the player who lacks funds you need to use the advantages offered by the Internet to level the playing field. You can only do that if your pricing strategy is sensible.

On the Web anyone with sufficient imagination can set the rules by which others play, but you have to be ready to play to win. That means getting your offering right, your service and quality right and your price right.

MINI CASE STUDY TWO

To give a general idea of the relationship between market dominance and profit you have only to consider the wide-ranging *Profit Impact of Marketing Strategies* study conducted by the Marketing Science Institute. Pre-tax profits as a percentage of sales for companies with 10–20 % market share were 3.42 %. They climbed steadily with market share so that at a market share of 40 % average pre-tax profits were 13.16 %. (Just in case your pre-tax profits exceed 13.16 %, please remember the old adage that an average is the best of the worst combined with the worst of the best, so many others are, like you, doing better than average.)

On the theme of loyalty there is strong evidence that firms who optimize their strengths, rather than going in for mindless dumbsizing every time the cards appear to be stacked against them, on average make profits five to six times as high as those of competitors who cut jobs rather than use their brains to overcome often transient problems. This is not to say that downsizing is never justified: sadly it is sometimes essential for survival. But it always carries costs.

The Internet allows you to do more with fewer people, but there is always much to be said for seeking to do more with what you have rather than firing people for a short-term market gain. Top companies ensure they have enough good, committed people to give top-quality service consistently.

Your pricing strategy must be right for your offering to the market place in relation to what competitors offer and the price at which they offer it. It also needs to take into account what customers are willing to pay and what exactly it is that they expect for their money. The world of customers has always been ready to pay for convenience. And they have always wanted value. There is always more than one way to skin a cat.

THERE ARE MANY WAYS TO SET A PRICE

☞ After you have done a thing the same way for two years look it over carefully. After five years look at it with suspicion and after ten years throw it away and start over

ALFRED EDWARD PERLMAN

To establish the right pricing strategy you need to know lots of things. Here is a list of a few:

- What the most worthwhile customers want of you.
- Where you are strong.
- Where competition is strong.
- Where competition is weak.
- Competition's pricing strategy (if they have one).
- The degree to which different segments, sectors, niches, or markets have different needs.
- What customer new desires and needs are emerging.
- Where to focus your initial marketing attack.
- Whether you need to make your attack openly or to conceal your intentions.

Remember Sun Tse:

66When strong, appear weak. When weak, be invisible. 99

- Which competitors' worthwhile customers you can win over through an effective pricing strategy combined with an appropriate offering and level of service.
- Which of your strengths need to be promoted by marketing and presented by sales people.
- How pricing relates to your overall marketing strategy.
- Your resources when compared to those of competition. (If they are rich you must be ultra smart.)
- Your costs.

A key tool for ensuring that you have this information available is a Comparative Analysis (Chapter 4).

Next you should conduct an Opportunity Analysis. Record all opportunities to build revenues, profits and resources. Take an entrepreneurial rather than managerial approach to assure that none are excluded as being 'impractical'. Brainstorm initially without concern for practicality and when the list is exhaustive screen for immediate exploitation by considering:

1   Do you have, or can you acquire, the necessary resources and people to exploit the opportunity effectively?
2   Is the exploitation of this opportunity likely to provide an adequate return on your investment of time, materials and resources?
3   Can you ensure that exploitation of this opportunity would not divert key resources or people from other more important activities relevant to the current business plan priorities or future strategic needs?
4   What pricing strategy will best help you to exploit this opportunity?
5   Is such a pricing strategy likely to grow the whole business profitably?

ACTION SUMMARY

- List every potential opportunity.
- Screen for your ability to exploit.
- Check feasibility now or in the future.
- Prioritize opportunities for exploitation.
- Establish a pricing strategy that reflects your strengths and competencies, customer expectations and market opportunities.

Perceived value is the complex interplay between the customers' perception of their satisfaction and your price. The higher the perceived satisfaction in general, the lower the concern about price and the stronger your competitive position. This is why the 'me too' followers in any market are vulnerable. Followers must provide at least as high quality and offer it at a lower price if they wish to overtake the leader. That is why they often lose money and withdraw from the field. Price wars are expensive. They are doubly costly when one party does not have to play the price-cutting game.

High price is a strategic decision in its own right. Not everyone who buys on the basis of price looks for low price.

The pricing policy needs to satisfy, at the same time, the need for an adequate return on investment and a clearly defined marketing objective. Some of the most effective pricing strategies now follow.

Differential or flexible pricing

Low prices are used in slack periods to generate sales and even-out fluctuations in demand. With intelligent shelves in supermarkets prices can nowadays be adjusted automatically to ensure an even flow of sales and little or no produce left on the shelves to pass its sell-by date. Pricing strategies must be careful not to 'prebuy' business you would have enjoyed regardless of any short-term price adjustment. Research suggests that in many cases although there is a degree of pre-buying to take advantage of temporary price reductions, the level of purchasing in general tends to increase marginally in the long run where flexible pricing is used intelligently to produce increased sales in the short term.

Discrete pricing

This is the nearest thing to licking your finger and holding it into the wind that professionals will countenance. Discrete pricing seeks to be neither high nor low, but by being aimed at the majority of customers' willingness or ability to pay it ensures an adequate return on investment by maximizing sales revenues. The ability to pay, however, is established by careful research or market testing and is not the result of unbridled hope or a wild guess. Since discrete pricing is dictated by the market rather than by the firm, the company's control of profit levels is limited to the degree to which costs can be controlled. The low cost of marketing on the Internet helps to keep costs down. Loyal customers and loyal employees help more. It remains essential that every employee is committed to the idea and the practice of exemplary service at lowest possible cost.

Discount pricing

Pricing is carefully used as a tool to attract volume business at a level where profitability is maximized through ease of distribution or economies of scale. Current technologies can be applied to minimize any edge gained by a competitor through economies of scale, but with the economics of distribution becoming increasingly important reductions of distribution costs should be always be sought. Fortunes will be made on the Web because 'no cost' distribution of some products (music, information, software) can be performed online.

Guarantee pricing

Prices are high, but so is the actual value of the product or service. This is only an option where you can provide Rolls Royce service at Rolls Royce prices. The customer's emotional feeling must be 'I am paying for, and getting, the very best available'. You, of course, need to identify a market with sufficient customers ready and able to pay for the best and then deliver better than any competitor to sustain a guarantee pricing strategy.

High-price maintenance

Similar to guarantee pricing, but in this case the superior value of the product may be more apparent than real, being based on a long and complex history of brand image building. For example a manufacturer may sell the same goods under different labels – one of them at a premium price. Unless you have already established a positive brand image you are unlikely to succeed with this approach.

Off-set pricing

Basic prices are low to attract customers, but 'extras' are heavily promoted and carry a heavy price penalty. When I was in the automotive industry many years ago it was common practice to offer a 'basic model' of a car at a highly competitive price. The dealers were not, however, expected to sell these value-for-money models. They were required to 'sell up' from them, a requirement which was often backed up by the manufacturer with stiff profit margin penalties to the dealer network if they failed to sell those cars that came complete with all the expensive extra bells and whistles.

Price lining

No company ought to consider this strategy in a world in which quality is king. It is the old trick of reducing product quality and standards of service to accurately reflect the level of the price. It is a case of building down to a price rather than up to a specification. John Fenton, in his advice to sales people on how to deal with the price objection used to say:

> Be proud of your price and justify it with the value of your product or service, but if the customer continues to insist, 'I can get it cheaper from X', try saying: 'X is a very professional firm who have a very accurate view of the worth of their product. So have we. Our price is what it is because we offer . . . .'

I have, for more than twenty years, considered that to be excellent advice that is typical of John's work.

Diversionary pricing

Also known as 'loss leaders', this is the concept of offering a limited range of products at a low price with the intention of giving an often false impression of low prices overall. How often do you hear the complaint 'Not everything is cheaper there you know', directed at a so-called 'discount store'?

Such a remark indicates a situation in which diversionary pricing has been tried with less than total success. Loss leaders can, however, attract customers to try your offering for the first time by reducing the risk of the initial purchase. A professional marketer will, of course, take advantage of the customers' perception of 'money saved' and high value to cross-sell other products or services.

MINI CASE STUDY

Proof that low prices can be a problem when marketing through the Internet is the sad case of Argos. This cut-price but by no means always cheapest retailer went on line apparently forgetting that its customers became its customers largely because they could not afford to buy such luxuries as home computers. According to independent research their first website had only 35 'hits' in more than a year.

Skimming pricing

Intentionally creating prices so high that they put the product or service out of the reach of the majority of the market to attract profitably those few buyers who seek to buy exclusivity at any price. There are customers who look for products and services that are priced this way, and they are not all rich individuals. 'Big name' consultants are able to make their astronomic fees a unique selling point in those corporations where it is believed that 'the label is more valuable than the garment'. So rife is the practice in buying consultancy on the basis of 'never mind the quality, feel the price' that my old mentor, Howard Shenson' used to advise those who were failing to attract enough business to see what happened if they doubled their price. Frequently what happened was that business increased to everyone's satisfaction.

NEVER LOSE SIGHT OF THE OBJECTIVES

By way of a final word on this subject, any pricing strategy is a good one if the objectives of the business are achieved. For many years we have been talking of SMART objectives. It is time to be thinking double SMART.

E-MARKET DOMINANCE OBJECTIVES MUST BE:

Significant:	They must make a solid business contribution to the strategy.
Specific:	They must state in clear terms exactly what must be done.
Meaningful:	They must be aimed at achieving profitable outcomes.
Measurable:	What you can't measure, you can't manage.

Achievable:	They must be feasible.
Accountable:	They must create challenge for specific individuals and teams.
Realistic:	They must be attainable with the resources that are available or easily accessible.
Raise Standards:	They must ensure that what you do well today you do better tomorrow and better yet the day after.
Time Framed:	They must be achieved by a predetermined date.
Taken up:	People must want to play their part in achieving the objectives.

WHAT YOU WILL HAVE LEARNED IN THIS CHAPTER

☞ Pricing is an important strategic issue.

☞ Pricing strategy must enable the achievement of objectives in every area of the business.

☞ Pile 'em high, sell 'em cheap is not the ideal strategy for customers who seek high quality combined with exemplary levels of service.

☞ The range of pricing strategies and how each might work for you.

CHAPTER THIRTEEN

TOMORROW THE WORLD

☞ The potential for the small company to become an international conglomerate online.

☞ How to manage virtually risk free entry into overseas markets.

☞ The readiness of countries and markets globally for e-commerce and e-business.

CULTURES AND INDIVIDUALS

To the company with limited resources, the Internet offers a unique business opportunity. As long as you can ensure service and obviate logistical problems you are, in effect, a global company as soon as you have a viable online presence. The international language of business is still English, so you have only a limited need to go to the expense of having a multilingual website. Anywhere in the world where business is taken seriously the potential customer will have taken steps to be able to conduct business in English. Consumers may be less accessible, but a website should enable even those who only make sales directly to the consumer to find local intermediaries and agents. In fact it is not a necessity to have your own website. Eager to build export trade, governments provide Web listings for would-be exporters usually free of charge. Take a look at www.tradeuk.net/ or www. ita.doc.gov/tic as examples in the UK and the US.

But wait a minute, you may be thinking, there is more to culture than language. Anthropologists make a good living telling us that people who live in different cultures have different customs, desires and needs. What is more, marketing gurus have always said you can't transfer a marketing strategy from one market to another. Surely there is more to having success in an overseas market than speaking English and understanding that the World Wide Web really is worldwide. You could be right, so let's look at a few facts.

Consider if you will the anthropologist. It may surprise you to know that some tell lies and others are the victims of often well-meant lies. Consider an example of each. Everyone knows that Eskimos have more than 200 (or is it 300?) words for snow. You can take your pick from the numbers because the statement isn't true, so it matters little which you choose. They may have a word or two we lack, but if you think of all the words we know (sleet, flurry, blizzard and the rest) it is actually a close-run thing. The Inuit snow thesaurus is a lie, but it is a lie that gains credence every time it is repeated by the – let me be frank – ignorant, lazy or untruthful.

The same is true of the Hopi having no concept of time or of the fabled wisdom of Don Juan (a novella, not a research report, in spite of fooling the academics for long enough to win the author his Ph.D.). All these and many more beside are what Josephine Tey called 'Tonypandy', myths that were invented and subsequently have been repeated with tenacious disrespect for the truth. (In case you are wondering, no starving miners were shot by police or troops in the Welsh valleys. The police were unarmed and the army never got within miles of the strikers.)

Probably the most famous anthropological dupe was Margaret Mead, of *Coming of Age in Samoa* fame. I remember being told in prurient detail when I was a student that the youth of Samoa lived a life of limitless premarital sex. The suggestion that the balance of decency was maintained by a taboo forbidding the sexes to eat together prior to marriage did nothing to cool the ardour with which I planned to get to South Seas while I still had youthful energy and appetites.

Sadly Margaret Mead and I were both misled. Dr. Mead was misled by a group of teenage informants who chose to invent stories they thought would interest and please the investigator. I in turn was misled by my professor who had swallowed the story whole when he read Mead's famous book – or being a professor, possibly read the notes or an essay passed to him by someone who might, just might, have read the book. (How many socialists or economists for that matter have actually ploughed through the turgidity of *Das Kapital*? I remember reading it in my youth and, recognizing the improvement in style and substance when Engels took over authorship, I might have wished Marx an earlier demise.)

The anthropologist William du Toit makes it clear that the apparent difference between cultures reduces the closer that you get to the individual. Take a distant view and you seem to see an alien culture. Move closer and you see many people deviating from that culture. Move close enough and you see an individual very much like you. The Japanese on average may tend toward an apparently exotic norm, but that norm is no more true of the individual than it would be true to call me a typical Englishman even if there were such a creature.

Fons Trompenaars in his fascinating book *Riding the Waves of Culture* administers 'opinionnaires' to very small groups of business people from a number of countries. He categorizes them on the crudest of arithmetical averages (anything over 50% and you're in the group) into descriptions of cultures where by definition anything up to half the subjects do not fit. This makes for a fascinating read, but I doubt the wisdom of building a business strategy on the findings.

So who can we trust? Psychologists have always found that people of different national groups have far more in common with each other than divides them through the political convenience of national boundaries. We all love our children, fight with our spouses, need security and love, look for social status, and seek to make the most of our talents and abilities regardless of the land of our birth. Of course there is something unique, something special about every human being – but that is the point. It is our uniqueness as well as our similarities that make the cultural myth unlikely. At best the much-vaunted national identity is a sad commingling of the best of the worst with the worst of the best and if the Internet enables anything it enables us to deal with individuals as individuals. The frequently misquoted Abraham Maslow did suggest that he who has only a hammer tends to treat everything as a nail, but with the Web we have a full toolkit. It would be a pity if myths denied us its proper use.

At the end of the day the businessperson tends to trust most those who literally put their money where their mouth is. Roper Starch Worldwide Incorporated could be throwing a great deal of good money after bad if global advertising turned out to be ineffective. They therefore had conducted psychological profiling of sample populations drawn from 35 countries in which they had commercial interests. They exhaustively tested 35,000 people and concluded that people are people and that national variation, although it existed, is far less significant than the traits that all people have in common. In short if you appeal to the deep needs and desires shared by all people your message will be very nearly as effective in Canton, Cairo or Camden as it is in Chicago. The difference will have less to do with national differences of attitude than it does with simple differences in buying power and accessibility of the customer.

Before going on to consider accessibility I would like to introduce you to the demographic typologies that the Roper Starch research suggested are common to all cultures. You should, whether you want to be a global player or stay in imagined safety at home, consider how you may best appeal to each of these types.

Strivers

These are people who a few years back would have been called 'upwardly mobile'. The difference is that many do not see advancement as being worthwhile for its own sake as the Yuppies did in the Thatcher and Reagan years. They want a better, more comfortable, more fulfilling life for themselves and those whom they love. They tend to be early adopters of products whenever they can afford to buy them and believe that they will help them or their children to make progress. They are open to new ideas and welcome information from those they trust. Educational products that will give their children a better start in life excite and attract them.

Devouts

Devouts are people who hold strong beliefs and values, neither of which is necessarily based on a religious faith. They do, however, tend to have high expectations of the financial probity and ecological responsibility of those with whom they do business. When they become convinced that a business meets the very high standards they believe in they are not merely customers for life, they become tireless advocates of the business.

Altruists

These are very likely customers for 'trade not aid' organizations and companies like Body Shop. They care about the welfare of others and contribute to that welfare to the degree they can. This does not imply they are necessarily anti-business. They dislike and mistrust the rapacity of the corporate world, but they often recognize that profit is an essential prerequisite of the redistribution of affluence.

Intimates

Such people seek close relationships in business as in life. Their family is often the absolute focus of their lives and allowing others to enter the family circle is conditional on trust. These buyers sometimes need a longer than average period of wooing before they are prepared to commit to a purchase, but once they decide to become a customer they become a friend and advocate.

Fun seekers

Fun seekers were once happily called 'swingers'. Sadly this word now has a different and less appropriate connotation than it once had. They tend to be if not young, then young at heart. They are in the market for hedonism and have epicurean tastes. If there is more than a passing touch of truth in the forecasts of an 'experience economy' the Fun seekers will lead the way.

Creatives

Peter Drucker once demanded of a self-styled guru why he snarled when he spoke the word 'people'. I come close to snarling when I hear the word 'creative'. I have spent a lifetime in business recoiling from those who never finish anything because they regard themselves, and their self-regard is massive, as 'creative'. If I think that way, however, I am doing these people a real injustice. The Creatives in this study are not people who drop any ball they are running with as soon as another bright idea hits them. Nor are they to be found among the denizens of the advertising agencies. Creatives in this sense are the people who are able readily to adopt products or services because they can clearly visualize how they can use them to meet their needs, often in unexpected and novel ways. Their imaginative approach to your message will lead them to become early adopters if you give them the room they need to think.

Types omitted by this study but which are also important include:

Nurturers

Nurturers who are often mothers in families where buying decisions are made on the basis of what is good for the children. These buyers have much in common with Strivers as described as above, except they have no wish to be upwardly mobile.

Economists

It is difficult to believe that any society lacks people who regard all products and services as being intrinsically the same regardless of competing brands and so buy only on price. These are the individuals who believe that all toothpastes clean teeth, all baked beans provide protein and dietary fibre, and that all cars transport you from where you are to where you want to be. On that basis their buying decisions are based only on price. Contrary to general opinion, research shows that these people are not in the majority, but they surely exist.

Wannabes

This sounds like a patronizing description of a fellow human being, but the Web is full of products, seminars, newsletters and the like that are so banal they could only appeal to dreamers happy to buy this or that panacea, knowing that when they make no effort to make it work another will be along in no time so hope can spring eternal in spite of the disappointments of inaction. The kind of people who sadly run the complete gamut from the Robbins fire walk to Jack Black and back again always looking for self-esteem and never using what they have been taught to find it. They are out there in huge numbers in every society. I include them for the sake of completeness.

MINI CASE STUDY Go East – Supermarkets

Supermarkets have experienced mixed results from online trading. The cost of picking and distributing relatively small and diverse orders have given them a major headache. The leading UK supermarket chain Tesco has persevered and gone to considerable lengths to re-launch its online grocery delivery service. Now that they cover 90 % of the British Isles they are looking to expand overseas. Online grocery is still very much in its early stages. Tesco's online revenues have recently topped £100 million, which represents only 1% of their overall sales. Early or not they are looking to online trading as a means of expanding in overseas markets. Their initial targets are Thailand, Taiwan and South Korea; in Thailand they have 24 stores and plan to open a further 16 within three years. This eagerness to look to the future and seek to exploit the realities has been typical of Tesco thinking in recent years.

Their stores in South and East Kent were losing sales because their customers preferred to take a cheap outing to France where alcohol and cigarettes carry far less tax. Some firms would have wrung their hands and screamed 'foul'. Tesco had a practical solution. They simply moved their tobacco and drinks outlets across the English Channel to Calais, where they could retain their customers and give them lower prices.

WHO IS READY?

When the Economist Intelligence Unit Business Forum investigated how countries rated when it comes to e-commerce readiness in May 2000, no one was surprised to hear that the US was confirmed as the world's most 'e-commerce ready' country. British and European e-traders should see this not as a threat, but as a golden opportunity. When I can I spend my time in the US and although I travel the length and breadth of the country I regard the Mid West as home away from home. Why do I love Illinois? It isn't for the climate. We enjoy, if that is the right word, summers in which the temperature climbs to the high nineties and stays there. We have rainstorms summer and winter that bend and sometimes even break the trees. In winter a snowfall of more than twenty inches in a day is unlikely to excite comment and of course we have the tornado season to give that little extra spice of excitement. On the other hand the women are beautiful. The booze is cheap and available from one morning until the next. The people are friendly, including the husbands of the beautiful women. And they love everything British. They want to buy our goods and services. It is a great pity that often we make it so depressingly difficult for them to do so.

In Chicago I worked with an American consultancy that had a small part of its business, but a huge part of its commitment, dedicated to helping British businesses to win orders from the US. I remember, not without shame, the frustration of my American colleagues when after interesting a potential customer in a British product or service they approached a British company for further information. Here was profit signed, sealed and all but delivered. All that our principals back home needed to do was to e-mail a price or delivery time to pick the lowest hanging of low-hanging fruit. Easy enough you might think. Please think again, and then, if necessary re-think the way your business is conducted. Time after time my colleagues' urgent requests were ignored for days or, in spite of numerous telephone calls, weeks. At last the call would fall to me. Some ill-tempered harridan of either sex would demand to know whether I was aware that it was Friday or why I was unable to deduce from a distance of four and a half thousand miles that the wilfully anonymous person that I 'needed to speak to' was on holiday. I mention this because the good news is that the EIU research indicates that we are relatively e-ready. So the relevant question is the degree to which we are willing rather than able to exploit our readiness.

Britain lies in sixth place behind three Nordic countries and the Netherlands. Wherever you may be in the world please consider this. Your Web presence opens your business seven days a week and twenty-four hours a day, but only if you have the will, the good sense and the infrastructure to give service throughout your new opening hours. When customers overseas ask for information they are politely requesting that it be despatched by return and by the quickest possible means, not when the sales director gets back from the Bahamas or even out of his pyjamas.

The EIU report looks at macro-economic factors and 'connectivity'. It tells you clearly where customers can be readily accessed and indicates their ability to pay for what they want. It could be a major factor in your strategic planning – and they have given it to us free. We should not look such a fine gift horse in the mouth.

The EIU report

The EIU evaluated two essential attributes of e-business readiness. First they looked at the general business environment of each country and measured or forecast 70 parameters, including the strength of the economy, political stability, taxation, and openness to trade and investment. Second they looked at connectivity, including dial-up costs and the literacy rate as well as the IT infrastructure. This approach to connectivity has been developed, tested and validated by Pyramid Research, the EIU's communications division. The combined results demand the most careful consideration by any entrepreneur or strategist who is even tentatively looking to the Internet to build and secure their business.

We will look at the results in detail, but first let us provide a little perspective by making some general points. The US heads the table as much for their openness to trade and their general economic prospects as for their technology. America scores the maximum for connectivity, but so do Sweden, Finland and Norway, who are barely behind the US in other measures. The Netherlands outscores all four of the leaders on the general economic and political measures and is less than 10% behind in their score for connectivity. Behind the Netherlands comes the UK, with Canada, Singapore, Hong Kong, and Switzerland completing the top ten.

The major players in the European Union are a little down the field, with Germany at number 13, France at 14 and Italy at 19. Ireland, Denmark and Belgium are all in the top 15. Nine countries in the top 10 (positions 1–9) are either English-speaking or have a strong tradition of English as a second language while the Swiss are no slouches when it comes to using English. So the customers in the top 10 e-business-ready countries talk your language.

Of those that may not, Japan is at number 21, immediately ahead of Spain, with Portugal at number 25, wedged neatly between South Korea and Argentina. Greece is at number 22, behind Malaysia.

In general the relative readiness of Asian countries is mixed. China is number 51 while India, which as a country produces some of the best computer software designers and mathematicians in the world, is only one place higher. Taiwan and Thailand are numbers 27 and 28. In general, Latin America tends to lag a little behind Eastern Europe, and unsurprisingly Iraq is at the bottom of the heap with Iran only two places higher. I take some personal pleasure in the fact that South Africa with all its problems manages a creditable place at number 36.

The measures look forward only five years, so countries with interesting e-commerce ambitions and liberal government policies are omitted. For example Jamaica has recently begun to invest heavily in e-commerce and information leadership. The Jamaican government has invested a substantial part of the limited resources of the island in technology and technological education and recently announced that all IT graduates will be found employment on completion of their studies. This enlightened approach cannot be expected to move a small island to dominance in less than five years, but all business people should be watching their progress with interest and goodwill.

For full details and interpretations of the scores you ought to visit the EIU website www.eiu.com/, which is crammed full of information that has interest and value to everyone in e-commerce.

SUCCESSFUL GLOBAL ENTREPRENEURING

That quick tour round the world of e-commerce prompts this reminder, for which I make absolutely no apology. Before you sally forth to conquer that world you need to have a number of things firmly in place at home. Such as:

1   A shared determination at the highest level to do whatever it takes to be the best of the best in the eyes of the customer.
2   A careful, even frugal, but adequate investment of resources.
3   A strategy aimed at delighting the customer, increasing your share of their total spend and keeping them loyal to you for life.

4 A 'big picture' of what the company is about that inspires every person in the team.

5 A clear understanding by every employee of what they get out of coming to work beyond a wage or salary, and an interface between the goals of the company and those of the people who will achieve those goals.

6 An attitude toward delighting the customer that is shared by every employee and is translated into action every minute of every day.

7 A top team that walks the talk of success all day every day.

8 A product or service range that reflects the customers' desires right now and will create and guide their wishes and expectations in the future.

9 A truly visitor-friendly website that attracts customers and makes them opt-in for further information, as well as stay and buy today.

10 Internal policies and procedures designed to support the customer and deliver delight at the end of every transaction.

11 Frequent and regular standardized contact from the top team with the customer to ensure that the top team knows the customer's current and emerging desires.

12 Superior distribution in any country where you choose to trade.

13 State-of-the-art online or offline after-sales support.

14 Systematic feedback, evaluation and review of performance.

For detailed market-by-market analysis of doing business overseas you can consult the website of the International Trade section of the US Department of Commerce, at www.ita.doc.gov/ita_home/itacnreg.htm.

MEASURING YOUR SUCCESS

Remember that old techniques may or may not work in a new and highly volatile economy. The Web is such an economy. Novelty is fraught with uncertainty because there is no way of knowing that the old approaches will still work as they once did. This means that in the world of e-commerce it is essential to exercise the discipline of measuring the return on your investment, even though that investment may be relatively modest.

The majority of financial managers have measurement and forecasting tools at their disposal that have served them well in the old economy and so continue to use them. This makes good sense to the extent that it is better to do something rather than nothing. But things move quickly in the new economy and unanticipated operating conditions can emerge quickly too. The effectiveness of a Web presence can be gauged by the methods recommended in other chapters, but the businessperson should never be seduced by new data into ignoring the need to continue simple measures of financial return on investment.

A substantial number of financial managers are now using benchmarking of competitors as well as the performance of the legacy business (the old bricks-and-mortar business) to evaluate financial returns. This approach to benchmarking is probably more useful than the old 'me too' approach that has dominated much low-quality marketing decision making in the past. If a competitor is making more money than you it is an indicator, a crude indicator perhaps but an important one, that they are doing something right where you are doing it wrong. In a fast-moving situation speed of decision making can become as important as the quality of the decision. For a time at least those who are fleet of mind will have an advantage over their more careful competitors.

It will become increasingly important to think creatively. There must be a point where experimentation and market testing have to stop and sub-optimal strategies have to be pursued with vigour. In the new economy there may be a period in which contribution is more important than profit and you are forced to consider unprofitable actions today to build future profit opportunities. If you do this remember that future profits can only occur if you are still around to collect them. When Peter Drucker said that profits are not just an objective of a business but an essential prerequisite to being in business he was not kidding.

A recent (June 2000) report by the Giga Information Group suggests that returns on their IT investment for some firms at least are better than older measures suggest. Whether this will prove to be true of e-commerce investment (the Giga report looks at total IT investment, which may or may not include e-commerce), is still to be tested by those who are in the front line. One area in the report that causes concern is that where old investment policies are used the company is likely to be getting a return on only a small part of total investment.

They suggest that some 75 % of IT investment in the firms studied was devoted to maintenance and operations, with 25 % allocated to creating the systems that enabled the businesses to streamline processes and exploit new market opportunities. On average, according to the report only one-third of changes prove successful – so only 8.33 % of total IT investment is actively generating a return. This cannot be extrapolated to the investment in e-commerce directly, but it clearly underlines the danger of allowing IT experts to lose sight of the fact that a Web presence is not a technological jamboree, it is a marketing and selling initiative.

It also directs attention to the need for new forms of measurement and much more carefully thought out resource allocation. IT is capable of delivering massive benefits, as is its small brother e-commerce. For example, growth in US productivity per worker has been double that of the UK for the last several years. During this period US investment in IT has been twice that of the UK. Contemporaneous happenings do not necessarily indicate cause and effect, but looking further back to a point where UK investment in IT was equal in terms of share of GDP with that of the US, the UK was able to hold its own in terms of productivity growth. A caused relationship does therefore seem likely.

So business needs to consider with great care the investment to be made in IT in general and e-commerce in particular. Only experience will identify the most useful new measures, but here are some guidelines that may be helpful.

1   Investment in a Web presence should be frugal. Fancy bells and whistles that offer little customer added-value should be avoided.
2   A programme of metrics based on well-defined goals should be developed and returns that are contingent on the achievement of those goals must be forecast. Some areas might include:
    - Increased revenue per customer transaction
    - Increased profit per customer
    - Increased lifetime value per customer
    - Savings in employee costs
    - Reductions in errors in shipments or order recording
    - Reductions in lead times
    - Reductions in gearing due to improved cash flow
    - Monetary value of time saved.

In the words of the report, 'measure, measure, measure, and communicate'.

3   Establish a frequent communication process to enable senior management to evaluate results, test new flexible strategies and invest in whatever is giving an acceptable return. When those with a vested interest, be they marketers, the IT department or advertising agencies, talk of 'jam tomorrow' you need to establish specific objectives and measure the contribution of the website to growing added value.
4   Emphasize those measures that prove reliable, but be creative about new forms of measurement.
5   Be ready to move quickly in a fast-moving new economy.

Traditional measurement tools and techniques may not be as effective in measuring performance when you look at many new-economy initiatives. There may be massive future value for example in expensively collecting immense customer databases today in order to benefit from them tomorrow, but if we use the tools we have and supplement them with new insights as these emerge, we will be more likely to survive long enough to enjoy tomorrow's proverbial pot of jam. If your financial people have doubts, listen to them. The gene that we have recently been told makes accountants dull may be a survival mechanism in the new economy as much as it presumably must have been in pre-history.

The Giga Information Group report is available online at Microsoft Business – Microsoft Business Home – Microsoft Corporation.

WHAT YOU WILL HAVE LEARNED IN THIS CHAPTER

☞ The Internet enables firms of any size to go global.

☞ Prospective customers overseas will be more accessible for the next five years in some countries more than others.

☞ Customers overseas have more in common than some culture vultures would have us think.

☞ Potential customers can be categorized on the basis of psychographics as much as demographics, and the marketing message can be targeted online.

☞ The old disciplines of measurement may be less than perfect in the new economy, but while they are all that we have they should be used, properly supplemented with informed insights.

CHAPTER FOURTEEN

PSYCHOLOGY IS STILL ABOUT PEOPLE

WHAT YOU WILL LEARN IN THIS CHAPTER

☞ There is an increasing body of knowledge about the online customers think and feel.

☞ This knowledge is essential if you wish to exploit fully the opportunities the Internet presents.

☞ With a little thought, you can use this knowledge to win business and avoid losses.

☞ The science is new so you will need to keep up to date.

THE PSYCHOLOGY OF CYBERSPACE

One of the most important gifts presented to business by science has been a clear and detailed understanding of customer behaviour. (For practical details of this sixty-year longitudinal study and specific 'how to' guidelines on its use please take a look at my book *The Power of Influence*.) Those of us who seek to prosper through e-commerce need to consider whether the Internet delivers potential and actual customers with strikingly different demographic and behavioural characteristics from those that are displayed in the so-called 'dirt world'.

The basic needs of people are common to all and are unchanging over time. But are they unchanging over space? We know that when we transplant an individual into a new environment, subtle but significant changes in behaviour are likely. Cyberspace is a very new environment, but already research is discovering some potentially deep consequences. For example, John Suler of Rider University has written a ground-breaking book *The Psychology of Cyberspace* (you can read it online at www.rider.edu/users/suler/psycyber/psycyber.html) on the behaviours that are specific to the often lonely and always restricted world of the computer. Another source of up-to-date information is The Psychology of Cyberspace Forum, located at the Behavior Online website, which is a lively and informative 'chatroom' where key ideas, research findings, hypotheses, and wild-ass guesses are exchanged.

How people actually use the Web has been the focus of research at the University of Wisconsin of Madison (my favourite state, city and campus in the US). Needless to say the research effort of the universities are being equalled or even exceeded by research bodies with a direct connection to commercial organizations. Xerox PARC (Palo Alto Research Center) has a proud history of research into the computer environment and effective development of technology; the scientists there invented the humble but essential mouse, without which the Internet would be inaccessible to those of us who find that a double click is a stretching technological endeavour. Today this research centre, which used to be dominated by the mathematicians, physicists and engineers on whom the development of technology depended, is teeming with sociologists, anthropologists and psychologists – further evidence that the exploitation of technology is increasingly being recognized as dependent on a clear understanding of human behaviour and customer desires.

This brief excursion can do little more than highlight a few findings of research and suggest what these mean for those who intend to use the Internet as part or all of their business strategy. But since we have committed ourselves in this book to providing a comprehensive guide to building online prosperity, we would be remiss if we failed to draw your attention to the growing understanding of the ways in which the online customer often has different expectations, desires and behaviours to the customer on the proverbial Clapham omnibus. The more you know about your customers, the more you may expect to build and sustain your prosperity, online or off it.

IS THE ONLINE CUSTOMER A DIFFERENT SORT OF ANIMAL?

Thinking about the Internet has routinely led too many into unproductive speculation about a menagerie of geeks and freaks. Who actually is using the Internet? Who are your online customers likely to be? Research suggests they are people just like you and me. That is, they are like you and me if we class ourselves as being among the better educated, more affluent, more articulate, more inquisitive, and possibly more acquisitive members of society.

We are also likely, though only just, to be male and American, but there are signs that both nationality and gender mix are changing. Two years ago approximately half the people online were American and almost 53% were men. More recent figures suggest that although the dominance of the US continues it will decline as the addition of people from other countries and cultures means that the world is truly moving into cyberspace.

Other demographics make it clear that contrary to the myth that the Internet is populated mostly by children, the largest single group is made up of 'thirty and forty-somethings' with money to spend. Six out of ten Web surfers are between the ages of 25 and 54 and six out of ten have disposable incomes of between $50,000 and $1 million. The majority, in the US at least, are college graduates with seventeen in every hundred having post-graduate degrees, a far greater proportion than in the population at large. To repeat the hopefully by now obvious, your customers and mine are bright and have the money to satisfy their desires. As marketers we therefore need to consider carefully how to win and retain a greater share of the life-time business of people who are not in general prepared or willing to play games.

Those who do like to play games, the under eighteens of limited means, constitute a little over 19 % of the population. They constitute a healthy proportion of the population, who are growing and regarding the Internet and all that it offers as a normal part of life rather than as a technological or marketing miracle. So those of us in business who get their Web strategy right and survive to prosper online will have a rapidly growing and maturing market that can sustain their businesses in the not too distant future, as well as having an affluent, mature market today.

AS OF TODAY THE AVERAGE INTERNET USER IS:

- Thirty-something.
- Married or in a stable relationship.
- A college graduate.
- In a non-technical occupation.
- Likely to have no better than average computer skills.
- Involved in sports, social or community activities.
- Concerned that he/she has less disposable time than disposable income.
- Likely to have close relationships beyond the family.
- Very articulate.
- Able to articulate needs.
- Not excessively religious.
- Mildly but not excessively introverted.
- Relatively comfortable with his or her feelings.

To prosper in e-commerce you need to bear in mind that your potential customer is not a nerd nor a geek. He and increasingly she combines smartness and affluence with concern for the well being of others.

PEOPLE STILL READ

One research project conducted by the University of Wisconsin made very careful observations of people's eye movements as they scanned Internet pages. As you might expect in a world in which generally speaking it is the better educated who use the Web, the subject's concentration was on getting and understanding detailed information. The expensive video streaming and other graphics beloved by the 'techies' who deliver expensive impractical websites to the unwary tended to be ignored, when they were not an annoying distraction. (In this research the subjects lacked the normal facility of being able to load 'text only'. The relative attention-grabbing propensity of text and graphics was the area under investigation.) It is still the message that counts rather than the entertainment. Your site may sing, dance and whistle to the delight of its designers, but your potential customers want information. If words remain the best way of conveying that information then words are what customers want. Where pictures do a better job they should be used, but be limited to conveying information and quick to load. Pictures only there because it is possible to show them become a distraction that can drive away potential customers, and customers driven off seldom if ever return to buy.

When people want to know, they want to know a great deal and they want to receive information in the easiest form for them to assimilate. For the present this remains the written word, presented clearly and fully with easy-to-read dark letters on a light background. I write 'for the present' because those children who have been weaned on graphic marvels may have different tastes and desires when they reach maturity. Only ongoing research will show us the best way to design things for the future. In the meanwhile the evidence is that clear and compelling messages presented without distraction is the best marketing strategy in the cyber world, as it is in the face-to-face business environment.

LOST IN SPACE

The design, not just of your site or mine, but of the Internet itself is a research priority at Palo Alto. Using the Web we can literally circle the world in our quest for information, entertainment, goods and services. We can move swiftly from site to site, and from country to country, without leaving so much as a footprint in the sand to indicate where we have been. Our world can have, and at the same time, the narrow dimensions of our computer screen and the almost unlimited depth of 75 million sites and billions of pages of information and entertainment. Technology has delivered miracles of opportunity, but an increasing number of scientists are concerned that it has done so with a cavalier disregard for the complexity of human experience. We are becoming increasingly disoriented in the tiny world of our PC screens.

We have only to point and click to move instantaneously through the 'info-sphere'. We jump from location to location. We zoom around the world in far less than Puck's forty minutes without ever touching solid ground. We do this without a roadmap, but without a roadmap even smart people can rapidly become lost and confused. We don't know where we've been and it is little more than a wild guess that leads us to decide where we should go next.

One of our most precious commodities, nowadays perhaps our most limited resource, is time. We risk frittering it away floating aimlessly through cyber-space. John Seeley Brown, the director of Xerox PARC, suggests that as we gape at the many wonders of the Net we are akin to someone peering at the world through two empty toilet tissue tubes. We lose the peripheral vision that anchors us in our surroundings.

It is that peripheral vision that prepares us for what may suddenly loom into view. On the underside of our brains are three small bumps. They are called colliculi, from the Latin for little hill. The detail of how these small lumps of dense neurons works is not clear, but yours have almost certainly saved your life.

You wish to cross the road. You look both ways to see the road is clear before you step off the kerb. As your foot touches the asphalt a truck, travelling far too fast, rounds the bend so close that it is on top of you before you know it. Consciously you would neither see nor hear the vehicle until it was too late, but unconsciously you automatically pull back out of its path and into safety. Your unconscious peripheral vision, mediated by those little hills under your brain, has saved you from serious injury or death. Evolution tends to ensure that something as vital to our survival as this cannot be ignored other than at great cost. Similarly, the lack of organization of the material on the Internet deprives us of something vital to our well-being.

The scientists at Palo Alto are designing and testing ways of adding the benefits of peripheral vision to our Web experience. The 'hyperbolic tree browser', for example, constantly rebalances the periphery to the centre by indicating the broad range of things that lie ahead and the things you have left behind as you concentrate on the information you need by focusing on the centre. It is a dynamic structure enabling the surfer to pull a page to the centre of attention without totally losing contact with the interplay of where you can go next and where you've already been. In this way it goes far beyond aping the sensory aspects of your perceptual system by incorporating a sensory motor system. The key to future website design will be that every page you or your customer visits will clearly indicate where you can most beneficially go next, whether it is forward or back to something you have just skimmed.

Until such approaches are generally available we need to make the best of what we have the capacity to do right now. When talking at conferences or seminars, I make no apology for quoting the Alta Vista research that says 83 % of potential buyers give up in disgust because navigating the site is too complex for them to place an order or is so byzantine that they cannot find out whether ordering on line is even a viable possibility. Imagine the cost of getting these customers to beat a path to our door only to send them away again empty-handed and disgusted with your clear lack of interest in their real needs. No amount of technical wizardry will compensate them for your want of thought or you for your loss of business. Common sense as well as psychological research demands we make it easy for the customer to navigate the site, get the information they require and place an order with confidence when they wish.

In Silicon Valley there is a discernible shift away from technology for its own sake and toward good design that takes full cognisance of human psychology, sociology and even physiology. We know we can handle a stream of information far greater than what comes to us through our PC screen. When driving on busy streets or strolling through a supermarket, we are subject to a thousand times as many visual and aural stimuli than our screen gives us, but we online get lost because the information is not well structured. So be sure that what you offer is well designed for customers not aesthetes, for buyers not surfers, and those customers and buyers will visit, stay and return to buy again and again.

Once you become aware that people have a deep need not just for information but rather for information that can be readily assimilated without confusion or loss of orientation, you will be able to design your website so that it will place you and keep you well ahead of the pack. Just as in the layout of an advertisement good design principles are business winners on line.

THE PSYCHOLOGY OF THE E-MAIL

My colleague has written more knowledgeably about the business uses of e-mail than I ever could, but perhaps I can dot a few of his 'i's' and cross one or two of his 't's' by looking at some of the psychological implications and what they mean to us in the online marketplace. Here I am again deeply indebted to the work of John Suler, I should add.

New expressions proliferate in new areas of thought and activity. In e-mail marketing, few are more redolent with meaning than the idiomatic 'TextTalk' coined by Suler. As my colleague made clear earlier (Chapter 7) e-mail provides a unique opportunity to transfer to text much of the informality and intimacy of face-to-face conversation. Not everyone feels comfortable enough to express themselves in writing (you should see the agony on my co-author's face as he works to polish his prose and ensure the clarity of his style), but the informal approach e-mail encourages has made it a medium through which friendships are made. People like to buy from people they like. More importantly here, people like to hear from (funny how we still use the word 'hear' when referring to letters or other written communication), those who care about them. That is why e-mail has the potential to create a whole new world of relationship selling.

We are social animals who pay great attention to face-to-face cues. I find it a little odd that people in my seminars frequently ask me to teach them something of body language. Research and experience combine to show we are all experts in the subject, having been given the gift or curse of being able to read other's true meaning from tone and posture with ease. As e-mail has proliferated writers have developed creative strategies for expressing the most subtle nuances of meaning through the typed text. Through the creative use of grammatical case to the invention of new signs and symbols, the lack of immediate personal interaction has been minimized and conversing through e-mail has become an expressive and sophisticated art form in its own right. Marketers can and should ensure their e-mail communications are as personal as a whisper if they wish to benefit from the sense of friendship that leads to life-long customer loyalty.

However, e-mails have a problem. The exchange of ideas, information, entertainment, and even intimacy does not take place in 'real time'. To use a little jargon, e-mails are subject to 'asynchronous interactions'. Or to put it more clearly, I write to you but then I must wait for your reply. Only by going online at the same time are we able truly to converse, and even then my lack of keyboard skills make the whole thing a cumbersome and frustrating experience. Psychologically this can be a problem. I may fire off an e-mail full of enthusiasm and wait impatiently for the reply. You may not share my sense of urgency. In total our conversation may cover a period of hours, days or even weeks, during which one party may experience agonies of frustration. To ease this situation you should do three things:

1   Make intelligent use of auto responders so the customer's desire for a speedy as well as personal response is satisfied.
2   After winning the customer's permission, initiate timely and relevant communications so it is you, rather than the customer, who is kept waiting for a reply.
3   Respect and maintain the confidentiality and sensitivity of the relationship so you never impose on the customer's good feelings toward you.

Research has been carried out into the effects of spamming. The more an individual uses the Internet the more they are inclined to view junk mail as anathema. To many of the old hands, the commercialization of their Web is an apocalyptic attack on the purity of cyberspace. Before you write these people off as fanatical geeks remember that they are often the people who control the search engines. They decide whether or not your website will be accessed by the buying public. Take their views seriously or their behaviour, though based on what you may see as their outmoded values, may well have serious effects for you and your business. Treat your customers' privacy with respect or you may find that customers are thin on the ground.

E-mail use

Experienced e-mailers tend to use e-mail more frequently than the tyro. The computer rapidly becomes the main factor in their communications. They download e-mail frequently and read it avidly. They become sensitive to the nuances of the concisely written word. They read between the lines – and often have the lines downloaded automatically at regular intervals in order to read between them. If they are anticipating a message from you they want it to be delivered on schedule. Reading e-mail is something I find I do several times a day, including immediately after getting out of bed in the morning. First thing daily and last thing at night I check my mail, though I am far from being as committed as the really seasoned professionals. So if you have an opt-in e-mail system or market through an online newsletter, make sure you hit your own deadlines. Be timely as well as personal and relevant.

Greetings friend or stranger

I think it was Jim Reeves who recorded a mawkish song called 'A Stranger's Just a Friend that You Don't Know'. In a way the psychology of the Internet matches the ill-remembered sentiments of that all-too sentimental song. Continued contact is aimed very specifically at turning strangers into acquaintances, acquaintances into friends and, if you are in business, friends into advocates. This is reflected in the salutation line of e-mails. I get a number of e-mails from readers of my books around the world and find the way I am greeted sits comfortably with current research.

- 'Dear Mr. Lambert' – formal, polite and something of a nod back toward letter writing. Ardent believers in the e-mail culture find the use of the word 'dear' too old-fashioned and frown upon its use in any circumstances. Such fanatics tend to look down upon the sender as being naïve when it comes to the social dynamics of e-mail.
- 'Dear Tom' – since book covers always carry given names and e-mail is a relatively informal medium, the use of the first name seems appropriate to most people. The e-mail nut, however, would still respond to the use of 'dear' with a sigh of sorrow or mild contempt.
- 'Hello Tom' – an approach used to set a tone of friendliness among peers that in polite society is usually reserved until at least the second communication
- 'Hi Tom!' – e-mailers seem to enjoy using punctuation marks that are rarely seen beyond the second-grade schoolroom. In part this is to make up for the lack of vocal and behavioural cues as mentioned above, but in

the main it is simply a sign of exuberance and enthusiasm. The combination of informality and enthusiasm is the equivalent of indicating with a broad smile and hand rubbing, 'have I got news for you'. If e-mailers want to turn up the volume of enthusiasm and add a dash of urgency they are likely to drop the 'Hi' and multiply the number of exclamation points: 'Tom!!!!'.

- 'Tom' – this is the e-mail equivalent of 'we are both busy people so let's cut to the chase' in conversation. The use of the given name retains a degree of friendliness, but there will be no wasting of words on niceties if the e-mail is consistent with the greeting.
- 'Hey there!' – very informal and generally restricted to correspondents whose friendship has blossomed to the point where names are no longer thought to be necessary.
- 'Yo Dude!!!' – this can only have come from a friend in the US.
- 'Greetings' – this is seen by the initiated as a sure sign of spam. To make matters worse, it is the most unacceptable form of junk mail where the sender knows nothing about me. They have not taken the trouble to find out my gender, my name or my wants. Like the wonderful Manuel in *Fawlty Towers*, 'they know nothings'. Such e-mails are deleted unread. The same fate awaits 'Dear Friend', 'Dear Colleague' and other clear warnings of junk to come.

We know about the body

Research into e-mail writing style and content emphasizes the need to develop and express empathy. Messages that are well received are in general those that accurately anticipate the needs and interests of the recipient. They convey anticipated, relevant and personal information, but they also ask relevant questions in a friendly manner. In this way a data bank of pertinent customer information can be built in the same way we build a mental data bank of the likes and interests of a friend. It is akin to the early days of dating: when a birthday or Christmas looms you try gently to discover what a new partner you know little about as yet would enjoy as a present.

Real professionals construct the body of the message with the reader firmly in mind. They use the whole of the keyboard to make their message visually interesting and easy to read. I have e-mail friends who use today's software to create attractive e-mail stationery. It takes a little longer to send and receive mail with a pretty background, but the effect can be enough to brighten a dull day.

Psychological research shows that apparent spontaneity is valued in e-mails. Some people plan in depth how to make their messages look and feel spontaneous. In purely social exchanges, spelling errors may be perceived as a sign of friendship and spur-of-the-moment eagerness to get in touch, but the businessperson needs to balance a desire for friendliness with professionalism.

Typed text must work very hard if it wants to convey feelings as would a smile, an eager or a downcast look. Some e-mailers have developed the sometimes engaging, but sometimes irritating habit of reporting feelings in parentheses:

- 'I wanted to tell you (feeling a little insecure here) that I ...'
- 'I completely forgot (slapping self on the forehead) ...'
- 'I know exactly what I am talking about (looking hopefully heavenward)'.

Psychologically these parenthetical comments combine the roles of body language and subvocal talking to oneself, but they can easily be overdone, becoming trite and unbusinesslike. You need to be unceasingly aware that what is cute in intimate correspondence is probably inappropriate when attempting to build a business relationship. At the same time it is important to realize that you are building a relationship for no better reason than that 'people like to buy from people that they like' and a little unveiling of feelings from time to time may be constructive in that way.

So for example the use of 'smiley faces' and the like has probably been so overdone that it is more likely to irritate than to charm. I would question whether any 'emoticons' have a place in business correspondence for the same reason: not because of any intrinsic shortcoming but because they have been used too much. In fact they have been used so much that only now do I discover that this software automatically turns the emoticon into an upright face. Time to be moving on from the smiley, the frown and the winky, I think. The same is probably true of the ubiquitous use of abbreviations. You may think it smart to inform a correspondent that you 'LMAO' (laughed my ass off) at something they said, but in the world of business it is passé as well as frequently not understood. The purpose of business communication is clarity so don't be tempted.

Sign-off and signature

People tend to like variety in sign-offs to personal communications, when they are not of that peculiarly intimate kind for which the same message is expected and desired. I may invariably add 'luv yer lotz' and 'HUGZZZZ' to the end of messages to my close friend TJ (she hates her given name) or Cathy the Dragon Lady in my beloved Roselle, but in general the business communication that seeks to appear personal needs to have a variety of endings. 'Warmest regards' today may become 'Best wishes' tomorrow. The important thing is that you can set up the address block to include all the information your customer may require, from your dirt-world address by way of telephone and fax numbers to your website address. Always use every opportunity to make a response easy. Regardless of the Internet, research shows time and time again that people are lazy. They like to have things made easy for them. Because all signature blocks have a pre-packaged feel to them you may want to turn them off when writing to a 'cyberbuddy', but they are essential to efficient business. In cyber psychology leaving off the signature is read as a curt, dismissive, formal and impersonal indication that 'I have had my say and if I were frank I might add that I don't give a hang what you think'. So remember to keep everything in place for business communication and vary your good wishes just a little.

BUYER THINKING

For many years the University of Columbia, New York conducted research into how buyers think. At the same time the Sales Analysis Institute of Chicago conducted practical research demonstrating what works in selling. The combination of their activities has led to the development of a cognitive map (a step-by-step analysis of general thought processes) of how we all think when faced with the decision 'to buy or not to buy'. The present state of research indicates no reason why this model should be amended. This is how your customers think when they visit your site. It is how your spouse thinks when you seek to persuade them to change their behaviour. It is how your neighbours and your children think when they have to decide whether you will be successful in influencing their actions or not.

The Internet is a great leveller. It gives all of us an equal opportunity to exercise influence while it strips power from the mighty. Think about your customers' known thought processes and design your marketing and sales messages with them in mind. The map below represents a total of more than 120 years of research. While human beings exist it will remain true. If you can structure your online and offline messages to satisfy the customer needs at every point and in the order given you will have a customer for life – as long as you deliver all that you promise.

A COGNITIVE MAP OF DECISION MAKING

I am important: Will my needs be treated as imperative or will they attempt a 'snow job' on me?

I have developed a point of view: Will my opinion be respected and understood, and will my valuable experience be taken into account in all dealings with these people?

I am a busy person: Should I really attend to this or just think of ways to say 'no' quickly and leave?

What is the idea?: What is the detail? How does it work? Would it work for me? Is it safe? Is it new? Is it attractive? Is it exciting? Is it fun?

Will this idea help me and give me what I want?: Does this person understand what I want? Is success guaranteed? Is there a rational case to buy?

Am I being unduly pressured?: Am I genuinely free to make up my own mind, or am I in danger of being pushed into something that I will regret?

OK – let's do it.

THE FUTURE

Have you ever had to face up to, or face down, an avatar? Your answer will be 'yes' if you have ever played any virtual reality games. An avatar is the electronic pseudo-human who is the hero or villain of such games.

University College London is using avatars to diminish or dispel for good the fear most of us feel when we must deliver a public speech. The student is costumed in the paraphernalia of virtual reality and gives his speech. The avatars respond with either avid attention or obvious boredom, according to the quality and quantity of the talk. They can lean forward, nod and take copious notes, or yawn, scratch themselves and hold whispered conversations. They can shout out abuse or indicate admiration. And it all seems very real. The psychologist in charge of the programme is presumably aware as anyone can be that the audience is not real. However when he tried to deliver a lecture to these electronic nothings he got a negative response that caused him to shout at the empty air: 'You have to take the exam not me, so if you don't want to listen you can sod off. I don't care.'

I mention this because it is almost certain that very soon the Internet will be able to use avatars to communicate with customers as credible human beings. Very soon the time will come when the perceived impersonality of the Web will cease to be a psychological or emotional problem. So, if you see an avatar with a shaved head and spectacles, it could be me.

Psychological and sociological research into cyberspace is a new science. It will mature over time, but more importantly knowledge will accumulate at a rapidly increasing speed. If you take business seriously you need to keep in touch with developments. The upside is that the Web makes this possible, and committed scientists like John Suler are there to help you. Visit his site from time to time. Constantly ask yourself the old question 'what is in this for me?' That way you will stay ahead of the pack.

WHAT YOU WILL HAVE LEARNED IN THIS CHAPTER

☞ We already have much useful knowledge of how the online customer thinks and feels.

☞ Future research will enable you take even more control of your destiny and prosperity.

☞ How to use what we know today.

☞ How to anticipate what we are likely to learn tomorrow.

THE SHAPE OF THINGS TO COME

Even Kondratiev, he of the famous long-term cycle, would have to admit that, in the ultimate scheme of things, the Internet is up there with the biggest. Even the Wall Street Crash was a blip in comparison to the effects the Internet revolution will have on all aspects of our lives. Our comfort, our prosperity, our safety and security, our entertainment, will all be affected.

So much has been written, both here and elsewhere, about how dramatically business will change as a result of the Internet that it seems clichéd to repeat any of it. But, it is not just business that will change. The infrastructure of commerce is being challenged, and many who perceive themselves as bastions of the industrial world today will feel the cold draught of competition coming from unexpected directions. One topical example of this is the MP3 discussions about the delivery of music over the Web. Napster.com has sent the music industry fleeing to their lawyers to try to protect their very existence in the future. My guess is that in the last resort money will prevail. The entrenched legions of Porsche-driving, red-spectacled music men will find a way of bringing the rebels into line. After all, despite its bright glow and obvious benefits, the everlasting light bulb no longer sees the light of day or even the darkness of night! And folklore has it that in the early part of the nineteenth century the big match companies bought up and destroyed the formula for the re-lightable match.

But the Internet is much more than a threat to single industries phenomenon. All industries are in the firing line. What effect will free, or nearly free, international telephone calls have on the big telecoms companies? How will publishers cope when co-operatives of writers gang up and begin writing only for the e-book and print-on-demand markets? Why will we need estate agents when all we have to do is post our property for sale on an international website, as there for a small fee we can expose our house for sale to millions of interested people? Where does the caring, sharing stock-broker fit in when I can buy and sell shares online with little or no human intervention? I don't even need them for advice, since the Web is jam-packed with would-be Warren Buffets all eager to share their thoughts and ideas, and differentiating the rubbish advice from the good was just as important when dealing with human financial advisors as it is online. However, human nature is thoroughly adaptable, and the large multi-national companies are led, in the main, by bright, resourceful people. They may be slow to recognize the advent of these changes, but once they do they will move heaven, earth and cyberspace in their efforts to consolidate, protect themselves and benefit from the new technology. If IBM can transmogrify itself so successfully from a mainframe dinosaur into a thoroughly up-to-date high-tech consultancy and services company, there is hope for the other industry-leading organizations.

Market dominance is no longer an option. It must be the objective. Fall short of that objective and you risk becoming an also-ran. Conventionally, organizations only begin to consider market dominance as an option when they actually are dominant in their market and want to consolidate that position. Rarely would a small organization have the precocity to declare market dominance as an objective. If they did it would be dismissed as mere advertising puff. That is not the case today. Because the Internet allows easy comparison of prices, service, quality and such decision-making factors, consumers and businesses are not constrained by geographic and other considerations. They are just as likely to buy from www.started-last-week.com as from a less attractive, more expensive dirt-world fossilized giant. The speed with which a start-up company can gain market dominance is dramatic and revolutionary. The financial constraints of history may well bring down many large, monolithic organizations because they are less able, or less prepared, to adapt than the fast-moving, uncluttered dot.com. The monolith has real-estate, infrastructure, people, ideas, and methods that were fine ten years ago – but will just not cut it today.

Factors such as an easily-remembered domain name or a well-designed and easy-to-use website can mean that Internet users will gravitate to that site to buy particular items. Why go to www.corner-bookshop.co.uk when Amazon can get you every book in the world? And they give you discounts and loyalty bonuses into the bargain. If market dominance is so vital to the survival of the twenty-first century organization, why has it been sidelined by so many companies who should know better? Maybe they think 'website today, e-commerce tomorrow, make profits next year, then we'll think about dominating our market'. Whoops, suddenly it is too late! www.jonny-come-lately.com has beaten you to it and no amount of advertising dollars will usurp them from their dominant position.

They set out from day one to dominate their market. They said so to their kindly venture capitalists, who thought that it was just more business-plan hype. They proceeded immediately to make sure their new and ever-evolving website got top positions on the search engines. They investigated affiliate programmes. They established dozens of appropriate links to sites worldwide. They gave visitors to their site good reasons to disclose e-mail addresses and their likes and dislikes. They compiled this information into a targeted e-mail database. They mounted an on-going campaign of communication with their clients and built one-to-one relationships designed to last for life. They made sure they over-delivered on promises. They adapted conventional wisdom with new-age ideas. And they prospered. It is just too embarrassing even to think about what the conventional organization was doing all this time. Probably paying lip-service to the concept by establishing a working party headed up by that guy who used to run the Azerbaijan sales office, and muttering to themselves 'that should keep the Chairman off our backs for a few months'.

But conventional organizations do not have to be so negative and resistant. They can be as positive and dynamic as new starters inspired by a great idea. The Internet presents wonderful business possibilities for both.

We have written this book to help anyone willing to do the work that will turn those possibilities into profitable realities.

UP-DATE FEBRUARY 2001

I suppose it was inevitable that, with the Internet market changing, growing, evolving and consolidating at a rate never before known in business, it would be impossible to be absolutely up-to-date between completion of any such book and its arrival on the shelves. Since completing the manuscript for *E-Market Dominance* we have, not surprisingly, discovered further new ideas, concepts, on-line business models and even business paradigms which will certainly change the ways we do business and how we approach the new technologies. Even in the past few months there have been some significant developments, both positive and not so positive. The down-turn in the stock-market and in high-tech stocks in particular has deflated the Internet bubble to the extent that people are looking at the situation more cautiously than a year ago. IBM summed it up rather succinctly in a recent advertisement:

> 66 The first chapter of e-business was an emotional one. It was filled with
> promise of wealth, the intensity of rapid innovation and the passion of
> entrepreneurship. It also showed a lot of Internet start-ups how devastating
> gravity can be. The rest of us learned that hype is not a business plan;
> that the fundamental business principles still apply. 99

On the face of it, it might appear that the doom-merchants who, for about six years, have been predicting the high-tech market crash have at last got it right. They can point to market statistics that range from positively negative to downright blood-curdling, and everything in between. They love to reflect on the demise of boo.com, the troubles of letsbuyit.com, and the slow-down in the growth of the online dealers such as e-trade. They wait with baited breath to witness the last minutes of lastminute.com. Nothing would please them more than to see the researcher's predictions proved true, that they expect that as many as 80% of dot-com companies will fail within the next 24 months. They and the fickle fund-managers in Wall Street and the City of London run scared when they see the results of a much-hyped gold-rush. The gold-rush they and their colleagues helped to fuel.

THE SUSTAINED PRE-EMINENCE OF E-MAIL

E-mail is the application which fueled the growth of the Internet. This basic truth has often been overlooked by analysts and market commentators. It is far more glamorous to write exciting and futuristic articles about e-commerce applications, Internet fraud and security, how to design the 'coolest' website or how to put your website onto a mobile phone. E-mail is just e-mail: not much to say about it! So many e-commerce commentators have missed the point. E-Mail is the 'killer application' much as word processing was in the 1980s and 90s. Despite this, the real power of e-mail has yet to be demonstrated. In fact many e-mail applications have yet to be thought of. The very fact that e-mail is at the heart of e-commerce means that a new business paradigm may well evolve with e-mail at the hub and all other CRM, management and control systems integrating with each other, with e-mail often being the information conduit. I will go into more detail shortly.

DOT-COM VS. CLICKS AND MORTAR

The massive growth of the dot-com company over the past five years or so has been tremendous fun to watch. It was almost as exhilarating to see the speed with which investors, venture capitalists, analysts dealers and the public shrugged off the thin cloak of shrewdness and caution to display the real animal beneath – green and greedy! Huge sums of their and other people's money was almost forced upon virtually any pimple-faced gonnabe or wannabe with a business plan. Their ability to set up and manage a business was considered less important than their ability to make a company logo spin, tumble and change colour. This was not a well-considered approach where seed funds would be provided on a 'suck it and see' basis. Many of these young dot-commers were given millions of dollars and pounds to throw at their ('world-beating' idea. They spent millions on brand awareness advertising, the hits on their websites went up, they made some money. Then hits on their website fell off; they made less money, they threw millions at brand awareness advertising the hits went up. ... This very expensive cycle was unsustainable. Even if the money they made had exceeded their expenses, which it mostly did not, a cyclical business of that kind, which is so dependent on advertising money, is unlikely to be sustainable.

On the other side of the tracks, in the 'dirt world', the conventional company was getting more and more rattled about this bloody Internet business. But mostly they were not absolutely sure why or what they should do about it. The Chairman of Oracle warned that all businesses needed to be e-businesses or die. Well he would say that wouldn't he? And all sensible IT managers saw and grasped the opportunity with both hands. After all, it meant Intranets, CRM systems to be integrated and the associated security problems. Web sites turned them into managers of new and unfamiliar functions such as design, editing and publishing. All in all, it just grew and grew their already substantial high-tech empires. Endless discussions took place about how Megabig Smokestack Inc. would manage the transition from a conventional to an e-business. Business processes were re-engineered, customer relations were managed, and the corporate logo tumbled, span and changed colour.

SURFERS' BEHAVIOURS HAVE CHANGED

Internet users are becoming more sophisticated. They know how to use the search engines to better and better effect. They are accessing the Net far more often but spending less and less time on pure surfing. The very fact of their becoming more familiar with using the Net means that it takes them less time to find and download what they want. E-mail is becoming more important to them. They are using it for both personal and business purposes, and they regard their e-mail box as private territory, even if it is provided by their employers. They are becoming less and less tolerant of what they regard as junk e-mail or spam. Conversely, they are becoming more tolerant of e-mail that informs or entertains them. They will quite happily receive and respond to an obvious advertisement provided they have agreed to receive it.

SPAM

As I said above, people and organizations are becoming far less tolerant of pure junk e-mail. Many systems are in place to identify, sideline or delete unwanted e-mail. The US already has a mish-mash of legislation to control the sending of pure spam. Sadly, all it does is confuse the issue. Any enforcement will need to grapple with the issues of which state issued the mail, which state received it and the relevant laws of each state. Most people will agree that the nuisance which can be caused by uncontrolled spam is an unacceptable burden on the recipient. For the business person the only safe and sensible approach is to avoid undertaking any transmission which is *or could be construed as* spam. Failure to do this could result in serious damage to your company, your brand, your image, and possibly your finances. Laws on such activity will only get stronger and more effective over time.

WAP

The Internet and e-mail delivered to the mobile telephone and personal organizers will enlarge the market many times over. Imagine you are passing a branch of Snow and Rock, and you have registered with them as being interested in climbing. Your mobile rings and a recorded voice informs you that only 20 metres on your right you will be able to buy Locking-Karabiners at half-price, and why not call in? What is more, on the LCD of your mobile is an image of the very Karabiners in question. What is your reaction? Are you furious? Or do you walk 20 metres and save yourself some money on your next equipment purchase?

But, hey! We ain't there yet. It is anyone's guess where this massive opportunity is going. My advice is sit tight and dabble but only get involved when we have decided in which direction we are being taken.

DATABASES

Marketers have been saying for years that 'location, location, location' has been replaced by 'database, database, database'. This has never been more true. Database technology is so powerful now that refining and accurate targeting is a real option which cannot be ignored. E-mail has enabled databases to be cleaned cheaply and accurately. All 'bounce-back' e-mails can be identified for removal or up-dating. With conventional direct mail, bounce-backs are minimal, just 1%. With e-mail it is 100%. Each campaign, whether for a sales or information, can refine your database. Eventually you will be able to sell to a database of one, millions of times over. Every recipient of your one-million address campaign will receive a slightly different message—and all at less than 10% of the cost of direct-mail. It is this person-alization factor which backs claims of a 75% response rate to an effectively targeted e-mail campaign. You are pushing at an open door.

CONSOLIDATIONS, MERGERS AND AFFILIATIONS

Apart from the glamorous mergers such as the Time-Warner/AOL marriage, there are many more smaller, but still significant, business consolidations in the pipe-line. The power of e-mail can enable differing and diverse businesses to co-operate in a way that benefits all parties to the transaction. This can mean that a conventional company can out-source all e-commerce functions until they are proven before integrating them into the main business. These functions can include marketing (JabCreative.com), fulfilment from one of the major international courier companies such as Fedex, DHL or UPS, secure payments from such organizations as NetBanx or QSI. Batch e-mail can be delegated to be dispatched by people like Accucast or E2 Software or Premier. These four functions are the key functions of a dot-com. Why shouldn't Mega Smokestack Inc. have MSI.com as a test-bed for its future e-commerce? There is no reason why not, and many companies have done just this. The secret of success in this is a well thought-out e-mail strategy. E-mail can glue diverse units together.

RICH E-MAIL

The term rich e-mail refers to the use of colour, animation, graphics and design. This produces a communications piece which is to text e-mail what the black and white TV is to digital, wide-angle Sony Trinitron stereo TV. In recipient's terms there is 'no contest' as to which they would prefer to receive. Even pure text messages look better when they are well laid out in appropriate styles and with sensible use of colour. (I still see websites with green back-ground displaying unreadable yellow text.) At the moment there are three types of rich e-mail. HTML e-mails with coloured text are not, strictly speaking, rich e-mail. Streaming is one method, attaching executable files is the next, and the latest and at present unique is the Jab Mail from Jab Creative a company which began in Brisbane, Australia but now has offices in Sydney, London, Boston and Los Angeles. Rich e-mail is interactive, which give it a much greater impact with the recipient. It is also a pro-active medium, unlike the website which requires off-line promotion to keep up the rate of visitors.

JAB MAIL

This unique concept from Jab Creative is founded upon the principle of 'prior relationship marketing'. This takes Seth Godin's 'permission marketing' one stage further. Jab say that you should have an existing relationship with the recipient. This protects your reputation and brand, and distances you from any possibility of being accused of spamming. The Jab Mail can be described as a mini-website *in* an e-mail. This means you can use graphics, animations, sound and even very small clips of video, as well as being able to include an effective response mechanism. But Jab Mail is not just a snazzy design service. In fact they plan to open their technology to large design groups so that organizations with established design relationships can have their designers trained by Jab. The exciting thing about this technology is not that they can get a very attention-grabbing design into an e-mail that can be as small as 200 KB, nor that their e-mail will penetrate 90 % of corporate firewalls because each Jab Mail has full Verisign certification (so that, in the unlikely event of it being tampered with, the recipient will be notified and warned). The exciting thing about this technology is that the marketers back-office system, which Jab call 'The Marketers Cockpit' can put an organization in total control of any of its e-mail campaigns. Once the campaign has been launched the marketer can see on-line and in real-time just how things are going. They can see how many mails were sent, how many have been opened so far, where the recipients are in the country or the world, how many mails have 'bounced', and how many have responded. In the case of a selling campaign they can even see the revenue being generated 'before their very eyes'. Never before has the marketing department been as measureable as the sales department. Never before has the marketing director had the power to say on Monday 'Let's have a product sale at half-price to get rid of stock. And, let's do it on Wednesday'. Her staff just use the Jab Mail templates to create the message required. They select the most appropriate segment of the database and send it for dispatch.

USEFUL WEBSITES AND NEWS GROUPS

These are just some examples of the kind of site that will be valuable to the online marketer. Whilst we have tried to be selective and to identify the most helpful sites, we have not evaluated any of the products or services outlined. You should use the normal commercial caution before entering into any agreements with any of the companies mentioned here.

ASSOCIATION OF CONSUMER RESEARCH

This is a list with the purposes of discussing consumer research. This list serves as a forum for researchers, practitioners and graduate students working in the interdisciplinary field of consumer research.

listerv@listerv.okstate.edu

ADFORUM

This list is about advertising education.

listserv@unc.edu

ADLAND

Adland is an e-mail discussion in digest format related to marketing online for those with a small or no budget looking for alternative solutions for their online business presence. To subscribe to Adlands' Digest, send the command

listserv@softfornet.com

ADMIN-HEERA

This list has been set up by HEERA (the Higher Education External Relations Association) to enable its members to discuss HEERA's areas of activity – public relations, internal communications, marketing development. Anyone interested or involved in these fields is welcome to join.

mailbase@mailbase.ac.uk

ADVERTALK

AdverTalk is an e-mail discussion group for small businesses to discuss issues and offer solutions related to small business marketing, including advertising, public relations, database marketing and sales channels.

dms_AdverTalk@fiestanet.com

AFMNET

AFMNet was created by the French Marketing Association. This list functions in the same way as ELMAR, which has been used as model. Messages can be posted in French or in English. For more information or to join the list, visit:

www.univ-pau.fr/~benavent/inscript.htm.

AFFILIATE PROGRAMS

Affiliate Programs are not appropriate for all online marketing. It is well worth considering them however, even if it is only to discount them at the end of the day. The reason for this is that they can have a massive impact on the numbers of site visitors. So if traffic is of greater importance to you than qualified visitors, your should look carefully at affiliate programs such as these I have shown here.

www.affiliatehelp.com/porters.html
affiliates.about.com/started.htm
www.i-revenue.net/
www.affiliatewire.com/
www.affiliatetips.com/

AIM

AIM stands for Asian Internet Marketing and has a web page at:

www.aim.apic.net/.

AMODLMKT

This list is for technical discussion of market modelling, and includes such topics such as GLS, simulated annealing, modelling books, asymmetric cross elasticities, and many others.

listserv@umslvma.umsl.edu

AM-POLITICAL-MARKETING

AM-POLITICAL-MARKETING: A Forum for all those engaged in political marketing research to share and communicate ideas, information, conference and event details. Political marketing as a topic includes lobbying, elections, referenda, and campaign communication. To join e-mail

AM-Political-marketing@mailbase.ac.uk

ARTS-HERITAGE-MARKETING

This is a forum for discussion and information exchange on issues related to arts and heritage marketing. It is a site for the discussion of marketing concepts, research methods and their application to arts and heritage marketing practice. Information available at

www.mailbase.ac.uk/lists/arts-heritage-marketing/

SITE BULLETIN BOARD

A bulletin board can add to the attractiveness of the site. You can operate it as a moderated area so that cyber-nutters cannot have a field day at your expense. It can be a good reason for people to re-visit your site. Make it fun, make it informative. Why not get a celebrity or a well-known industry personality to act as moderator for an hour a week? They can do it from home after all.

www.ultimatebb.com/

CRM-L

CRM-L is for researchers interested in issues in relationship marketing.

listserv@emuvm1.cc.emory.edu

DM-DIGEST

This list is to discuss database marketing and relationship management. To subscribe, send e-mail to

majordomo@lexiconn.com

with the only message line being:

subscribe dbm_rm

The website for the list is at:

www.argo-navis.com/competence

E-COMMERCE

These sites include e-commerce software packages and companies who will advise and implement on e-commerce projects and strategies.

www.ecommercetimes.com/
www.microsoft.com/technet/ecommerce/ecseries.asp
www.webdeveloper.com/ecommerce/
tech.irt.org/articles/commerce.htm
www.quadrantinternet.co.uk
www.ecommerce-scotland.org/
www.iserver.com/products/ecommerce/
www.ibm.com/e-business/ecommerce/
www.icat.com/services/
www.intershop.com/
www.zygon.com/index2.html

E-MARKETING

This list discusses electronic marketing techniques. Subscribe by visiting the E-Marketing website at:

www.webbers.com/emark/

Ethical e-mail marketing will be part of life very soon. In many ways it will be much less intrusive than direct mail has been and certainly less intrusive than domestic telesales campaigns. The main attractions are the low cost and the high response. An online marketing person's Holy Grail perhaps?

list-advertising.com/opt-in/
www.emailmarketing.com/
www.maildrive.com
www.email-marketing.net/
www.worldataexchange.com/

E-TAILER

E-Tailer's Digest is a resource for retail on the Net, and is published in a moderated digest form every Monday, Wednesday and Friday. The E-Tailer's Digest topics include any and all subjects that pertain to retailing. Such subjects might include, but of course not be limited to: Interaction with customers, Psychographics, Point-of-sale software solutions, Point-of-purchase displays, Security issues, Effective merchandizing and open-to-buy, Mail order issues, Shipping and tax issues, Accounting and legal issues, Public relations, Promotions and advertising, On-line marketing, Differentiation, Doing business internationally, and Effective website design.

www.gapent.com/etailer/

EURO-BUSINESS

Euro-Business has a Web page with subscription info and extensive documentation. Euro-Business is a moderated forum for discussing, exchanging, commenting on news, views, issues, opinions on practices, customs and conducting business in modern Europe.

majordomo@primenet.com

EVENTWEB

The EventWeb mailing list is a discussion list that also includes monthly mail out of a digest. The EventWeb discussion list addresses the interactive marketing needs of meeting, conference and trade show promoters, educators, organizers and Webmasters.

www.eventweb.com/

FRANKELBIZ

FrankelBiz is the Web's only listserv devoted exclusively to doing business on the Web, instead of talking about it. List members exchange reciprocal discounts, offer business leads and do business with each other. Sponsors offer products and services at discounts to members.

www.robfrankel.com/frankelbiz/form.html

GB-INTERNET-MARKETING

The GB Internet Marketing Discussion List deals with all aspects of Internet Marketing relevant to the UK. Subscribe by sending a blank e-mail to:

subscribe@digitalnation.co.uk

GINLIST

GINLIST has its own Web page. GINLIST stands for Global Interact Network mailing LIST and focuses on discussion of international business and marketing issues. The list is owned by the Center for International Business Education and Research. Send e-mail to:

listserv@msu.edu

GLOBAL_MARKETING_DISCUSSION_LIST

This list is a forum for the discussion of issues relating to sales and marketing in the worldwide Internet marketplace. The issues of language, culture, currencies, payment mechanisms, and trade barriers are especially keen in our consciousness, if we are to make the world a truly single market that can be worked through the Internet. Subscribe by sending e-mail to:

global-marketing@glreach.com

HEALTHCAREBUSINESS

HealthCareBusiness is a moderated list dedicated to discussing programs that health care business professionals can use to gain competitive advantage. Participants are invited to share suggestions, questions, and experiences on business initiatives that they are undertaking to improve health care quality, decrease cost, or otherwise attract new members and providers.

healthcarebusiness@world.std.com

HTMARCOM

HTMarCom has its own Web page. The list is dedicated to discussing the marketing of technology products.

majordomo@listserv.rmi.net

I-ADVERTISING

This list offers a moderated discussion on all aspects relating to Internet advertising, including online media planning, media buying, campaign tracking, industry trends and forecasts, creative development, cost estimates, advertising sales, and other aspects relating to the promotion of a business on the Internet through an ongoing new media campaign. The Web page is at:

www.internetadvertising.org/.

Send e-mail to:

listserv@guava.ease.lsoft.com

IESS LIST

IESS stands for Internet Entrepreneurs Support Service. This list is a discussion group for entrepreneurs and businesses doing business on the Internet.

majordomo@ix.entrepreneurs.net

IMAFDI-E

IMAFDI-E is a mailing list for students on Marketing on the Internet.

majordomo@lists.lrz-muenchen.de
www.diplomarbeit.com/imafdie.htm.

IMALL-CHAT

This list discusses Internet Malls. Send e-mail to:

listserv@netcom.com

IMARCOM

IMARCOM is a platform to learn about and participate in the further development of marketing on the global Internet. It will act as a central resource to the marketing professional and a magnet to attract a community of shared interest.

listserv@internet.com

INDUSTRIAL-MARKETING

This list links you to a global network of marketing professionals, with a broad range of experience in a variety of industries. You can ask the marketing questions you've always wanted to ask and have your questions taken seriously.

practitioner-request@izzy.com

INTERNATIONAL BUSINESS LIST

The International Business List is a moderated public Internet mailing list that seeks to provide a bridge between business people in all lands and provide them with a way to make contacts, find new trading partners and share resources.

www.earthone.com

INTERAD

This name refers to Internet Advertising. The purpose of this list is to promote discussion and exchange ideas on the use of the Internet for advertising. For example, discussion might include Internet and website strategies, advertising on popular sites, and cross-media promotion of websites. Interested participants are advertising agencies, new media developers,

Internet presence providers and consultants, and corporations who are either already on the Net or are considering an Internet presence. To subscribe to this list, please e-mail:

interad@iponline.com

with the words – 'subscribe Interad' in the subject line or message body.

INTERNATIONAL-BUSINESS

Discusses topics that concern business owners and marketing professionals as they relate to the Internet and the Web. Send e-mail to:

majordomo@globalbiz.com

INTERNET-SALES

Internet Sales has its own home page. The goal of the Internet Sales Moderated Discussion List is to provide meaningful and helpful information to those engaged in the online sale of products and/or services.

join-i-sales@gs2.revnet.com

INTERNET RESEARCH

It behoves the ambitious Internet marketer to keep up to date with what is happening on the Web. Even if things are not appropriate for you today, they may well be tomorrow. WAP or its equivalent technology will be part of every commercial website. It is not appropriate for most sites today because of the poor quality of the transmission and the data. Video and online TV will change the way we need to do things. Keep abreast by visiting and perhaps subscribing to some of these sites:

www.jup.com/home.jsp
www.forrester.com/Home/0,3257,1,FF.html
www.resourcehelp.com/index1.htm
www.afn.org/~afn05660/search.html
www.vanguard.edu/rharris/evalu8it.htm
www.irdc.com/
websnapshot.mycomputer.com/

I-SHOP

The I-Shop community discusses topics from both the merchant and consumer perspectives. Sign up via

www.audettemedia.com/I-Shop/shop.html.

ISI-L

This list was created by Interpretive Software Incorporated for the discussion of classroom simulation and marketing education software. Send e-mail to:

70401.2062@compuserve.com.

ISP-AUCTION

This list is for the ISP or Web provider who is or has implemented auction websites. It includes discussions about auction website software/hardware. This list is NOT for the end user, but rather for the Auction WebSite Developers, webmasters, and owners.

join-isp-auction@sparknet.net

ISP-MARKETING

This list is exclusively for Internet Service Providers who wish to discuss marketing. There is a URL for the list at:

www.isp-marketing.com/.

JOBS-SLS

JOBS-SLS is a moderated mailing list of employment opportunities for sales and marketing jobs, including advertising, customer service and public relations.

jobs-sls@execon.metronet.com

MARKET-ECRES

Market-ECRes is an e-mail discussion list for the discussion of Marketing Research on Electronic Commerce. Market-ECRes is an unmoderated forum for the discussion of electronic commerce for marketing faculty, doctoral students and practitioners. The topics range from inquiring about a research source to testing a new research idea.

Majordomo@volition.com

with the following command in the body of your e-mail message:

subscribe market-ecres

MARKET-L

Market-L is the oldest Internet e-mail list on the subject of marketing. A partial list of topics discussed on Market-L would include pricing tactics, distribution, promotion and advertising, segmentation, surveys, service quality, marketing planning for non-profits, positioning, exporting, market models, product design, marketing information systems and decision support, channel structure, relationship marketing, database marketing, marketing ethics, branding, and salesforce compensation.

listserv@amic.com

MAILBASE

Mailbase has a collection of business e-mail lists:

www.mailbase.ac.uk/category/N.html

MEDIAPLAN

MediaPlan is a discussion arena for professionals working in the planning departments of both traditional and new media agencies, and it is also for marketing professionals and academics who have an interest in media planning, buying and research. MediaPlan was established to encourage discussion of advertising media management issues. Planning, buying and media research are the broad topical areas. Discussions may cover new media, rate trends, strategic analysis, syndicated audience measurement methodology, traditional versus high-tech approaches, planning and buying techniques, information sources, planning software, media sales, reps and media computer services. To subscribe send e-mail to:

listserv@amic.com

MKTRSRCH

MKTRSRCH is an open, unmoderated discussion list covering the topic of primary and secondary market research. Primary market research topics such as survey design, sample size determination, statistical and other analysis tools, industry software, the conducting of focus groups, and implementation techniques (e.g. telephone, paper, personal interview, mall intercept, Web surveys) are likely to be discussed. Send an e-mail to:

listserv@listserv.dartmouth.edu

MKTSEG

The purpose of the list is to allow and encourage an exchange of ideas and information relating to advertising and marketing to target segments. These include but are not limited to ethnic segments, lifestyle and lifestage segments, and interest group segments. Topics might include advertising creative material, media issues, research, data base marketing, direct response, promotions or education relating to all the above, and other segmentation information resources.

maiser@mail.telmar.com

MKTSHARE

Marketshare (MktShare) is a moderated list provided by Northwestern University focusing on the theoretical and applied aspects of relationship marketing, brand management and integrated marketing communications. Current membership is open to anyone and includes university faculty, Ph.D. candidates, graduate students, practitioners, and editors of academic and commercial publications from around the world. Send e-mail to:

listserv@piranha.acns.nwu.edu

MKTTEACH

MktTeach is an unmoderated list for the discussion of teaching issues in marketing education. MktTeach was established by the Teaching Special Interest Group of the AMA Academic Council.

majordomo@hawk.depaul.edu

MT-L

Marketing with Technology is an unmoderated list. Send e-mail to:

listserv@uhccvm.uhcc.hawaii.edu

MRKT-PHD

This unmoderated list focuses on topics of interest to doctoral students in marketing. Send e-mail to:

listserv@vm.sc.edu

NETMARKETING

NETMARKETING is a moderated discussion list in the German language related to all matters of online advertising, banners, webpromotion, etc. To subscribe send e-mail to:

majordomo@horizont.net

NETMARKET-L

The NetMarket-L list is unmoderated. It is for entrepreneurs, webmasters and pioneers, those of us who are testing new ideas and marketing concepts on how best to promote our business, products and services on the Internet. The goal of the list is to brainstorm new marketing concepts and help each other test them. To subscribe send e-mail to:

listserv@citadel.net

NEWPROD

NEWPROD is a mailing list devoted to the discussion of new product development in both product and service industries. New product development touches a number of different disciplines. Marketing, market research, management science, R & D, quality, and organizational behaviour all have a role in the new product development process. The latest management research recognizes the cross-functional nature of the process and the importance of teams in creating successful new products. Send e-mail to:

majordomo@world.std.com

ONLINE-ADVERTISING

This list is sponsored by the Tenagra Corporation. The Online Advertising Discussion List focuses on professional discussion of online advertising strategies, results, studies, tools, and media coverage. It also welcomes discussion on the related topics of online promotion and public relations. The list encourages sharing of practical expertise and experiences between those who buy, sell, research and develop tools for online advertising, as well as those providing online public relations and publicity services. It will also serve as a resource to members of the press who are writing about the subject of online advertising and promotion. To subscribe, use the online form at:

www.tenagra.com/online-ads/

ONLINE PAYMENT METHODS

Getting paid is the object of running an e-commerce site. Even in a site where the receipt of money is not the prime objective, there can be ways to off-set the costs of running the site by providing something of value and making a charge for it. There is a range of payment options and some of these are given here.

www.cybercash.com/
www.internetact.com/
www.cybank.net/
www.brokat.com/int/netnews/online_payment_costs.html
www.prologiccorp.com/
www.microbanker.com/eleccomm.html
www.netinvest.co.uk/ncr/netbanx/
www.secpay.com/
www.ibill.com/web900.html

ONLINE-PUBLISHERS

The list is a resource for marketers who want to use e-mail newsletters to promote their business. It covers topics such as managing, distributing, promoting, and editing an online newsletter.

www.ideastation.com/ subscribe@ideastation.com

ORG-MARKETING

Org-Marketing exists to focus communication on the subject of marketing for non-profit and not-for-profit organizations, in response to several requests from members of high-traffic marketing discussion lists. An archive of Org-Marketing is maintained at:

www.amic.com/forums/.
listserv@amic.com

Put in the BODY of the e-mail:

SUBSCRIBE Org-Marketing

PORTALS

These sites will give you an overview of some current portal sites. It may be useful to review these sites if you have an idea that you might want to use some of this technology to turn your own site into a portal. Revenues can be generated from a portal site by various means, including sponsorship, advertising, subscriptions, and sales of products.

www.traffick.com/
www.emarketer.com/elist/t10portals/top10portals.html
www.govtech.net/publications/gt/2000/may/portals/portals.shtm
www.earthportals.com/earthportals/
www.brillscontent.com/next/bw_portals_0499.html
www.algonquinc.on.ca/lrc/search/portals.html

RETAILER-NEWS

The Retailer News Digest mailing list is a moderated discussion list for retail business owners, managers, and salespeople. It is only available in digest form. The list is archived. It is published by the Retailer News Online magazine:

RetailerNews.com/

You can subscribe at the website. Send e-mail to:

majordomo@mailing-list.net

RITIM-L

This list is for the discussion of telecommunications and information marketing. Send e-mail to:

listserv@uriacc.uri.edu

RTL-MGMT

RTL-MGMT exists to facilitate communication about retailing and retail management practices, policies, plans, and procedures. Send e-mail to the server:

mailserv@UToledo.EDU

SEARCH ENGINE INFORMATION SITES

Knowing how to use search engine technology can be very useful to the online marketer. The ability to use the major search engine's more advanced search techniques will speed up and improve your online research. You may also want to use the technology on your own site. This will be particularly useful to your visitors when the site is large or contains a lot of textual information. See also the next entry.

cui.unige.ch/meta-index.html

www.searchengineguide.com/
searchenginewatch.com/webmasters/work.html
websearch.about.com/internet/websearch/msubmenu12.htm
home.sprintmail.com/~debflanagan/engines.html
www.searchengineshowdown.com/multi/

SEARCH ENGINES FOR YOUR SITE

bridges.state.mn.us/custom.html

SITE PERFORMANCE MONITORING

One of the huge benefits of online marketing is the audit trail left by visitors to your site. Like the shiny little lines left by a crawling snail, the clever and inquisitive online marketer can glean a mass of information from the use of an effective tracking software. There are a selection of different options here.

www.web-stat.com/
www.freestats.com/
www.graycorp.com.au/ssleuth.htm
goldstats.com/
www.casystat.nct/
fishclix.com/

SMBIZ

The Small Business Discussion List is for all small-business owners, workers, marketers, and developers. This list is for networking, sharing ideas and information and open discussion about business problems and issues. Submit with the message: smbiz-list-request@dandyweb.com

www.dandyweb.com/smbiz/.

SOC-MKTG

This is a list for those particularly interested in social marketing. The list is a place for those in academia, in research, and in practice to exchange information to advance the field.

listserv@listserv.georgetown.edu

SITE PERSONALIZATION

Site personalization and customization will become more and more important as competition for the return visitor increases. The technology to customize your own site is already available and need not be cost-prohibitive.

www.personalizing-e-commerce.com/e-commerce/b2b-
  e-commerce.htm
guidezone.com
www.ence.umd.edu/~caseymj/av/489lec5/sld022.htm

SEARCH ENGINE POSITIONING

The search engines do a really great job for us in locating information. They are up against some really tough challenges, including the many site owners who want to 'cheat' the engines into listing them more highly. This will eventually result in better and better technology that will enable the engines to present better and more relevant sites on any given search. There is no need to resort to cheating tactics. You need only buy the submission software and carry out the painstaking task of presenting your site the way the engines would best like it presented. Alternatively you can use one of the submission services, some of which guarantee their work.

www.searchenginewatch.com
www.webposition.com
www.searchenginecommando.com
www.coastalsites.com

SALES-CHAT

The Sales-Chat List was formed to provide a discussion forum for people involved in selling or interested in selling: account managers, sales reps, inside sales reps, sales managers, etc. Topics for discussion can be, but are not limited to, sales automation products, motivation, success stories, horror stories, travelling hints/tips, sales presentation hints/tips, customer satisfaction, recent books, selling yourself, networking, sales meetings, time management, generating leads, handling job stress, etc.

sales-chat-request@listserv.direct.net

TRADENET

TradeNet is a moderated announcement list featuring international trade contacts, products and services from around the world.

List@TradeNet.org

WEBCONTENTSTRATEGY

This list is for Web-based content business owners and advisors to discuss strategy and funding issues. Subjects discussed are strategic or financial, rather than trading or operating in nature. They include:

- How to find and negotiate with syndication or other partners.
- Evaluation and referrals of advisors.
- Web content business structures and models.
- Issues around raising or making equity investments.
- Guerrilla financing.
- Strategic investor relationship issues.
- Lessons from relevant success/failure stories.
- Business planning questions.

Visit the official website at:

www.fourleaf.com/
join-webcontentstrategy@lists.fourleaf.com

WTB

The Women-Talk-Business list is set up as a discussion list for business topics. It was formed as a moderated list due to the tremendous number of women on other lists. It focuses on business topics and is open to anyone, although it will primarily target women. Subscribe at:

www.listhost.net:81/guest/RemoteListSummary/WTB

WTZ-INTRADELEADS

WTZ-INTRADELEADS is an unmoderated International leads list. On an average day, the list will receive and re-distribute 40–60 trade lead posts from subscribers. You can visit the website at:

www.worldtradezone.com/

Subscribe using:

wtzadmin@worldtradezone.com

GLOSSARY OF TERMS

ADDRESS

An address in a unique identifier assigned to a Web page. The address is more commonly referred to as the URL (Uniform Resource Locator).

ADN

Advanced Digital Network. Often refers to 56 kbps leased line.

APPLET

A multimedia application written or embedded in the Java language, such as animation or sound. Viewable only in a Java-enabled browser such as Netscape 2.0 or HotJava. See also: HotJava, Netscape.

ANONYMOUS FTP

Users may gain access to a remote server using FTP (File Transfer Protocol) without actually having an account on that server. The user's e-mail address is usually given as a password and the user name 'anonymous' is assigned to the user by systems supporting this service.

ARCHIE

A database of anonymous FTP sites and their contents, 'Archie' keeps track of the entire contents of these sites and allows users to search for files on those sites using various different kinds of filename searches.

ARCHIVE

Often compressed, archives are usually large files containing several smaller files. Commonly used archive file formats are ZIP, TAR, ARJ, LZH, UC2.

ARCHIVE SITE

Contains archived files of many kinds, available for users to download either by FTP or e-mail.

ARJ

Allows the user to store one or more files in a compressed format in an archive file. This saves space both in the compression and in saving of disk sector clusters. Particularly strong in compressing databases, uncompressed graphics files, and large documents. Named after the creator, American programmer Robert Jung.

ARPA

Advanced Research Projects Agency. US governmental organization responsible for creating an experimental network which heralded the beginning of the Internet. Now known as Defense Advanced Research Projects Agency.

ARPANET

Network created by ARPA in 1969, primarily allowing data transfer between government laboratories. Now defunct.

ASCII

American Standard Code for Information Interchange. A file containing only text characters: numbers, letters, and standard punctuation.

ATM

Asynchronous Transfer Mode. A new communications standard that is currently in the later stages of development. ATM is designed to transfer voice, video and other multimedia data requiring short bursts of large quantities of data that can survive small losses but must be broadcast in real time.

ATTACHMENTS

Multimedia files that are 'attached' to an e-mail. Can be text, graphics, sound, video, spreadsheet, database, or even an entire application.

BACKBONE

A central high-speed network established by a company or organization for connecting independent sub-networks.

BANDWIDTH

In simplistic terms, bandwidth is the amount of information travelling through a single channel at any one moment in time.

BAUD RATE

Speed at which data travels through a modem, measured in bps (bits per second). Most modems today range from 2400 to over 50,000 bps.

BBS

Bulletin Board System. A computer system usually run by local users making files available for downloading and setting up electronic discussion forums.

BINARY

Binary data is a direct representation of the bits stored in RAM on a computer. Much more compact and accurate than ASCII.

BIT

Binary DigIT. The smallest unit of computerized data, comprising of either a 1 or 0. A combination of bits can indicate an alphabetic character, a numeric digit, or perform a signalling, switching or other function. Bandwidth is usually measured in bits per second.

BODY

In e-mail terms, the part of the message containing the most textual content, sandwiched between the Header and the Signature.

BOOKMARK

Virtual bookmarks work pretty much the same as the real ones. They record a URL or Web page to enable you to refer back to at a later date.

BPS

Bits per second. Speed at which data transfer is measured.

BROWSER

Often called a 'Web Browser'. Allows the user to search the Web and other Internet facilities using a Graphical User Interface. Examples are Mosaic and Netscape.

BYTE

A unit of data, generally formed from eight bits. Example: 01101010

CERN

(Conseil Européen pour la Recherche Nucleaire) A laboratory located in Geneva, Switzerland, where the concept of the World Wide Web was first developed.

CGI

Common Gateway Interface. An interface-creation scripting program that allows you to make Web pages on the fly based on information from fill-in forms, checkboxes, text input, etc.

CLIENT

In a client–server relationship, the client is a computer running programs or applications from the server, or accessing files from it.

COMPRESS

The act of discarding redundant or semi-redundant information from a file, thereby making it smaller.

COMPUSERVE

US Internet service provider; one of the oldest and biggest.

COOKIE

A piece of software which records information about you. It holds this information until such time that the server requests it. For example, if you are browsing around a virtual shop, each time you place an item in your basket the information is stored by the cookie until you decide to buy and the server requests the purchase information.

CYBERCAFE

A cafe or bar allowing customers to explore the Web whilst having a drink or snack. Usually charged per half-hour of usage.

DAEMON

A program that runs in the background whenever needed, carrying out tasks for the user. They 'sleep' until something comes along which needs their help; most commonly found on Unix systems. See also: Unix

DIALUP

'Dialup Access' or a 'Dialup Account' is when a modem is used to gain access to the Internet via a network. See also: Modem.

DOMAIN NAME

Unique address identifying each site on the Internet. Usually of two or more segments separated by full stops.

DOMAIN NAME SERVER

Computers connected to the Internet whose job it is to keep track of the IP addresses and domain names of other machines. When called upon, they take the ASCII domain name and convert it to the relevant numeric IP address. See also: IP Address.

DOMAIN NAME SYSTEM

Allows users to relate to computers on the Internet by using textual addresses (eg. www.theplanet.net) for ease of use, rather than the IP address system.

DOS

Disk Operating System. Simple operating system developed by Microsoft, allows extensions by other programs.

DOWNLOAD

When you transfer information off a remote machine connected to the Internet onto your local machine, you are downloading data. See also: Upload.

ELECTRONIC MAIL OR E-MAIL

Method of communication whereby an electronic message is sent to a remote location and received by another user at a specific e-mail address. See also: Attachments, Body, Header, Signature.

EMOTICONS

These are the sideways smiles and frowns used in e-mail to indicate emotions. e.g. :-) would indicate a smile and :-(would indicate a frown.

ETHERNET

A type of network cabling allowing theoretical data transfers of up to 10 Mb per second.

FAQ

Frequently Asked Question. Lists of frequently asked questions (and their answers) covering all manner of topics can be found across the Web, allowing the user to search for a query that somebody has already found the answer to.

FDDI

Fibre Distributed Data Interface is a standard for transmitting data through optical fibre cables at a rate of around 100 million bps. See also: Bandwidth, Ethernet, T–1, T–3.

FILENAME EXTENSION

Commonly a three or four-letter extension on the end of a file name designating the file type. There are hundreds already in existence and new ones frequently being invented. Examples are: .txt (text file), .gif (Graphics Interchange Format).

FINGER

A Unix program which displays information about a particular user or all users logged on the system, or a remote system. See also: Unix.

FIREWALL

Secures a company or organization's internal network from unauthorized external access (most commonly in the form of Internet hackers).

FLAME

An insulting or derogatory message usually sent via e-mail as punishment for breach of netiquette. There have been instances of 'Flame Wars', when other people join in the heated exchanges. In either case, not recommended. See also: e-mail, Netiquette.

FORMS

Certain Browsers support electronic fill-in forms. A form on a Web page can be filled in by users all over the world and the information sent electronically to the relevant domain site. See also: CGI, Browser.

FREEWARE

Software allowed to be distributed free by the author, but often with certain conditions applying (i.e. the software cannot be modified, etc.). See also: Public Domain, Shareware.

FTP

File Transfer Protocol. One of the main ways files are transferred across the Internet. An FTP site is provided by a company or organization as a depository for all kinds of files which users may download. See also: Download, Protocol.

FTPMAIL

The process where e-mail is used to access FTP sites. See also: e-mail.

GATEWAY

The interface between two opposing protocols. By means of software and hardware a gateway allows connection between otherwise incompatible networks. See also: Protocol.

GIF

Graphics Interchange Format. Developed by Compuserve, GIF is a platform-independent file format, used extensively throughout the Internet for graphics files. Compresses files using a 'lossless' method which ensures picture quality is not diminished. See also: Compuserve.

.GIF

Graphics Interchange Format (GIF) filename extension.

GIGABYTE (GB)

A thousand megabytes. See also: Megabyte.

GOPHER

Internet Gopher is a distributed document search and retrieval system. It takes a request for information and then scans the Internet for it. The protocol and software follows a client–server model, and permits users on a heterogeneous mix of desktop systems to browse, search and retrieve documents residing on multiple distributed server machines. See also: Protocol.

HEADER

In e-mail terms, this is the part of the message indicating who the sender is and some other brief details, such as the subject of the message. See also: Attachments, Body, e-mail, Signature.

HIT

As used in reference to the Web, 'hit' means a single request from a Web browser for a single item from a Web server; thus in order for a Web browser to display a page that contains three graphics, four 'hits' would occur at the server: one for the HTML page, and one for each of the three graphics.

HOME PAGE

On the Web, this is the main navigation page owned by a company, organization, university, individual, etc. from which hyperlinks are made to other pages on the site (or other sites). See also: Hyperlink.

HOST

Usually you connect to a host computer whenever you use the Internet.

HOTJAVA

A Web browser developed by Sun Microsystems expanding traditional browser capabilities by allowing dynamic functions instead of just static text and images. See also: Applet, Java.

HTML

HyperText Markup Language. The tagging language used to format Web pages. Allows pictures and text to be combined to create Web documents, and the most important feature – hypertext – making it possible for links to be made between different documents. See also: Gif, Jpeg, Tag, World Wide Web.

HTTP

HyperText Transport Protocol. Used on the Web since 1990, this application-level protocol is essential for the distribution of information throughout the Web.

HYPERLINK

In Web pages, hyperlinks are highlighted text or images which, when selected (usually by clicking the mouse button), follow a link to another page. Hyperlinks can also be used to automatically download other files as well as sounds and video clips. See also: Download.

IMAGE MAP

An image with clickable 'hot spots', allowing several hyperlinks from a single image file. For example, the image could be of a country, split into different areas, each of which could be clickable and hyperlink to a larger view of that specific area. See also: Hyperlink.

INTERNET

When spelt with a lower case i, it is a group of two or more networks connected together.

INTERNET

With a capital I, it is the collection of all the interconnected networks in the world, and is often simply referred to as the 'Net'.

IP

Internet Protocol. The main protocol used on the Internet. See also: Protocol.

IP ADDRESS

Unique four-number code designated to every domain on the Internet. Each domain also has a domain name as well as an IP address to make site addresses easier to remember.

IRC

Internet Relay Chat. Real-time world-wide electronic chat program allowing the user to communicate with other people across the globe.

ISDN

Integrated Services Digital Network. Digital telephone line allowing faster data transfer rates than existing analog lines. Allows simultaneous transfer of voice, data and video information.

ISP

Internet Service Provider. A company or organization, such as Planet Online, dedicated to providing businesses or home users access to the Internet, usually for a fee.

JARGON

Like all other specialized subjects, the Internet has its own jargon – a somewhat cryptic language describing technical details. Some jargon is explained in this glossary.

JAVA

Developed by Sun Microsystems, Java is a Web programming language supporting online multimedia effects, such as simple cartoon-like animation, background music and continuously updated information in Web pages. See also: Applet, HotJava.

JPEG

Joint Photographic Experts Group. A standard of image compression developed especially for use on the Internet. Most photographic images can be highly compressed using this method, without greatly diminishing image quality.

.JPG OR .JPEG

Filename extensions given to JPEG graphics files.

KILOBYTE

1024 bytes, usually rounded down to a thousand bytes for simplicity.

LEASED LINE

A rented, high-speed phone link for private use, available 24 hours a day.

LINK

Link puts the hyper in hyperlink. Links are the connections between hypertext pages. Every time you click on highlighted text to go to another page you are following a link.

LOCAL AREA NETWORK

Usually referred to as a LAN, this describes a group of computers commonly in the same building, connected by network cables.

LOGIN

When a user tries to gain access to the Internet through their host computer, they must Login with their password and User ID.

MAILSERVER

The computer (and software running on it) that allows sorting and retrieval of e-mail messages. See also: e-mail.

MEGABYTE (MB)

The unit of measurement for a thousand kilobytes; a million bytes. See also: Gigabyte, Kilobyte.

MIME

Multipurpose Internet Mail Extensions. A format designed originally to include images, sounds, animations, and other types of documents within Internet mail messages.

MIRROR SITE

An FTP site containing exactly the same files as the site it is mirroring. Sites may be mirrored several times, often in different countries around the world. They relieve the load that can be placed on a very popular FTP site, making it easier for users to gain access and download files faster. See also: Download, FTP.

MODEM

MODulator-DEModulator. Allows the transmission of digital information over an analogue phone line.

MOSAIC

Web browser written by a group of people at NCSA. Provides a Graphical User Interface for accessing data on the Web. See also: Browser.

MPEG

Motion Picture Experts Group. Video compression format used for movie or animation clips on the Web.

.MPG OR .MPEG

Filename extension for MPEG movies.

NCSA

National Center for Supercomputing Applications. Powerful organization that launched the Mosaic Web Browser in 1993 for Windows, x-Windows and Macintosh platforms.

NETIQUETTE

Informal, largely undocumented set of rules designed to make the Web a polite and civilized 'society'.

NETSCAPE COMMUNICATIONS

Creators of Netscape Navigator, one of the most popular Web browsers. Became notorious after introducing several HTML 'extensions' that were unsupported by other browsers. See also: Browser.

NETWORK

Two or more computers linked together and able to share resources constitute a network.

NETWORK TIME PROTOCOL

Internet protocol ensuring that the correct time is transmitted. See also: Protocol.

NETWORK TIME SERVER

Using Network Time Protocol, you access this machine to get the right time.

NEWSGROUP

Thousands of Newsgroups exist, distributing information on different subjects using Usenet.

NEWSREADER

Program that allows the user to read Newsgroup messages via Usenet.

NIC

Network Information Centre. The location where all the data is organized for a certain network.

NNTP

Net News Transport Protocol. Usenet news uses this transfer protocol for shifting files around the network. See also: Usenet.

NODE

Any single computer connected to a network. See also: Network.

OFFLINE

When your computer performs an operation while it is not connected to any other computers, it is working offline.

ONLINE

Your computer is working online when it performs an operation while it is connected to other computers.

PACKET

Information moves around the Internet in 'packets'; chunks of data each with its own destination address. Think of packets as sealed envelopes containing data, with addresses written on them. They all go through the system and usually end up at the correct destination. The more envelopes the system must handle, the slower the process becomes.

PAGE

A Web page is the name given to a basic Web document, such as the one you are viewing at any one moment.

PKZIP OR PKUNZIP

Utilities for easily compressing and uncompressing DOS and Windows files. They use the .zip filename extension.

PLUG-IN

There are many things that your browser can do, such as displaying images and Web pages. Other things are beyond its capabilities and that is where plug-ins are introduced. Shockwave and RealAudio are examples of plug-ins required for audio and video.

POP

Post Office Protocol. Provides a store-and-forward service, intended to move e-mail on demand from an intermediate server to a single destination machine, usually a PC or Macintosh.

PPP

Point to Point Protocol. A kind of Internet connection that allows a computer to use Internet protocols to become a part of the Internet. Requires a modem, a standard telephone line and an account from a service provider.

PROTOCOL

Method by which computers communicate to each other over the Internet in order to provide a service. See slso: FTP, HTTP, IP, NNTP, POP, PPP, SLIP, SMTP, TCP.

PUBLIC ACCESS PROVIDER

An organization that provides Internet access for individuals or other organizations, often for a fee.

PUBLIC DOMAIN

Refers to software that anybody can use or modify without authorization. See also: Freeware, Shareware.

RESOURCE

A particular object of information provided on the Internet. Can be anything from a picture through to a video or application.

ROUTER

A special-purpose computer (or software package) that handles the connection between two or more networks. Routers concentrate on looking at the destination addresses of the packets passing through them and deciding which route to send them on. See also: Network.

SCRIPTING LANGUAGE

Series of programmed commands that designate how one computer communicates with another computer.

SELF-EXTRACTING ARCHIVE

An archived file with the filename extension .exe, indicating that when downloaded and run it will be extracted by the decompressing program around it, without user intervention.

SERVER

Within a network, a server makes files available to client programs located on other computers, when requested.

SERVICE PROVIDER

Freeserve are currently the largest Internet service provider in the UK. The role of a service provider is to provide subscribers a gateway to the Internet.

SHAREWARE

Software distributed freely, but with certain conditions applying to it. The software may be released on a trial basis only, and must be registered after a certain period of time, or in other cases no support can be offered with the software without registering it. In some cases direct payment to the author is required. See also: Freeware, Public domain.

SIGNATURE

The automatic addition of a few lines at the foot of an e-mail. These usually consist of the sender's e-mail address, full name and other details. See also: Body, e-mail, Header.

SLIP

Serial Line Internet Protocol. Like PPP it lets you use a modem and phone lines to connect to the Internet without connecting to a host computer. See also: PPP, Protocol.

SMILEYS

Characters often used in news messages, e-mails and on Web pages to offer some degree of character or emotion. An example is :-)

SMTP

Simple Mail Transport Protocol. Often referred to as sendmail, is designed to allow the delivery of mail messages to Internet users.

SNAIL MAIL

Write a letter. Buy a stamp, put stamp on letter. Walk to the postbox and post letter. Wait a day or two and hopefully it will have reached its intended destination ... that's s n a i l - m a i l.

SURFING

A popular metaphor used for describing someone exploring the Web.

TAG

In HTML terms, a 'tag' is used for marking-up text in various ways so that it is formatted in a Web document. They are sometimes called 'Markup Tags'. See also: HTML.

T–1

Network link used on the Internet allowing speeds of up to 1.54 megabits/second. See also: ADN.

T–3

Higher speed (45 megabits/second) network link used on the Internet. See also: ADN.

TCP

Transmission Control Protocol. Works in conjunction with IP to ensure that packets reach their intended destinations. See also: Packet, Protocol.

TCP/IP

Transmission Control Protocol/Internet Protocol. The two fundamental protocols which form the basis of the Internet. See also: Protocol.

TELNET

Terminal emulation program allowing an authorized user to access another computer on the Internet and use that computer as if it were local, when in reality it could be several thousand miles away.

TERABYTE

1000 gigabytes. See also: Byte, Kilobyte.

TERMINAL

Piece of hardware that allows commands to be sent to a computer, usually by means of a keyboard and display unit.

TERMINAL EMULATOR

Allows a PC to emulate several terminal types.

THREAD

In a Usenet group, this is a list of messages loosely relating to one another (using the same 'thread').

TIMEOUT

The facility whereby after a certain period of inactivity the connection is dropped.

UNIX

An operating system typically written in C and designed for multi-user environments. It has TCP/IP built-in and is therefore one of the most popular operating systems for servers on the Internet.

UPLOAD

Transfer of files off a local computer up to a specified remote computer. As opposed to download, where files are pulled off a remote machine. See also: Download.

URL

Uniform Resource Locator. Resource addressing scheme of the Web. Assists in locating and identifying of multimedia resources or multiple copies of resources.

USENET

Specialized network linking thousands of newsgroups covering every subject under the sun.

VERONICA

Very Easy Rodent Oriented Net-wide Index to Computerized Archives. A resource-discovery system providing access to information resources held on most (99 % +) of the world's Gopher servers. In addition to native gopher data, Veronica includes references to many resources provided by other types of information servers, such as Web servers, Usenet archives, and Telnet-accessible information services. See also: Gopher.

VIRUS

A virus is virtual evil. It can hide anywhere a computer stores information. Viruses have the ability to transfer from computer to computer using the Internet and various other networks. A virus can do a number of things to a recipient, such as reformatting hard drives and so destroying data.

WAIS

Wide Area Information Servers. An architecture for a distributed information retrieval system. WAIS is based on the client–server model of computation, and allows users of computers to share information using a common computer-to-computer protocol. See also: Protocol.

WIDE AREA NETWORK. WAN

Group of computers located geographically apart, usually belonging to a single company or organization, connected together using dedicated lines or by satellite to simulate a local network.

WINSOCK

WINdows SOCKets. Windows utility program allowing users connected by SLIP, PPP or other direct connection to communicate with other computers on the Internet by TCP/IP. See also: PPP, SLIP, TCP/IP.

WORLD WIDE WEB

Usually abbreviated as WWW or 'the Web'. Specialized Internet service allowing users to connect to remote sites, with information presented as text with hypertext links. These links can be used to refer to almost all other resources on the Internet. Graphics can be embedded in Web pages, but can only be viewed using a graphical Web browser. Other applications supported are sound files and movie files. See also: Browser, HTML, Internet.

WORM

A search utility on the Web that locates resources following user-determined guidelines.

XMODEM

A popular but slow file transfer protocol.

YMODEM

Another file transfer protocol, slightly faster than XMODEM.

.ZIP

Files that have been compressed using the PKZIP program have this filename extension. They can be decompressed using the PKUNZIP utility.

ZMODEM

The fastest and most popular file transfer protocol, due to its efficiency and crash recovery properties.

INDEX

In essence this book is about customers: finding them, delighting them, keeping them, and establishing the rules by which others who want to sell to them must play the game. Charles Revlon said many years ago that the purpose of the business is to create and keep the customer. Some things at least never change.

Common sense and experience combine to show that it is impossible to dominate any market unless the customer is central to the strategy. As a result the word 'customers' appears on virtually every page of this book. We index customer references therefore only when it is strongly advised that the reader should use the material to think even more deeply than usual about the steps they intend to take to create and sustain customer pleasure and satisfaction.